ADVANCE PRAISE FOR *RUINED*

Riveting. . . . Forthright, compassionate, and expertly crafted—everything readers should want from a memoir.
—*KIRKUS REVIEWS*

Ruined is one of those memoirs that sticks to your heart, helps you understand the power of a story, and gives you a framework to understand God when terrible things happen. Honest and beautifully written, Ruth's story will help readers discover the love of God in unexpected ways.
—MARY DeMUTH, AUTHOR OF *WORTH LIVING*

Mostly I wish this book never needed to be written. But it did, it was, and it's powerful. With heart-wrenching honesty and a refusal to leave the chaos, Ruth Everhart shows us the raw courage necessary to emerge both wounded and healed. Alternating between fury, hurt, fear, and rage, we journey with her to find God and her way back to life.
—NANCY ORTBERG, AUTHOR OF *LOOKING FOR GOD* AND *SEEING IN THE DARK*

Ruined

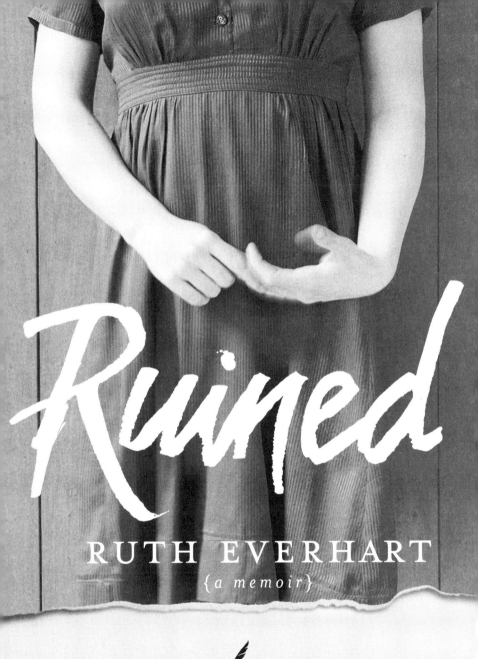

Ruined

RUTH EVERHART

{a memoir}

Tyndale House Publishers, Inc.
Carol Stream, Illinois

Visit Tyndale online at www.tyndale.com.

TYNDALE and Tyndale's quill logo are registered trademarks of Tyndale House Publishers, Inc.

Ruined

Designed by Dean Renninger and Julie Chen

Edited by Stephanie Rische

The author is represented by Chip MacGregor of MacGregor Literary, Inc., PO Box 1316, Manzanita, OR 97130.

Library of Congress Cataloging-in-Publication Data
Names: Everhart, Ruth, author.
Title: Ruined / Ruth Everhart.
Description: Carol Stream, IL : Tyndale House Publishers, Inc., 2016.
Identifiers: LCCN 2015045856| ISBN 9781496413925 (hc) | ISBN 9781496413161 (sc)
Subjects: LCSH: Everhart, Ruth. | Christian biography. | Rape victims—Religious life. | Rape—
    Religious aspects—Christianity.
Classification: LCC BR1725.E925 A3 2016 | DDC 277.3/083092—dc23 LC record available at
    http://lccn.loc.gov/2015045856

Printed in the United States of America

22   21   20   19   18   17   16
7   6   5   4   3   2   1

To Doug, who believes that nothing is wasted—
a belief that works on a person like love, like water.

To Hannah and Clara, our children, in the hope that these pages
enlighten where they came from and with the prayer that their
own stories never include such dark and violent passages.

And to all victims of sexual violence.
There are too many of us.

*The universe is under no obligation
to make sense to you.*

NEIL DEGRASSE TYSON

*Do not remember the former things, or consider the
things of old. I am about to do a new thing; now it
springs forth, do you not perceive it? I will make
a way in the wilderness and rivers in the desert.*

ISAIAH 43:18-19, NRSV

CONTENTS

PUBLISHER'S NOTE

Dear Reader:

The story you are about to read is true. The events depicted include violent situations and vulgar language that typically don't appear in books we publish. But after careful consideration, we decided to include some descriptions and dialogue that, though potentially offensive, are accurate, help to capture the intensity of the events in an authentic way, and give a truthful illustration of the human condition.

Some of the names have been changed to protect the identities of those involved.

PART 1

THE CRIME

November 5–6, 1978

*Yea, though I walk through the valley of the
shadow of death, I will fear no evil.*

PSALM 23:4

*Even in the valley of the shadow of death,
two and two do not make six.*

LEO TOLSTOY

1

It happened on a Sunday night, even though I'd been a good girl and gone to church that morning.

My older sister, Mary Lynn, had picked me up and then dropped me off after the service. She went home with her husband and young son, but I couldn't join them. I had studying to do. I was working on a paper about Buddhism for my World Religions class. The problem was that I couldn't grasp what I was reading. At the center of all things there is a great emptiness? I could hardly conceive of such a thought. Wasn't God at the center of all things? I'd been taught for as long as I could remember that God was sovereign—that nothing happened outside His will. I had no pocket in my mind that could hold a concept like Buddhism.

I lived in a house off campus with five friends: Marty, Teresa, Cheryl, Karen, and Lisa—all of us seniors at Calvin College in Grand Rapids, Michigan. After supper some of us housemates sprawled across the living room, talking. Thirty-seven years later, I can't say with certainty what we talked about. We may have ranged from Spinoza to Descartes, because Marty and Teresa loved philosophy.

No doubt Cheryl talked rapturously about Spain, because she was planning to spend her spring semester in Seville. And I'm sure I at least mentioned the name Jim—casually—since I was trying to figure out if he and I were friends or something more. Karen and Lisa had each spent the weekend with their parents, who lived in the area. At some point that Sunday Karen returned, but Lisa called to say she was staying with her folks one more night and would see us on Monday.

We were a talkative, opinionated bunch. We cooked and ate supper together most nights and discussed every subject imaginable. Could radical Christian community actually work? Would the Bob Dylan concert be worth the ticket price? What happened with the recent Camp David Accords anyway? And whose turn was it to buy groceries?

On that particular Sunday night, in our house on Alexander Street, we must have talked about groceries, because our cupboards were bare, and that mattered. The intruders were hungry. But I'm getting ahead of myself.

It was early November. I was the youngest of the group, not quite twenty-one. Graduation was still safely distant, some six months in the future. My main goal was to leave every door open. Everything seemed possible.

My bedroom, which originally had been a sunporch, was just off the dining room. Between my bedroom and the dining room were double French doors with window glass—the kind of doors you could throw open in a dramatic way if you were in the mood for that sort of thing. The room was small, but that was part of its charm. It was big enough to hold everything I needed and nothing more: hooks where I hung my second pair of jeans and a few tops, a desk where I stacked my textbooks, and a single bed with four posts, covered by a flowered yellow comforter.

Best of all were the windows on every side. During the day they bathed the room in light, and every evening I pulled the shades closed. I never thought to be nervous about those windows surrounding me as I slept. All that breakable glass. Those flimsy window clasps.

That night when I clicked off my bedside lamp, I had no idea that my room would never again feel full of light—not from the gooseneck lamp or from sunlight streaming through the abundant windows or from conversation and laughter drifting through the double doors.

I was sound asleep when I heard Marty screaming. My first thought was that she and Teresa must be clowning around. I sat up in the dark.

At the same moment, I felt someone beside me on the bed— a body pushing against me and pressing something cold and metallic against my temple. He was breathing hard and hissing words in a high-pitched voice. He sounded young and nervous and angry and black. I couldn't comprehend his words, but I could comprehend the danger.

A black ski mask covered the man's head. The whites of his eyes glowed. His dark lips were visible through the mouth hole.

"Get down, b—, get down!"

Time stopped as I tried to think. This wasn't a dream. This was really happening. This man had broken into our house. This man who had broken into our house meant to harm us.

"On the floor, b—!"

What was he saying? What did he want?

Upstairs, Marty had stopped screaming. Someone turned on the kitchen light, which shone through the double doors into my room. I could see Cheryl standing there in the kitchen, all six feet of her. Her hand was still in the air, grasping the pull-chain for the overhead light. She must have heard the screaming and come up from her basement bedroom. Without thinking, I pushed the intruder away, scrambled out of bed, and ran to Cheryl. She hugged me as I let out a strangled cry, my voice high and terrified.

The intruder followed me into the kitchen, yelling. He grabbed me from behind and shoved the gun into my side. The pull-chain was swinging wildly around our heads, and he cursed until he got a hold of it. He gave it a firm tug, and everything went dark.

I heard, rather than felt, a sharp crack. It occurred to me, almost as if I were wrapped in many layers of gauze, that the sound had come from his gun connecting with my skull.

"Get down!" He was furious.

Cheryl and I dropped to all fours. We were both whimpering. He kicked us. "Move!"

We crawled forward, shoulder to shoulder, like animals. My long flannel nightgown kept tripping me, and I had to pull the fabric away from my knees so I could keep crawling. At the doorway we jammed up, so Cheryl went first and I followed. We passed from the worn linoleum of the kitchen onto the rough carpet of the dining room.

"Get down!" This command came from a different voice, one strangely low and rough.

I looked up to see our other housemates—Marty, Teresa, and Karen—enter the dining room, followed by another masked man with another gun. The women looked ghostly in their nighties, barely visible in the faint streetlight that filtered through the curtained windows. The man was as dark as a shadow, dressed all in black, with a ski mask over his head.

"On the floor! Face down!"

My friends dropped to their knees. The two intruders moved around us, kicking our feet and bodies. They would yell "Move!" or "Stop!" at the same time—directions that were impossible to hear and comprehend and follow, so we crawled blindly around, as terrified as insects running from a boot.

"Shut up!" they yelled over and over, even though no one was talking.

When one of them pushed me down with his heel in the middle

of my back, I crumpled where I was. I could hear my own blood pounding in my ears. I buried my face in the carpet, which smelled faintly like soap. We had shampooed the carpets with a rented machine just a month before, for our first party of the semester.

I could hear ragged breathing beside me. We seemed to be lying in a row like sardines, alternating heads and feet. I thought Marty was on one side of me and Cheryl on the other, but I couldn't be sure.

The intruder with the rough, low voice said slowly, as if he were making an important announcement: "This is a robbery. We ain't gonna hurt you."

When I heard those words, with my face pressed into the carpet's worn nap, I was flooded with relief. They would take our money and leave. Before we knew it, we'd all be in the campus coffee shop telling the story. Everyone would say how lucky we were.

Or maybe we'd never tell anybody. Not even the police. Why should we? So what if they took our money? We had so little—what would it matter? If they would just leave quickly, we could go back to sleep. We could pretend this never happened. Maybe this wasn't happening. Maybe this was only a dream.

I've always been a dreamer—both daydreams and night dreams. I construct whole worlds in my head and live there. When I was seven years old, I had a dream that was so thrilling, and at the same time so comforting, that I cultivated it night after night. I assumed everyone did this—that this was why sleep was so wonderful. Each night I would breathe deeply and slowly until my sleeping body would rise and pass painlessly through the knotty pine ceiling of my bedroom. I would float above the housetops, gazing down at the lit-up boxes where people went about their mysterious lives.

I would rise farther into the night sky until a genial older man appeared at the end of a long table, its gleaming surface stretching between us. The man was dressed like an old-fashioned theater usher or perhaps Captain Kangaroo, wearing a dapper suit with piping along the edges of the lapel. He had a quill pen, and in each dream, he wrote something in a ledger.

Then I would rise still higher, to the rear of a great cathedral, where the dream deposited me onto plush carpet. I would lay there listening to magnificent organ music and feeling a sense of great peace until a kindly man in a black robe approached me and said, "My child." When I rose to follow him to the front of the cathedral, I would invariably wake up.

As I lay sardine-style on the floor that night, I wanted nothing more than to rise out of my body and escape through the roof. But what about Marty and Cheryl and Teresa and Karen? Even if I *could* levitate, would I escape and leave them in jeopardy?

The rough, low voice that had announced the robbery spoke again. "In case you're wondering, it's for real."

I heard shuffling movements, punctuated by thumping sounds. When it was my turn to have my head cracked with the gun, I was surprised how much it hurt. Maybe the shock was wearing off.

Then the rough voice said, "You." There was a stir as someone got up farther down the line—probably Teresa or Karen.

"Don't move, or she's dead," the low voice said. I scrunched my face into the carpet.

Oh God!

But I needed to do better than that. I needed to actually pray. I tried to construct a prayer, but the same words spiraled through my mind, down and down and down—a descent with no bottom. *Oh God, oh God, oh God!*

It was a cry of terror and a plea for mercy. It was also wordless repentance for whatever I had done to bring this on. *Oh God!* As the minutes dragged on, I tried to think of other words and to force those words into order, into sentences.

Oh God, no shots . . . God, please . . . Yea, though I walk . . . Oh God, please! . . . Yea, though I walk through the valley . . . God, where are You?

I tried to focus on Psalm 23 and recite it all the way through, as if it were a key, a magic phrase, a talisman that would protect us. With an effort, I began at the beginning. *The LORD is my shepherd, I shall not want . . .*

What came next? It was an act of the will to begin again, to keep trying to get through the whole psalm. I couldn't do it properly. The words and phrases twisted out of order, and I felt no solace from them. *He makes me to lie down. . . . Yea, though I walk through death . . . through the shadow . . . through death.*

The intruder still hadn't come back with Karen or Teresa—whoever he had—so I tried again. If I could keep it up, surely all would be well. He would bring her back. Take our stuff. Leave. Any minute now.

The LORD is my shepherd. The LORD.

"You." The voice was unexpected, loud. He kicked my shoulder. "In here!"

I raised my head. It was the first intruder, the one who had accosted me in bed. I couldn't see well in the dim light, but I could tell he was gesturing toward the open French doors, his gun glinting.

Oh God. He knows this is my room.

"Get up!"

I got to my feet. He pressed the gun into my ribs and pushed. I walked backward through the dining room and into my bedroom until I was perched on the edge of the bed. He sat beside me and clamped his arm around my shoulders. The polyester fabric of his jacket was dark and slippery. There was a vaguely chemical odor about him that I didn't recognize. When I shrank away, he tightened his grip. With his other arm, he pointed the gun at my friends on the floor in the other room.

What does he want?

2

Growing up, I had very little contact with black people. My world was almost entirely populated by pale-skinned people of Dutch descent. Such isolation is astounding in any time and place, but especially so when you consider that I grew up in urban areas in the sixties and early seventies.

My family lived in the Chicago area when I was born, and we moved to northern New Jersey just before I began fifth grade. In both places, we were part of a religious and ethnic subculture that revolved around the Christian Reformed Church. This small denomination is a Dutch version of Presbyterianism, with the same Reformed roots and Calvinist doctrine. Its forebears came to the United States from Holland beginning in the mid-1800s. They were staunch farmers who knew how to persist through difficulty.

Running through their stoicism was a deep intellectual vein and the belief that faith touches every aspect of life. Accordingly, the denomination ran its own school system. These two institutions, church and school, were the pivot points of our family's life. My parents both worked in the Christian school system—my father as a principal and my mother as a teacher—and my four siblings and I attended Christian schools from kindergarten through high school.

In my graduating class of 120, there were only 2 black students. One was a girl who'd been adopted by well-meaning parents who spoke with a Dutch accent; the other was a boy with a single mother, another fact that highlighted how atypical he was. Most of my classmates had last names that showed Dutch roots, beginning with *Van* or *De* or ending with *a* (*-sma*, *-stra*, or *-ga*), as mine did. In my world, no one had trouble pronouncing *Huizenga*.

The nearby city of Paterson was crime ridden, and on the local evening news I frequently saw mug shots of men who had been apprehended. Their faces were dark skinned and sullen. I was fascinated by the height markers behind them, which seemed to be forever taking their measure, and by their names, which sounded to me like strung-together syllables rather than proper names.

The talk at our family dinner table often touched on various "home mission" efforts organized by our denomination. One church worked with ex-offenders, another with drug addicts. My father's school, Eastern Christian Junior High, was located in Prospect Park, a community adjoining Paterson. He faced severe criticism for leaving the gates to the school's parking lot unlocked after hours so local youth could play basketball there in the evenings.

Dad told us, "People say they're worried about security. But they wouldn't complain if those boys were white. The fact is, they're Negro."

"Don't say *Negro*," my older brother, Tim, said. "Say *black*."

"On the farm my uncles said much worse! They called them darkies, 'coons—"

"That's enough, Nick!" my mother warned. "Don't repeat the rest of that poison. There are big ears in the cornfield."

I remember watching these exchanges and taking in the power of language. But to me all the words—*Negro, black*—really meant the same thing: *other*.

The intruder and I were perched on the bed, one of his arms squeezing around me like a vise, the other training a gun on my friends.

"Get your money," he told me. "But no funny business, or one of them gets it."

My whole body was trembling. I pulled away from him and went to get my purse from the spot where I always kept it: hanging by its strap from the back of my desk chair. But it wasn't there. Then it hit me: I must have left it in my sister's car after church. My heart skipped a beat.

"I don't have my purse," I told him. "I misplaced it."

"F— what!"

"I always hang it right here, on this chair. But it's not here." Through the eyeholes of the ski mask, the whites of his eyes followed me. "There wasn't much money in it anyway," I said. "A couple of dollars. I think three dollars."

He swore again, which frightened me. I wished I had a lot of money just lying there so he would take it and leave.

His voice rose into a command. "Get your jewelry. And get the f— back here."

The miniature cedar chest where I kept my jewelry was on my desk. I grabbed it and brought it to him. With his free hand, he dumped the contents onto the floor, in a patch of street light. He kept the gun trained on the huddled figures in the dining room as he pawed through the little pile of necklaces and earrings. None of it had any value.

I realized that he was distracted. Maybe I could get past him.

How many steps is it to the back door? Does the dead bolt turn left or right?

He finished rifling and said, "Get your pot."

"What?"

"Get your pot!" This was clearly a command.

"I don't have any pot." As soon as I said the prim words, I regretted them.

His tone was suspicious. "You sayin' you never smoked pot in your life?"

"That's not what I said."

He wasn't listening. "I go out there and axe your friends, do she smoke pot? What they gonna say?"

"I said I don't *have* any pot."

"Booze then. Liquor."

"There might be a beer in the fridge," I said, knowing there wasn't.

From upstairs I heard a thumping noise. *The other one is up there. With the other gun.* Suddenly the utter futility of the situation hit me. There was no way we could escape alive—not all of us, not alive.

He jerked me to my feet and shoved me back into the dining room. The other intruder was returning, and I could see that he had Karen. He was pushing her from behind with his gun.

In his rough voice, he yelled, "Why you got her up?"

He's the one in charge. The leader.

"She ain't got nothin'." The one who was holding me spit out the words in disgust. "No money. No pot."

The leader shoved Karen onto the floor at the other end of the room. The other one pushed me down with a similar show of force. Then he kicked me, for good measure. My skin goose-fleshed. I wondered what else he might do to please the one in charge. I buried my face in the comfort of the clean carpet.

"Get up." It was that rough, low voice again. This time I thought it was Marty who moved.

Oh God, not Marty.

⁓

Marty and I had a complicated relationship. We met in fifth grade when my family moved from Illinois to New Jersey for my father's new job as a principal. Things didn't go well for me in elementary school, with my Midwestern accent and outdated clothes. In contrast, Marty was one of the cool kids. She and her best friend had blonde hair that hung so straight it might as well have been ironed. They spent their summers in vacation cottages, waterskiing. After Christmas break they laughingly pushed aside those blonde curtains to display midwinter sunburns in the shape of ski goggles. I tried hard to be invisible—to them and to everyone else.

In seventh grade my class entered Eastern Christian Junior High, where my father was the principal. I suppose I could have made this work to my advantage, except that I was hopelessly unsophisticated.

During our eighth-grade year, my father disciplined Marty's best friend for a minor infraction. Furious, the girl's parents pulled her from the school. The loss made Marty hate my father and, by proxy, me. I might have sympathized with her if I'd known what was going on, but my father never said a word about such things at home. All I knew was that Marty bellowed "Ruuuth Mooose" at me during recess, the taunt blowing across the school yard as the winter wind wrapped my skirt around my legs. The nickname stuck. I was already the new kid, the principal's daughter, a goody-goody. Now I became a pariah.

In high school, Marty and I were both tracked as college bound and placed in all the same classes. We spent hour after hour together: algebra, history, English, Bible. But it was the easy class, typing, that brought us to a truce. We were assigned to the same double desk, each with our own manual typewriter.

The typewriters had silver handles that we struck at the end of each line to return the carriage and begin a new line. The carriage made a thwack as it slammed across the page, and a bell dinged. It was obvious who was typing faster by the frequency of those dings, so the two of us had breathless races. But if we typed in a spurt, out of rhythm, the levers would sometimes cross paths and get hung up on each other. Then we'd have to pry the little hammers apart with our fingers in order to keep going. Sometimes we had to do goofy things like balance a sheet of paper on our knuckles to keep us from peeking at the keys we were pressing. Marty sputtered and steamed and cursed. I delighted in her invectives, since they were no longer aimed at me. My dings outpaced hers.

The reason I was in the class was because my mother believed a girl should be able to earn her own living. "The world always needs a good secretary," she'd say. "What's good for the gander is good for the goose." I repeated my mother's words to Marty. We laughed at the funny phrase but analyzed it as our fingers raced beneath the fluttering edges of notebook paper. We agreed that we should be able to support ourselves. But should women be content to simply type words that were written by men? We both wanted more.

———

While Marty was gone, I gave up on Psalm 23 and switched to the Lord's Prayer, which was easier to keep straight. *Our Father which art in heaven, hallowed be thy name.*

I was always dutiful. Diligent. I did what was expected of me. In this situation, facedown on the floor, I knew praying was the expected thing, so I kept it up. I could do that for Marty. I could do that for all of us.

Before long the leader brought Marty back, then took Teresa. *The prayer is working. Just Cheryl now, right? Then they'll have everyone's stuff. They'll leave.*

But Teresa didn't come back as quickly. My prayer loop began to fray. Still, I kept going. I began to count the repetitions on my fingers. When I got to ten, I began tracking by tens. I was counting to stay focused. At least that's what I thought I was doing. I realize now that I was doing something more complicated on that dining room floor. I was acting out a certain theology: *God loves good girls, so be good. Even now. Especially now. Be good, and you will be rewarded.*

Eventually the other intruder—the one who had asked me for

my pot—got tired of waiting. He asked Cheryl where her room was, and she told him it was in the basement. He yelled at us to get up and then marched us down the wooden steps, single file.

The basement was unfinished except for Cheryl's room. He made us lie down on the bare concrete floor, and then he went into the bedroom with Cheryl. The cold seeped into me through my flannel nightgown. I wished for the worn carpet from the dining room.

It's almost over. Cheryl is the last one. They're almost done, and then they'll leave.

But they weren't, and they didn't.

The intruder finished ransacking Cheryl's belongings, but instead of marching us back upstairs, he had Cheryl lie down on the concrete floor beside me and Marty and Karen. Then he kicked my feet and told me to get up. He took me just inside the doorway of Cheryl's room and had me stand next to him. He pointed the gun toward my friends on the floor. He slid his other hand up under my nightgown. His hand was hot and slick on my skin. My heart raced, and I felt bile rising in my throat.

They said this was a robbery!

He felt me all over, especially my breasts. He kissed the side of my neck and my cheek. The pillowy feel of his lips was foreign to me. I felt repulsed. I turned my body away even though I was afraid of making him angry. He hit the gun against my temple, a reminder of his power.

I heard footsteps thumping down the wooden stairs—a hollow sound that made me both relieved and terrified. Relieved because the intruder pulled his hands from beneath my nightgown. Terrified because the leader was shoving Teresa in front of him. Teresa's face was unreadable in the darkness.

"What you doin' down here?" the leader barked. I noticed that the rough tone of his voice sounded almost put on, like a kid in a play who was instructed to sound sinister. But none of this was pretend.

The leader shoved Teresa onto the concrete floor. The one who was holding me followed suit, pushing me down as if I were a dog.

The intruders exchanged words, but I couldn't hear them. Maybe I'd ceased trying. What did it matter? I couldn't do anything. None of us could. All five of us were prostrate on the dirty basement floor, cold, exhausted, and terrified. We were unable even to offer consolation to each other.

Then they made us stand up again. They tied our hands behind our backs with some kind of cord—maybe a phone cord. As the criminals went down the line, I snuck a glance at my friends. Marty was visibly shivering. She didn't have a flannel nightgown like I did. When we were bound, the leader pulled Karen out of the line and pushed her up the stairs.

Karen again? What more do they want? Oh God!

3

WHEN I WAS GROWING UP, my father liked to teach us things. One time he took my younger sisters, Beth and Susan, and me with him when he was delivering something to a home-mission church in Paterson. It wasn't far—less than four miles—but a world away. After completing the errand, he drove us to the Great Falls on the Passaic River. We got out of the car to peer over a rusted, wobbly railing. The churning water of the falls was so full of garbage and brown foam that it looked like sewage. I had never seen a natural site so defaced. The riverbank was lined with crumbling, graffiti-covered buildings, their broken windows like blank, blind eyes.

"Girls, those are abandoned silk mills," my father said. He went on to tell us about the silk industry and how it had once been Paterson's economic engine. He described how "the Negro people" came up from the South to get the mill jobs, but the working conditions were terrible. There were strikes and picket lines and riots, but the city always sided with the mill owners.

"What shut down Paterson's silk mills wasn't justice," my father said. "It was polyester."

Then he drove into the inner city, detouring down side street after side street until I was nervous that we'd never find our way home. Did my father really know his way around these neighborhoods? Children playing ball in the streets had to stop so our car could pass. They watched us watch them, our faces separated by the car windows.

"These children have nowhere to play," my father said, his voice filled with emotion. "Look at all the broken glass in the streets."

During high school I learned more about the history of Paterson: that the people who worked in the silk mills represented many nationalities, including some Dutch people, and that it was rayon that replaced silk decades before polyester did. But even as a child, I knew that my father was trying to teach us something more than facts. Awareness. Compassion. Gratitude. I understood all that, but I also felt a vague sense of guilt. I wished the poor people would all just move away from that awful place. What was I supposed to do about it?

As I got older, I began to understand that faith demands a response to human misery. To be a Christian, a citizen of the Kingdom of God, I must do my part to clothe people and feed people and help people. At the very least, I must love them—must keep my mind and heart open to them. The song we learned in Sunday school meant something: "Red and yellow, black and white, all are precious in God's sight. Jesus loves the little children of the world."

All of this—as inarticulate and naive as it sounds—was part of the reason my friends and I had moved into one of the downtrodden neighborhoods in Grand Rapids. Not only was the rent cheap, but we had the hazy idea that our presence was somehow beneficial. We weren't exactly the shining light on the hill that John Winthrop, our Calvinist forebear, extolled, but maybe we would be, someday. Meanwhile, our presence showed that we, white Christian college students, didn't think we were better than our black neighbors.

The leader had taken Karen. The rest of us were tied together like prisoners, in one long chain. The other intruder marched us up the stairs.

Our feet were bare, and the shuffling noises they made sounded piteous. I was almost glad to take my place in the dining room again, in sardine formation, on a carpet. This time I noticed how much floor space we took up. How could we be so many and yet so helpless? I also saw that the phone had been disconnected. I hadn't even thought about the phone as an escape route, only the door. My foolishness pierced me. They had caught us unaware and unprepared. No wonder they could prey upon us as they liked.

Events began to blur together. Over and over, one of the intruders would return to the dining room with the latest victim and choose the next. I could no longer catalog it all, like a dream that drags on. Each moment is so unreal, so intensely colored that you think you'll never forget it. But that very intensity pushes the previous moment out of mind.

My prayers lessened to a trickle. I could no longer hold everything in my mind at once. And what was the point? So I was a good girl. So what?

At one point I smelled cigarette smoke and turned my head to watch a red circle of ash travel through the darkness.

At another point an intruder brought Cheryl into the kitchen, saying he wanted a sandwich. I heard the refrigerator door open. Then came the angry shout: "You ain't got nothin'!"

"There's peanut butter," Cheryl said diplomatically.

"I don't want no peanut butter! Ain't you got baloney?"

"There's no baloney in this house," Cheryl said. "We don't eat processed meat."

Decades later, I remember that line exactly, along with her prim tone of voice, because wouldn't you?

At some point the leader kicked my feet and said "You" in that creepy, rough voice. I was instantly alert. I got to my feet and followed the prodding of the gun—up the stairs and into the large front bedroom that Karen and Lisa shared. He asked me which bed was mine. When he finally understood that my room was downstairs, he sprawled out on one of the beds as if he were going to take a break.

"What's your horoscope sign?" he asked.

"What?" I'd understood him, but I couldn't believe what he was asking.

He asked again, more forcefully this time.

I told him: Sagittarius.

His mask was still on, but I could see his lips protruding through the mouth hole. Then he pointed his gun at me and spit out one word: "Strip."

I pulled my flannel nightgown over my head and shivered.

"The rest," he said.

I peeled off my underpants.

He made me turn around. Then he told me to put my clothes back on and marched me back downstairs.

⁓

This is hard to admit. When he made me pirouette for him naked, I was overwhelmed with shame at the immodesty and utter violation of the situation. Still, I sucked in my stomach. That's right. I held in my stomach so I could look more attractive to the man who might rape me. That's how thoroughly I had internalized the fact that a woman should make herself attractive to the eyes of a man.

This single fact haunted me for years, which is why I tell it. It's a snapshot of the forces of submissiveness and shame and never-being-good-enough that shaped me, as they do so many women.

It seems especially ironic that the pressure to look pleasing to a man was so deeply instilled in us, given that we girls were also taught not to be vain. Our church's girls' club had a motto that we chanted at each meeting: "Grace is deceitful and beauty is vain; but a woman that feareth Jehovah, she shall be praised. Proverbs thirty-one verse thirty."

No one explained what the Bible verse meant. "Beauty is vain." I thought the word *vain* meant beauty pageants. Makeup. Gold jewelry. Fine clothes. Worldly things.

But that isn't the only definition for the word. *Vain* also means vanishing. Disappearing. Transitory. Fleeting. That night I learned about many things that are vain—things that vanish. Not just beauty, but also certainty. Hope. Faith. Even the future itself.

———

When I got back to the dining room with the leader, the intruders conferred. Then the other intruder marched me upstairs again with his gun in my back, this time to Marty's bedroom, at the back of the house. He sat on the bed and pointed his gun at me. He said the same thing the other one had said: "Strip."

Somehow this time felt different.

I took off my nightgown and underwear and waited, shaking. The shaking angered him. "Quit shaking, or I'll blow your brains out!"

"I can't help it." I couldn't stop crying either.

"Lay down on the bed," he said.

I crawled onto the bed, trembling. I couldn't see him clearly in the dark, and I didn't want to see him. I only wanted it to be over with.

Was that the faint scent of blood? I remembered the two tampons I had inserted before bedtime. Hours ago. A lifetime ago. I had my period, heavy flow. Now I wondered where the tampons would go and if they could pierce anything, and whether that would hurt.

He climbed on top of me. He had taken off his pants and jacket, but he was still wearing a pullover shirt and the ski mask. He moved awkwardly. I noticed the strange chemical smell again—a scent I couldn't place. His skin was hot and smelled like sweat. It occurred to me that the intruders were wearing much warmer clothes than we women were.

He kissed my breasts. "Do you like it when I do that?"

I didn't respond, so he repeated himself, more angrily.

I shrugged, but knowing he couldn't see me, I made some disgruntled noises.

"I got the gun right here," he threatened. "And I can let the other guy at you. I ast' for you special."

Finally I forced myself to speak. "I don't like it," I said.

"Why not? Don't you like it when your boyfriend do this?"

"I don't have a boyfriend."

"How come a pretty girl like you ain't got no boyfriend?"

Maybe I had a boyfriend. At least, I had a male friend who might be something more. His name was Jim. He was a funny guy, a drama geek. For the past year, he had spent huge amounts of time hanging around with me and my housemates. One evening six months earlier, right before our house disbanded for the summer, Jim and I had spent time together, just the two of us—an evening that included some sweet kisses.

Then I went to Wyoming for the summer, to take a seasonal job at Yellowstone. I worked in a kitchen and was part of a volunteer team that conducted Sunday worship services at the Old Faithful Inn. While I was gone that summer, Jim and I wrote to each other. His letters confirmed that he was everything I hoped for in a husband: kind, funny, adaptable. And he was a Christian, but not a nut job about it. So if he wanted to take things between us slow, I wouldn't push. Mostly because I didn't want to jeopardize the relationship, but also because of my housemates. Everybody loved Jim. Our group had wonderful camaraderie. If a dating relationship went bad, that would botch things up for everyone.

My rapist was obviously enjoying himself, grunting repeatedly. "That's good, that's good."

I spent most of my energy trying not to think, but the slightly metallic scent of blood invaded my mind. Everything felt slick. I willed myself to float up, to hover in the air over the bed instead of having to lie in it.

The rapist paused in the act, as if to prolong it, to savor it. The pause seemed particularly inhuman. I wanted it to be done so I could let out my breath and resume living. But I could only wait. I continued to hold my breath, but it didn't stop me from crying.

"Why you cryin'?"

I ignored him.

He stopped altogether and awkwardly wiped the tears from my cheeks. I couldn't help but notice the pinkish underside of his hand. His strangely tender gesture intensified my tears, adding confusion to my anger and pain. Why was he doing this? Was I a person to him or not? I hated him. I wanted to feel nothing but hatred. I didn't want to smell his sweat mingled with my blood. I couldn't bear the vulnerable pink of his palm. I didn't want him to be a person. To have a soul.

I concentrated on the gun beside my head, lying on the pillow. Could I feel it, cold and metallic beside my temple? Yes, I could. I focused on that bit of steel, that immediate bit of metal just outside my body, and stopped crying. Everything slowly stopped spinning. It turned out that the fear of dying, not just in the abstract, but in an immediate, proximate way, focused my mind.

I might die. I might cease to exist.

These weren't logical thoughts that my mind laid end to end. They were heartbeats, and each one held in itself the possibility of cessation. *This one, right now, might be my final heartbeat.*

I breathed in and out so I wouldn't float completely away from my heart.

When he was finally done, he climbed off me. He sat on the edge of the bed and got dressed, the gun between us. Then he looked through Marty's jewelry box in a desultory way and found some hard candy. He held a piece out to me, the plastic-wrapped globe in the center of his pink palm.

For a moment I considered taking it. What would it matter? Sugar to salve the pain. It was Marty's candy after all, not his. And then it hit me that everything in this room was Marty's. I had been raped on her bed. It was a fact. Unchangeable. It had happened and could never be undone. None of this night could be undone.

This was not how I wanted to be connected to Marty. This was not the bond we had cultivated. We were friends, a hard-fought friendship, already multilayered. What would our bond be now? Fellow victims? Perhaps I sensed, already, that this bond was too charged, that it would generate a rupture between us.

The rapist unwrapped Marty's candy and sucked on it. He told me to get dressed, watching my every move. I thought about the candy. I was thirsty. My mouth tasted bitter.

4

WHEN I WAS IN SEVENTH GRADE, I found a book on the coffee table in our living room, a slim volume with a heavy paper cover. The title was something like *Two Shall Become One*. I remember that my face felt hot as I held the book in my hands, studying the cover art. I scoffed at the picture even as I devoured the details. A tall man stood beside a short woman. The area where the female shoulder overlapped the male midsection was transparent, as if the two bodies merged there, approximately where the man's rib cage surrounded the woman's throat.

I knew immediately that my father must be considering this textbook for our school's health and PE curriculum. Perhaps he even meant for me to find it. Why else would he have left it lying there? I could imagine him handing it to our tall, gangly gym teacher, a single woman. Would she be condemned to cover this material with us? We would all die a thousand deaths.

I opened the book. For all my eye rolling, I didn't know exactly how two bodies became one. I had only the haziest idea of a boy's "thing" hanging down there. I skimmed the text rapidly. Anatomical details were lacking, but one point was clear: when two people join in sexual union, that bond is unbreakable, intended to last a lifetime. In the eyes of God, not only have two bodies joined, but so have two souls. Nothing besides death can split them apart.

The book's cover art seemed sobering, even ominous: when the male ribcage surrounds the female throat, that union can never be undone.

———

The intruder propelled me down the stairs with the gun pressed into my back. But I had lost interest in the gun. I had lost interest in the events of the night. I lay on the dining room floor where he cast me down.

I willed myself up and away. I left my body behind. I left my prayers lying beside my body, as helpless as I was. *Yea, though I walk through the valley of the shadow of death, I will fear no evil.*

Bullsh—.

At some point I heard a noise that brought me back into my body. The criminals were conferring. Suddenly I felt a thud beside me, someone being pushed down. Marty must have been taken out and returned while I was floating on the ceiling. Then one of them had me move into the living room, away from the others.

I lay facedown on the floor again, and he bound my wrists behind my back with some kind of cord. He hissed into my ear that if I moved, he would make the knots tighter. The explicit instructions brought me back to life. What did this lowlife know? As soon as he left, I tried to pull my hands apart so I could slip the knot the way they do in TV crime dramas. Instead, the cords tightened and bit into the skin of my wrists.

When we were all trussed up, the criminals collected their loot. They carried both of Marty's brown vinyl beanbag chairs out of the house, and they used our blankets to wrap up armloads of stuff.

I didn't pay much attention. They could have taken everything I owned. They already had. I just lay there, not praying.

Eventually the leader made an announcement in that creepy voice: "We're coming right back. So don't move." Then he left.

To me it sounded like a bluff. I sometimes babysat my younger sisters, so I knew those kinds of bluffs. As soon as the door shut, I sat up and began talking, but my friends hushed me. Chastened, I lay down again.

Eventually Teresa and Marty managed to untie each other's knots. Then they got a knife to cut the rest of us free. We worked silently. The cords around our wrists turned out to be speaker wire, not phone cord. The rotary phone had simply been unplugged. We relayed this information to each other quietly.

The emergency number for the police was on a sticker on the phone. Teresa dialed the seven digits carefully, each number spinning itself out. I didn't listen to what she told them. I was too busy thinking, *It's really over.*

We sat on the floor waiting for the cops. Marty said she was going to call her mother. Teresa said she should wait until the police came, in case they needed the phone. The two of them dickered, but quietly, until Karen interrupted. "Nobody's calling anyone!"

"I'll wait," Marty said. "But as soon as I can, I'm calling my mom."

"But if you tell yours, then I have to tell mine," Karen said. "Let's not tell anyone. This was stupid. So stupid!"

A wave of surprise washed over me. Could we really not tell anyone? It was an appealing thought. If we didn't tell, maybe this hadn't happened after all. Still, I was struck by Karen's word: *stupid.* I turned it over in my mind. Was this night stupid? To me it felt anything but. This night felt life altering. Irrevocable. It was the end of something. Maybe it was the end of everything. But it wasn't stupid.

Teresa said, "Karen's right. If one of us tells, we all have to tell. It'll get out. You know mothers."

"Fine," Marty said. "Do what you want. But I'm telling my mother."

Cheryl spoke up. "Of course we'll tell. Why wouldn't we?" She punctuated her proclamation with her trademark laugh, a throaty *ha-ha-ha* that shrugged off all further discussion.

———

Why did we consider not telling? In a word, because of shame. We hadn't named it yet, but we grasped it, like the tail of a great beast, never guessing how well acquainted we would become with it in the months and years ahead. We had no way of knowing how shame would manipulate us and twist us and thwart us, how it would cast a shadow over us and create a valley between us and all the women who had not been raped, how it would divide us even from one another.

Decades later, I can still look down from my spot on the ceiling at those exhausted young women surrounded by scraps of speaker wire as they argued about who to tell, and when. They were becoming theologians. They were asking, *Why did this happen to me? Where is God? Whom can I tell?* Like the biblical Tamar who was raped, they were crying out, *Where can I carry my shame?*

It's painful to know that they would continue to ask these questions for years, with an urgency never felt in Sunday school or catechism class or youth group or Bible class—questions that would rise like prayer from dark places, questions that would bounce off the ceiling and ricochet endlessly.

Until that night, I thought theological questions were beautiful and abstract, the place where interesting subjects inevitably led. I was the kind of student who pondered the meaning of redemption while I studied literature, my favorite subject. When I lived in Yellowstone's geyser basin, I mused about those strange, exploding water jets. So our majestic God favored a bit of surprise, did He? To me, thoughts about the nature of God were a source of deep comfort and security. My belief in God told me who I was and where I belonged. I believed the catechism lessons I'd been taught: that I belonged to my heavenly Father, who so cared for me that not a hair could fall from my head but by His holy will.

In high school, Marty and I had been in the same Reformed Doctrine class, which everyone called Ref Doc. I didn't want anyone to know how much I enjoyed that class. We were assigned papers on topics such as "What Man Can Become in Christ." I can still recall the teacher's graying curls, which jutted out from her head an inch before curving downward, their cylindrical shape a memory of the pink foam rollers she must have slept in. I can recall the platinum sheet of Marty's hair, which swayed when she made impassioned arguments. I can recall my own rippling reddish-brown hair, which I anchored at the temples with bobby pins to frame my pale face and eight-sided tortoiseshell glasses.

I still have the papers I wrote for Ref Doc, a surprisingly thick stack of yellowed notebook pages. It's been instructive to reread the theological thoughts of my seventeen-year-old self. One paper, titled "The Nature of Man," has the central question printed across the top: "Man, like every other animal, is born, breathes, eats, sleeps, and dies. What is it that sets him apart from the animals and makes him uniquely human?" In the four-page paper, written in my careful script, I quoted seven Scriptures, which I labeled "biblical passages," and three theological books. My last paragraph says, "In summary: man is made in the image of God. He consists of two parts, body and soul. He is totally depraved and therefore commits sin."

What strikes me now is not only the gendered language but also the fact that I knew what each of these words meant—and had never questioned any of them.

The teacher's red ink is still legible on the yellowed pages. She circled the words "biblical passage" and wrote, "If you capitalize your book titles, you should do the same with the Word of God!" It is the only comment on any of the four pages. The grade was an A minus. I'm sure I didn't give that grade another thought at the time—it was my usual grade in that class. Now the minus seems rather niggling. It is acceptable practice to use lowercase for the adjective *biblical*. In hindsight, I think the minus was actually an affirmation of the paper's central point. If total depravity is your baseline, nobody ever deserves a straight A. We will always fall short of perfection.

It was Teresa who opened the door for the police. They arrived quickly, two white men in blue uniforms. They brought the ordinary world back into that house of horror. We all began to cry and then to wail. The two officers took in the scene, their faces going carefully wooden.

Someone turned on more lights, revealing the disarray of a house that had been ransacked. One officer went through the rooms, his hand on his gun. The other officer pulled out a pocket-sized notebook and began asking questions and jotting down our answers. How many perpetrators? Race? Height? Build? Clothing?

My housemates answered quickly. I was amazed at their poise.

"Okay," the officer said. "As soon as I call this in, we'll begin a manhunt. Any idea how they got in?"

"Through the dining room window," Marty said. "That's my theory."

The dining room window? Wait . . . Marty has a theory?

The officer wrote something down and flipped his notebook shut. Then he went into the kitchen to make a call on his radio. When he returned, he said, "They're sending the crime lab truck. And we're alerting the hospital. You'll go there first. When you're finished there, you'll come to the station and we'll take a complete statement."

I didn't want to do any of that. I wanted to go back to sleep. No, I wanted to wake up from this nightmare. I wanted to undo what had been done. I wanted to erase everything, including all these tangled sensations. Shock. The residue of fear, like something burnt on my tongue. An almost giddy relief. An unaccustomed rawness between my legs. The beginnings of an anger so deep that it terrified me.

Meanwhile, the house filled with chaos and noise, but it was all in slow motion, as if this were a movie rather than real life. More officers arrived. Multiple conversations were going on at the same time. Some officers were on their knees looking at patches of carpet. Other officers spoke to me, but I couldn't take in what they were saying. I couldn't quite think to the end of a thought.

What's happening? What day is it?

Time had slipped a cog, and I was staggering in a sort of in-between world, like a car thrown out of gear, or maybe like someone knocked over by the surf. I couldn't get my legs under me.

We were told to get dressed and bring our nightclothes to the officers.

"Can we pee?" one of my housemates asked.

"No. Yes. Just try not to wipe. That's evidence."

I went into my bedroom to get dressed. It was the same windowed room I'd loved the day before. Now it was a scene of savagery. Items from my jewelry box were strewn on the floor. My bed was a tangle of blankets. I stared at it for a few moments before I realized that someone had been raped there—someone other than me. Karen? Yes, Karen. In a kind of twisted reciprocity, I had been made to pirouette naked while a rapist reclined on Karen's bed, and Karen had been raped on my bed.

I realized in that moment that I would never again sleep in this bed. But where would I sleep? Where would I live? What was going to happen to us?

Police radios squawked from the dining room. Someone in uniform was examining the area around the phone. I needed to get dressed. Needed to go to the hospital. Needed to move. But my closet seemed far away. I stepped over the jumble of jewelry and grabbed a turtleneck and jeans—the same clothes I would have worn to class in another lifetime.

But where could I get dressed? I couldn't take off my nightgown with the doors to the dining room open and an officer right there. But I didn't want to shut the doors and be alone in this bedroom. This crime scene. I went through the dining room, through the kitchen, toward the tiny half bath tucked beside the back door. With new eyes I regarded that door and its window, where two months before I'd hung a curtain in a cheery rose-colored print. I'd sewn the curtain myself in a flurry of activity just before I returned to school—it was an artifact of my happy anticipation of the year ahead. Now I didn't see the rosy curtain but the window glass it covered. I studied the door's ancient dead bolt. The criminals hadn't entered through this door, but couldn't they have? The door with its merry curtain suddenly seemed pathetic.

I went quickly into the half bath and pulled the door shut. To my relief, I could still hear the squawk of the police radio. I pulled off my soiled nightgown and panties. These weren't just laundry; they were "evidence." The underwear was trash, as far as I was concerned. But not the nightgown. I wanted to stuff that bundle of flannel in the washing machine and wash the night away. I loved that nightgown. I'd sewn it myself, imagining the late-night conversations it would hear. The pattern hadn't been simple to sew. It mimicked the popular Laura Ashley look, with a heavily gathered yoke, full sleeves, and abundant lace trim. I chose a bright-blue flannel printed with tiny sprigs of white flowers. I had to use my mother's buttonholer to make the front placket. When I was finished, I proudly turned the garment inside out so my mother could admire the craftsmanship of my French seams. I didn't want to think about a detective turning the garment inside out, looking for . . .

I brought the wadded-up clothing into the living room. A uniformed man crammed it into a bag and attached a label.

"I'd like that nightgown back when you're done," I told him. "But you can keep the underwear."

He nodded and made a note on the tag. He pointed toward another officer. "Talk to him. Tell him where the perpetrators touched something."

I went into each room with the officer and pointed at things. My wooden jewelry chest. The top of Marty's night table. Her jewelry box with candy.

"That's it?" the officer asked.

I nodded. "Mainly he touched the gun. And me."

"You're trembling," the officer commented. "Are you cold?"

I had forgotten I didn't have to be cold anymore. I went back into my bedroom to snatch my chamois shirt from its hook. The shirt was sage green, soft and oversized. It felt good to be warm and enveloped. Then, because I didn't want to be anywhere alone, I grabbed my hairbrush and stood in the living room, in the middle of the hubbub, brushing my hair.

In my teen years, my grandmother chided me for excessive hair brushing, saying it was a vanity. I never spoke back to her. But I remembered how Amy in *Little Women* protested when her sister Jo cut and sold her hair: "Oh, Jo, how could you? Your one beauty." Even the sober March family allowed women that small measure of vanity. So why couldn't I have at least this? My hair was thick and wavy and auburn. Brushing it calmed me.

I brushed my hair and looked in the mirror over the fireplace. The mirror reflected the officers working in official jackets, the letters backward. The mirror reflected my housemates getting ready to leave for the hospital. And the mirror reflected me. I was still there. But who was I? It had been a question even before this night changed everything.

5

"The woman problem."

That's what church people called the controversy over whether or not a woman could hold church office as deacon or elder. Although, as my mother muttered darkly, "It's not the women who are the problem."

I observed my mother walking a fine line. As the wife of a Christian-school principal, she was expected to be a model for others. And she was. All five of us siblings were in church every Sunday morning, properly dressed and shiny clean. We four sisters wore dresses that our mother had sewn. After church she served a roast beef dinner in her apron, often for guests. On Sunday evening we were all back in church. What made my mother unusual was that she had a career on top of all that. Fortunately, teaching in a Christian school was an acceptable choice for women—one of the few available.

One Sunday a visiting minister came to dinner. He praised my mother's roast beef, and then, when she brought up the role of women in the church, cut her off. "I don't like it any more than you do, but women are excluded from church office—that's clearly what God intends."

I remember the tone he used—a jailer's tone, at once stern and conciliatory, as if he'd been charged with enforcing a rule he hadn't made. He was only thinking of our own good.

"It's simply not God's will for women to serve in a church," he said.

"Anything other than coffee, you mean," my mother retorted.

I was surprised by her comeback and proud that she was not cowed. My mother was willing to question what was, and what wasn't, God's will. Especially for women.

Few of my friends were as interested as I was in "the woman problem"—except Marty. In college, she and Teresa and I had bonded over our discussions on the subject. One evening during our sophomore year, the three of us had walked across campus to Calvin Seminary to hear a lecture by a trailblazing woman named Marchiene Rienstra. She had earned a master of divinity degree at the seminary, but she couldn't get a position as a minister because the denomination refused to ordain her. After some preliminaries, Ms. Rienstra walked to the lectern, an ankle-length black dress swirling smoothly around her legs. For the next hour and a half, she worked her way through the "problem texts" regarding the role of women. She read the Scriptures without flinching, even the epistles' troublesome words about male headship—the words that seemed to lock us women inside a box.

I took notes as she quoted famous theologians, notes I still have. Some names were familiar—Augustine, Martin Luther, John Calvin—but others were new to me: Dorothy Sayers, Mary Daly, Rosemary Radford Ruether. I wrote as quickly as I could: "Christianity is a liberating force" and "Christianity has been used as a tool for patriarchal domination." I didn't fully understand the phrases I wrote or their implications, but I knew these ideas would be important to my life.

I was already passionate about equal rights for women. Teresa and Marty and I all were. Wasn't it obvious that guys should help wash dishes? That men and women should be paid equally for equal work? But I'd never applied these concepts to religion. The possibility seemed both tantalizing and radical.

Walking back to our dorm on that cool evening, with dry leaves underfoot, we were in such high spirits that we almost floated. Teresa held out her arms and spun around, saying, "Did you hear what she said? Women are whole people. We don't need a man to complete us."

I loved Teresa for homing in on that and saying it aloud. I wanted to believe it too—that I was complete without a man. I still wanted to get married, don't get me wrong. But I glimpsed a purpose that went beyond cooking a roast dinner on Sundays. What would it be like to wear a cool monkish dress and discuss theology in a public gathering? Maybe we really could have it all! I whirled around beside my friends, carried by the cool breeze.

It's a sweet memory. Isn't this youthful vision the kind of thing that binds friends together for a lifetime? These glimpses of liberation, these visions of a larger world.

———

Marty's brother, Pete, showed up while the police were taking pictures and dusting for fingerprints. Pete was almost a decade older than Marty, a bearded, bear-like guy. His very size was reassuring. I suppose Marty must have called him, though at the time I simply accepted his presence the way a child accepts a parent appearing in a sickroom.

Marty, Teresa, Cheryl, and I piled into Pete's ancient Buick to ride to St. Mary's Hospital. Karen was with her older sister, who had also appeared. We drove in tandem over hissing, wet roads. Apparently, while we were lying on the floor in terror or in beds being raped, God had sent rain to cleanse the streets of Grand Rapids.

I watched the glistening streets glide beneath the car. I listened to the rhythmic slapping of the wipers. They were like a metronome, measuring something. Maybe they were marking out the tempo of our new life, the tempo of *after*.

At stoplights I stared into other cars, at people who drank coffee out of travel mugs. To them, these were just wet roads, and this was just a rainy Monday morning. I was jealous of their lousy day. They still lived in *before*.

When we pulled into the emergency room entrance, nurses were waiting for us. They ushered us into examining rooms. Marty and I were put in a room that had two beds and was divided by a curtain. Someone handed us hospital gowns. Marty snapped that she was tired of being cold. I agreed. I didn't want to take off my chamois shirt.

Reluctantly, we undressed and put on the gowns. We got into the side-by-side beds and scooched under the thin sheets for warmth. A nurse came in and closed the curtain between us. Marty hopped out of bed to open the curtain, yanking it along its metal channel. The next person who entered the room pulled the curtain shut again. Marty hopped up and flung the curtain aside again.

The nurse, or aide, said something about protocol, but Marty would have none of it. Instead of dressing the person down with her usual verbal polish, Marty simply yelled, spitting profanity at the nurse, at all hospital personnel, at the hospital itself, at all hospitals everywhere. Even her scalp went red beneath her white-blonde hair. Her hospital gown flapped open, exposing her naked rear end. I laughed, but my laughter came out in strange little explosions, more like sobs.

A nurse appeared beside me and held my hand. Her hand was dry and warm, like my mother's. She spoke to me in a low voice. I had to gulp some air and settle down in order to hear her.

She asked if I would want to douche once the pelvic exam was over. She could get things ready. I told her I didn't think so. I'd never douched before. For that matter, I'd never had a pelvic exam before. I read the little brass nameplate pinned to her uniform: Nurse Terpstra. I read and reread that name, like a lifeline.

Two other nurses were scurrying about. They opened cupboard doors and laid instruments on two carts, one for Marty and one for me. They stopped to read directions and add more items. They kept conferring with each other.

"These are brand-new rape kits," Nurse Terpstra explained, still holding my hand. "It's our first time using them, and the instructions are complicated. You'll have to forgive us if we're slow." I just clung to her hand. The term *rape kit* struck me as beautifully bald, a plainspoken use of an unspeakable word.

When everything was finally ready, the doctor showed up. He was looking over the cart when he was called away again. For long stretches of time, absolutely nothing happened. Nurse Terpstra stood there holding my hand. The other nurses disappeared, came back, and left again.

There was nothing to do and nowhere safe to look. Various medical charts and diagrams were posted all over the walls. I expended considerable mental energy ignoring them. I didn't want to see any organs. No vaginas. No uteruses. No penises.

Finally the doctor returned. He said other patients had arrived with more urgent needs and he was sorry. I noticed that he had stubble on his face. He'd been working long enough to have stubble. He was young and handsome and exhausted. I felt sorry for him. He needed a nap. But of course he was called away again.

We waited, gowned, for another hour or more. At last the doctor was ready for us. He took care of Marty first while I tried to close my ears and eyes. I didn't want to know what would come next. I concentrated on handling this precise moment, no more.

At last they were done with Marty. She disappeared to get dressed, and the doctor came to the foot of my bed. The bustling nurses wheeled the tray into place and hovered behind the doctor. Nurse Terpstra was still at my side, near my head.

"The first step is to comb your pubic hair," Nurse Terpstra said. "To look for stray hairs. Evidence."

"Do I have to put my feet up?" I asked, thinking of movies I'd seen.

"Not yet," she said, squeezing my hand.

Later, at the trial, I would hear more about the hair and semen samples they gathered that day. But in 1978, the world of forensic evidence was unknown to the general population. The grittiest crime drama on TV was *Quincy, M.E.*, and that was still new. It would be eight years before DNA testing was used to solve crimes, twenty years before *Law & Order: Special Victims Unit* pulled back the covers on prosecution for sexual assault.

The doctor stood at the side of my bed with a comb and focused on his work with great intensity. The nurses stood on the other side of the bed. Three heads were bent low over my pelvis. The indignity of the situation flooded me with embarrassment.

As the doctor fished out hairs, he slid them into a paper envelope. When he was finished, he straightened up. "Who knows?" he said. "Maybe we'll be lucky. Maybe one of these will help them catch those . . . clowns."

Clowns? I was surprised by his word choice. I knew he was tired, but what kind of word was that? The police had called them perpetrators. Nobody said rapists, which was what they were. The word was truly unspeakable.

With a clang, the nurses assembled the stirrups. When I saw the metal grips, I willed myself to go numb again. This was the dreaded pelvic exam. I felt a hand grip my heel and guide my bare foot into the cold metal holder. A nurse coached me to slide down toward the doctor while someone draped a sheet across my knees.

I whispered to Nurse Terpstra that I didn't want the sheet—I wanted to see what they were doing.

"Of course." She pulled off the sheet, to the consternation of the other nurses.

After that, the doctor narrated everything he was going to do. He took his time. "This is called a speculum. It might feel cold."

That was an understatement. When he inserted the metal instrument, it felt like a gallon of cold water was being poured into my body.

I whispered to Nurse Terpstra about the tampons. She leaned over and said something to the doctor, then resumed her station near my head.

The doctor glanced at me and asked for a vial. Then he extracted a soiled tampon, the blackened string hanging uselessly from the clamp. The other nurses gasped, which made me hate them. The doctor dropped the tampon into the vial. Then he pulled out the second one, similar to the first.

When the bloody business was safely sealed away, he adjusted his light and peered between my legs. I imagined the black-red blood that coated my insides. Was there some kind of wound, some evidence of what had been done to me?

"Everything looks fine," the doctor said simply. He put down his tools and peeled off his gloves.

The nurses shot glances at me as they switched off the lamp and tidied up. Nurse Terpstra helped me into a sitting position.

She suggested again that douching might be a good idea. Again, I wavered. She assured me that she would take care of everything—I just needed to sit on the toilet.

"Can you do that?" she asked.

"Yes," I said, in barely more than a whisper.

She guided me to a bathroom and got everything ready while I sat on the toilet. Then she stood beside me holding a clear plastic bag. The liquid ran down the tube and into my vagina and back out again. The tears ran down my face. Neither of us spoke until it was done.

"Now you're all clean," Nurse Terpstra said.

Am I? I didn't feel clean. I felt ruined.

6

Now I wonder about the timeline of feeling ruined. Did the feeling begin that night, or had it taken root years earlier, when I came to believe I could never be good enough? Maybe the rape, and the despair that followed, gave me the words to describe the way my Calvinist upbringing sometimes made me feel.

One of my earliest church memories comes from the end of second grade. Each of the students had to meet with the minister individually before we could progress to the next grade of Sunday school. The reverend was a terrifying man, tall and gaunt, with bushy eyebrows and a thundering voice. After church one Sunday, he ushered me into an empty classroom for my inquisition. He was wearing his preaching suit, dark colored and sober, and I was wearing my Sunday dress, pastel and poofy. I looked up from my patent leather shoes, past his eyes, and focused on those eyebrows. The individual hairs cast shadows on his forehead. I knew that this was what Moses looked like. Maybe it was even what God looked like.

His voice rumbled: "Ruth, tell me. Why do you love Jesus?"

I said the first thing that popped into my mind—a line from a hymn: "Because He first loved me."

"That's right. He died on the cross for you." The reverend grabbed one of my hands and drove his index finger into the center of my palm. "He loved you so much He had *nails* driven into His hands for you."

I wanted to pull my hand away but didn't dare.

"Without Him, you are nothing, do you hear me? Nothing!"

———

After douching, I got dressed and was told to go to the waiting room, where the rest of our group had gathered. Before I pushed open the door, I looked through the small window in the top half. Across the expanse of linoleum, I saw Karen and her sister in an embrace. Lisa, our absent housemate, was talking to Marty. Teresa was with her boyfriend, Sam. Cheryl was paging through a magazine. Marty's brother, Pete, was sitting stoically in a chair, and beside him was Jim. My Jim. My heart beat faster. I hadn't presumed to call him. How did he know I was here?

I pushed open the heavy door. Jim saw me and rose from the molded plastic seat. I wanted to rush to him for a bear hug, rough and warm. I wanted to feel enveloped and safe. But I believed it wasn't proper for a woman to make the first move, so I walked slowly toward Jim. We hugged awkwardly.

Pete had appointed himself our shepherd. He gathered everyone and announced that it was time for breakfast. His voice boomed through the waiting room. "Who's hungry?"

We caravanned to a Big Boy restaurant on Michigan Street. Normally I loved going out for breakfast with a group, but I have no recollection of that meal—what we ate or what we talked about.

"You can't talk about the crime, not until you give your statements to the detectives," Pete told us. "The police were very clear about that. After breakfast we'll go to the police station for fingerprinting. It's all standard procedure." Pete spoke with reassuring calm, as if he'd done all this before. I didn't even stop to wonder how he knew what he knew. "But the detectives are backed up for a couple of hours, so why don't you go get some sleep first? God knows you must be tired. Ruth, you can go with Jim."

By now the rain had turned to drizzle. Jim drove me to the house he shared with another college student, in a bad part of town. I wondered if Pete had asked Jim to take care of me, but I didn't dare ask.

Jim led me into the basement, saying it might be easier for me to sleep where it was dark. He assured me he'd be just upstairs if I needed anything.

I lay down on a mattress on the floor and tried to sleep, but I was too exhausted and unnerved. Occasionally I heard a noise like a plop—the sound of water gathering and falling just outside the basement windows. I told myself it was nothing, to just tune it out. But I couldn't. Then I heard footsteps—an intruder! I cried out, sitting bolt upright. But it was only Jim, coming down the stairs with a cup of tea. He apologized repeatedly for frightening me.

I didn't care much about the tea, but I sipped it. I wanted Jim to stay. I wanted him to lie next to me. But I didn't know how to ask. I didn't know what it would mean if I did ask. So I lay on the mattress on the floor, wide awake, and listened to his footsteps retreat up the stairs.

Sleep would not come. Finally I gave up trying and went upstairs. Jim was sitting at a table by the front window in the living room. He was staring out at the gloom and smoking a cigarette.

"I didn't know you smoked," I said.

He extinguished it. "I don't. These are my housemate's."

"So what?" I told him. "Smoke away."

"Can't you sleep? Want something to eat?" He seemed happy at the thought of feeding me.

"Sure."

He rummaged in the fridge and found some eggs and a single onion. "I wish we had some cheese," he said. "But what can I say? We're pretty primitive here—just a couple of guys."

I sat at the rickety kitchen table and watched him cook. There was something reassuring about his matter-of-fact movements, as if this were just a day and we were doing the things a person did in a day. First Jim chopped some of the onion finely and fried it in butter. When the onion turned golden, he scraped it into a bowl and set it aside. He beat two eggs and poured them into the pan. He lifted the edges of the egg so it would cook evenly and, at the right moment, added the cooked onion. Then he folded the omelet and slid it onto a plate. At the time, I worked as a waitress at a breakfast restaurant on the weekends. I'd watched many cooks make countless omelets. But I'd never watched anyone make an omelet with such care.

"I really wish I had some cheese," Jim repeated as he set the plate in front of me. Then he sat down to watch me eat. Neither of us spoke as I ate that sacrament of onion omelet.

I wanted it to be enough, but Jim was right. Cheese would have been nice.

When it was time to meet the others at the police station, Jim drove me there. I had mental images of how it would look, based on episodes of *Dragnet*. But real life is different from TV. The police station didn't look like a bastion of efficiency and justice. It looked like a mobile trailer.

Several police officers stared at the five of us victims as we filed in. There were no words of welcome. The officer who took my fingerprints did the job roughly, without speaking. He grabbed my hand and manipulated it to isolate my thumb; then he pulled my thumb toward an ink pad, rotating it against the blue-black sponge. His next move was to yank my blackened thumb toward a piece of cardboard with marked-off boxes, where he rolled the inky digit in the appropriate spot. He repeated the process nine more times. He made the movements jerkily, as if he were angry about having to do this.

Well, me, too.

We met our detectives, two of them. One was big and talkative and fatherly; the other was compact, quiet, eagle-eyed. They knew we'd been up all night and were exhausted, so they interviewed us as a group, to speed things along. The first thing they asked about was the weapons the perpetrators used. I immediately felt like I'd failed a pop quiz. I should have gotten a better look at the guns. It had been so dark. And when either gun was close to me—trained on me or touching me—I'd gone blank. Now the detectives' simple questions filled me with self-incrimination. *Why did I hide my head and pray when I could have been useful?*

Teresa asked, "Have these guys done other crimes?"

Maybe they had. A whole string of them. But we couldn't discuss that.

The detectives asked us to recount the chain of events, including as much detail as possible. "Start at the beginning. What's the first thing you remember?"

By this point, we'd been awake some thirty hours. We were exhausted. We were in shock. Now, as a group, we needed to reconstruct a detailed timeline for events that had unfurled over a span of hours. Hours of confusion and darkness. Hours we wanted to forget.

"The first thing I remember?" Marty had been the first to see a masked intruder. She caught a glimpse of him in the dining room when she headed to the kitchen for a midnight snack.

"I'm always hungry," she explained with a rueful laugh. "Always."

She continued, "I saw someone in the corner. I couldn't even scream, I just turned around and ran up the stairs and into Teresa's room—"

"Stairs?" the detectives asked.

And so it went. Every sentence required a rewind button. Whose room was whose? Where was the staircase?

Then we began the story again with the other intruder, the one in my bedroom. I told about the kitchen light coming on, seeing Cheryl come up the stairs—

No, the other stairs. The basement stairs.

It took forever to get us all into the dining room and on the floor—a circumstance that in real life had taken just minutes. It was like trying to explain plot points to someone who walked in during the very last scene of an episode of *The Rockford Files*. To make matters worse, we could hardly tell the main characters apart. We needed some way to keep the intruders straight. Since it was dark and they were masked, we went by their voices. We called the one with the rough, low voice "the leader" and the other one "the accomplice." Because that's how it had seemed to all of us.

Our timeline was complicated, because with two intruders and five victims, events overlapped. We went forward and back with the intertwining story lines. We kept losing our place. Who was taken out when? By which one? To which room? I wanted to cry in frustration and exhaustion. Mainly I just wanted to be done talking about this. I wanted to forget it, forever. I told myself we needed to tell the story this once. Get it right. Then never talk about it again.

Because it was bad. Even worse than I'd thought. It turned out that Marty, like me, had been raped by the accomplice. So had Karen and Teresa. But Karen and Teresa had also been raped by the leader. They had each been raped *twice*. Which was so disturbing that I hardly knew what to do with that information. My friends had suffered doubly.

Just as shocking, perhaps, was that Cheryl had not been raped at all. In fact, she hadn't realized what was happening to the rest of us. When she heard our stories, her eyebrows raised and her mouth dropped open in surprise.

Under ordinary circumstances, the word I'd use to describe Cheryl is *imperturbable*. I'd known her since seventh grade. Even then she was probably five foot ten. When we were sophomores in high school, she once persuaded Marty and me to tromp into a fancy French restaurant in New York City with her, even though we were wearing jeans and clodhopper boots. She ordered snails and proclaimed them "Sublime!" while the tuxedoed waiter looked on, unamused.

But now even Cheryl looked agitated.

Of course I was glad that she had been spared. But did she really not know what was going on in those bedrooms? Could she possibly be that naive? By some strange logic, I both scorned and envied her naiveté. She had lived through the same night as the rest of us, but not really. I suddenly saw that innocence is a privilege, granted only for a time, only to a few—a privilege I hadn't known I had until it was taken from me.

I wasn't the only one who wondered why Cheryl had gotten special treatment. The detectives probed at this. They acknowledged that her height might have made a difference. Cheryl was taller than either of the assailants. But the detectives zeroed in on a single moment in each of our stories—a scrap of dialogue, an especially bizarre interaction in the midst of a surreal night. It was the moment the leader asked each of us our horoscope sign.

"Do you think that mattered?" one of my housemates asked.

"I think it did," the detective said. "Tell me again, Cheryl. What sign are you?"

"Virgo." She let out a throaty laugh. "Was that the right answer?"

"It must have been," the detective said.

There was a moment of stunned quiet as that soaked in.

"Golly," Teresa said with a choked laugh, "I wish I'd known to say Virgo."

"So you think they treated us by our sign?"

"I do," one of the detectives replied. "Though it's just a theory at this point. And who knows how far it goes. But they were certainly rougher with some of you than others."

So our fate had depended on our answer to a single fruitcake question? It was incomprehensible. I refused to believe it. And even if we'd somehow guessed the question's significance, we still couldn't have known the right answer.

The right answer was *not* Sagittarius. That much was clear.

By the alignment of the stars, quite literally, Cheryl had gotten the answer right. She won the jackpot. She strode through even the valley of the shadow of death unscathed. Was that God's doing, or random luck? If it was God's doing, why Cheryl? Why was she alone spared?

As much as I cared for my friend, I suspected that this would change our relationship forever. I had trouble looking at her creased brow or listening to her exclamations of pity.

⌒

Around four o'clock, the detectives gave us a break. We talked about where we would spend the night. Teresa said I could stay with her, at her sister's house. But of course I had a sister too. I just wasn't thinking. I used the station phone to call Mary Lynn. I told her where I was and what had happened. She was shocked. We'd been together just the day before. Hadn't we? It seemed impossible. Time had no meaning.

"Anyway, can I stay with you tonight?"

"Of course. I'll come get you. Tell me where you are again."

The five of us reassembled, and the detectives resumed their questions. Even after we'd mapped out the events of the night, there were so many things they wanted to know. Tiny details, each one requiring focus. Every defining characteristic about the assailants. Each one's clothing. Bodily features. Smell. Any facial features we could detect through the masks. Exactly what they said, both the words they used and their tone of voice. The relationship between the two of them, and why, exactly, we thought one was the leader. What type of knots they used to tie us up. The items they carried out of the house. What they used to carry them. Which door they left through. The sound of the getaway car.

By this time we'd been answering questions for about four hours. Just tracking with the interrogation took tremendous effort. First to follow the detectives' questions. Then to digest my housemates' responses. To sort out what was the same, or different, from my experience. What could I add? What might make a difference? It seemed critical to help the detectives. What smidgeon of information might be the one that caught the criminals? The stakes seemed very high.

The detectives wrote down snippets of dialogue, word for word. Cheryl said the leader had asked her, "Where's your TV?"

She laughed as she recounted her response: "We're college students—we don't have a TV. But we have plenty of books!"

"You certainly kept your sense of humor," one of the detectives commented.

"Do you think that's why they didn't rape her?" someone asked.

"Could be. Could be."

As the possibility hung in the air, I felt its unintended accusation on the rest of us—we who had gotten raped, we who had been so humorless.

Meanwhile, our relatives had arrived to pick us up. Still, the detectives were loath to let us go. They were in hyperdrive, hyperfocused. "Just one more question, okay?" We all tried to help. But I was keenly aware of how much I had failed to take in, how many details I had blocked from my awareness.

Sometimes you hear about crimes on the news and you think, *How did that happen?* You know you'd be so smart, so brave, if it happened to you. You'd alert the police somehow. You'd outwit the bad guys. Maybe you'd talk them out of it. But no. When it happened, I just ground my face into the carpet and waited for it to be over. No heroics from me. No humor. Just survival.

7

WHEN THE DETECTIVES DISMISSED US, my sister Mary Lynn was waiting for me. I asked her to take me to the Alexander house so I could get my overnight things before heading to her place. The drive to the house—the crime scene—wasn't long, maybe fifteen minutes. I have no memory of it. My sister, however, remembers that drive vividly. Thirty-seven years later, she was able to recount the details of our conversation and the circumstances around it. For her, it capped what had already been a life-changing day.

That morning Mary Lynn had received long-awaited news about her son's medical condition. Danny was eighteen months old, and it was clear that something was wrong with his development. He couldn't walk yet, or even crawl. Tests had been done, and Mary Lynn and her husband, Roger, had gotten the doctor's report that very morning. The news wasn't good. There was no exact diagnosis, and the cause was unknown—other than lack of oxygen to the brain at some point in utero—but the doctor was quite sure that Danny's condition would be lifelong. He might never learn to walk. He might be completely dependent for his entire life.

Although I didn't know it, Mary Lynn had listened to the doctor explain these facts while I watched the rain fall and collect outside the window in Jim's basement. Life would never be the same for either my sister or me again. Our different but equally devastating crises had happened in synchrony. To this day, I find it astounding that both of these life-altering events occurred in the same twenty-four-hour period. Should that timing be chalked up to coincidence, or was it divine Providence?

Looking back from a safe distance, I better understand that moments like these are precisely when life takes shape. This is when we exercise our free will. Call it making sense of things, if you like. Call it making meaning when things don't make sense. It's what humans do. It's perhaps the most human thing we do. We make meaning. We soldier on.

Over the next months and years my sister and I did exactly that, but in very different ways. The gulf between us widened, painfully. It helps me to remember how young we both were when our crises transpired: Mary Lynn was just a week past twenty-six; I was not yet twenty-one.

⸺

I left the police station and climbed into my sister's car. I told her the bare bones of what had happened: the attackers, the hours on the floor, the rape. They were shocking events, of course, but I'd been thinking about nothing else for hours. Mary Lynn says that I spoke with absolute calm, almost robotically. We were both in a state of shock, although we didn't realize it. Maybe that's why I said what I did. As she tells it, I said, "It's not that big a deal. It's not like it's the first time I've been raped."

Then I told her something that had happened to me the previous summer, when I was working in Yellowstone. It's not much of a story—at least, I didn't make it into one. I told her I'd gone backpacking by myself when I had some days off. I met two guys who seemed like good guys, so we hiked together. It seemed safer than being alone. That night one of them made a pass at me. "He wouldn't take no for an answer." Those are the words she repeated back to me more than three decades later.

I am amazed at the clarity of my sister's memory. I don't remember telling her the story—and in fact, I'm surprised I did tell it. I must have been brimming over with guilt and the need to confess. Because of our five-year age difference, Mary Lynn was something of a mother figure to me. She and I were both raised to be good girls and believed what we'd been taught: that it was of supreme importance for a woman to be sexually pure.

Whatever my reason for telling her all those years ago, I trust my sister's recall of the conversation. Those are exactly the words I would have used. I would have spoken in code, in innuendo, in language avoiding blame. *He wouldn't take no for an answer.* That language hardly conveys what actually happened. I woke up with that man in my sleeping bag, on top of me, inside of me!

Decades later, I would like to be more truthful and wipe away the shilly-shally. That "good guy" took advantage of my naiveté and trust. He broke the unspoken social contract that exists between acquaintances, the contract that says to do no harm while a person sleeps. Not only was I easy prey and unable to fend him off, but my shame kept me silent. I blamed myself for hiking alone.

He wouldn't take no for an answer. My words reflected my beliefs. That it's normal for men to attempt rape. That it's up to women to make men stop. That women are unable to make men stop. My former self believed all those things, God help her.

But perhaps that's one of the gifts of doing any kind of sustained, prayerful self-reflection: taking an unflinching look at who you used to be, and then loving yourself anyway.

When Mary Lynn and I arrived at the Alexander house, all was in chaos. All the victims plus assorted relatives were there, moving through the rooms. In the kitchen, someone had the refrigerator door open and was emptying its meager contents into a garbage bag. Fingerprinting powder covered every flat surface, a layer of filth. In the dining room, pieces of severed speaker wire still littered the floor. Our possessions were strewn everywhere—clothing and jewelry and knickknacks—things the criminals had evidently rummaged through and not taken.

I tried to focus on what I needed for the next day: my toothbrush, schoolbooks, clothes. Mary Lynn helped me gather things into a pile. "I lost my purse," I told her. "I have no idea where it is."

"Oh, I know! It's at my house. You left it in my car. I found it yesterday when I got home from church."

Church was yesterday? My life was like an episode of *The Twilight Zone*. We had somehow stepped outside normal time.

"I guess forgetting it turned out to be a blessing," Mary Lynn said. "Thank the Lord for his care for us."

I stared at my sister's face, so smooth and oval, so much like my own. She wore a soft, eager smile. Even in that moment, I recognized that she was trying to find something positive to say about this awful situation. I would need to forgive her for saying this. This wasn't the Lord's care. This was something different. Maybe I could forgive her later. But at that moment, what I understood was that we had very different notions of God, and of God's care for us. I felt a sense of panic. Where was He, anyway? I felt so utterly alone.

Teresa went past, her arms full of belongings. She looked unflappable and calm. I grabbed her arm. "Come with me to my sister's house."

Teresa looked at me with dry eyes. We were both years older than we'd been twenty-four hours before.

"Okay, Ruthie," she said. "As long as there's a bathtub. The doctor says I need to soak."

"Why?" I asked.

"Lacerations," she said simply.

———

Teresa had never been to my sister's house, so I rode with her to tell her the way. Teresa's beater car was broad and beige and banged up, oddly comforting. We didn't speak, except when I gave directions.

Lacerations. I suddenly realized that I'd had it easy, that the menstrual blood had made everything slippery. I felt a pang of gratitude for that fact, but also guilt, since my friend had suffered more than I had.

When we arrived at my sister's house, she had already gotten out bath towels and Epsom salts for Teresa. The small bathroom was spotless. Mary Lynn asked if there was anything else we needed. I knew I could have asked her for anything at all and she would have given it to me. My sister was doing her best to love me in this impossible situation, and I did my best to love her back.

While Teresa soaked in the bathtub, I perched on the closed toilet lid. We talked about the next day, about logistics. We were used to coordinating schedules for rides and meals. Teresa squirmed a bit in the tub.

"Do you hurt?" I asked.

She shrugged it off. She was never the fragile-flower type. "Just cramps. From the pill they gave us, I guess."

"What pill?"

"Some kind of morning-after pill," Teresa said. "Didn't they give you one?"

I felt a sense of narrow escape. "I guess I didn't need it. I'm on my period."

So that was another reason to be glad for my womanly blood. I'd been spared any internal debate about taking such a pill. It was all too much to think about right now. I couldn't even form the word *pregnancy* in my mind.

———

I left the bathroom to give Teresa some time alone. Downstairs, Mary Lynn was waiting for me. She asked if I was ready to call our parents. "It's time," she said. "It's after five, so it's evening rate."

"I almost never call them," I said. "It's so expensive."

"I've called a few times recently, about Danny. Actually, they're expecting me to call tonight."

"Do you want to talk to them?" I was unaware of the news the doctor had delivered earlier that day.

"No. Not now. Tonight is your news," Mary Lynn said. "And if they ask about Danny, don't say anything. There's plenty of time for that."

Even though I'd been anticipating this conversation all day, I didn't feel ready for the phone call. How long ago had Teresa cut the cords that the rapists used to bind my wrists? How long ago had all of us discussed whether or not to call our parents? I just needed to get this over with. This conversation. This day. This nightmare.

How do you tell your parents news like this?

I asked if they'd heard anything. They had not. In as few words as possible, I told them the most basic facts. Our house had been broken into by two men with guns. I had been raped. We had all been raped. Well, most of us had been. It was complicated. Yes, we had called the police. We had gone to the emergency room. I was with Mary Lynn now.

"I'm all right," I said by way of summary.

After a brief silence, my mother asked if there was any news about Danny. I said I didn't know. Mom asked to speak to Mary Lynn. I held the phone out to my sister, who shook her head and gestured for me to keep talking.

"But Mom asked for you." I shook the phone at her. "Really."

"They're in shock," Mary Lynn said. "Of course." She took the phone from me, the long cord stretching between us. I listened to my sister's side of the conversation.

"It's not as bad as it could be, but it's bad enough." Pause.

"It's really hard to know." Pause.

"We'll just have to see how things develop." Pause.

"Yes, I know this is God's will, and I trust Him for all things." Pause.

My sister looked tense. One hand held the phone to her ear, and the other twisted the telephone cord around and around. When I caught her eye, she shook her head slightly and turned away. I might as well leave the room.

8

PEOPLE OFTEN SAY THAT WE CHOOSE OUR BELIEFS. The image that comes to mind is Internet shopping, where it's possible to scan the alphabetical list from asceticism through Zoroastrianism, dragging the most appealing beliefs and practices into a shopping cart.

Or maybe there's an element of critique to it, like watching a movie and pronouncing, "This plot is full of holes. This deity character makes no sense. The whole thing needs a few more laughs." As if one might then shelve it, a doctrinal system to hold in reserve until something better comes along.

Or maybe this idea of choosing theology is a sampling process, like tasting a flight of wines. "I don't find that doctrine particularly palatable," someone might say, wrinkling his or her nose. "Give me something sweeter." Or "I'll skip the full-bodied reds altogether. Too heavy." We take the mixed case only if we can choose each vintage.

But that's not the way I came to my beliefs. In the Christian Reformed Church, there was no shopping, no critiquing, no sampling. No shelving, no mixing, no choosing. My—*our*—theological system was inherited as a package deal, a complete way of understanding the world.

Here's the Reformed worldview in a nutshell, meant to be ingested in one swallow. The sovereignty of God means that God is supreme and rules over all. Nothing can happen apart from God's will. Total depravity means that we are sinful in every part of our being. Redemption means that despite our sinfulness, God loves us and saves us. Well, some of us anyway—the ones who are elected to salvation, which is referred to as limited atonement. Predestination means that God has already chosen the people who will choose Him. Perseverance of the saints means that once a person is saved, there's no going back; it's a forever deal. Bottom line: if you believe in God and are saved, then you're chosen, and so are your children. That's called "covenant theology," although there's more to the covenant, of course. Still, the family package is the spoonful of sugar that makes the whole system go down.

This belief system was my birthright. My indoctrination into it started early and never flagged. Every day, Monday through Friday, the school day began with Bible class. On Sundays my family went to church both morning and evening, plus an hour of Sunday school. In late elementary school we added a midweek catechism class after school, which prepared us to make a public profession of faith. Our girls' club met on Wednesday evenings, and the boys had their own club too. During high school, both girls and boys converged into youth group on Sunday evenings. Within this busy cocoon of church and school, learning the Bible and doctrine reigned supreme. Our belief in Calvinism set us apart from the rest of the world, both because we paid so much attention to it and because its teachings ensured our position as covenant people: fallen and depraved, but God's elect.

Although it was never a conscious thought, I simply assumed that we Dutch people were better than everyone else. In our church's parking lot, cars sported the bumper sticker "If ya ain't Dutch, ya ain't much." Maybe it was supposed to be a joke; maybe it wasn't. But I felt sorry for anyone who wasn't us. Not that I really knew anyone who wasn't. We didn't mix much with the world.

———

I began attending our church's girls' club in fifth grade, when we moved to New Jersey. The name of the club was Calvinettes, which seemed perfectly natural to me. Every Wednesday evening after supper, I put on a white-collared blouse, a true-blue skirt that my mother had sewed for the purpose, and a triangular scarf with badges. My mom drove me to church.

As with most church-related activities, I both loved and hated Calvinettes. I dreaded one more opportunity to reveal how uncool I was, a Midwestern girl who pronounced long vowels. I couldn't say a word like *radiator* or *roof* without being laughed at. I avoided saying my own name aloud, with its pesky long *u*. But I loved eating snacks and earning badges and talking about God. All the while, the club motto rang in my ears: "Grace is deceitful and beauty is vain."

One particular Wednesday evening stands out in my memory. We were sitting in the usual circle of folding chairs, including the leader, who was a teacher from the junior high. Since I sometimes helped my father in the school office, the teachers were familiar to me. In that context I saw them as individuals, but when I was in public, I pretended I didn't know them. I continued the pretense that night at Calvinettes, even though I felt sorry for the teacher. She had just moved from the Midwest too and talked the way I did. She also looked as unhappy as I felt. I worried about her. She was single and overweight. How would she ever find a husband, or happiness?

From her metal chair, the leader laid out the lesson: some people are destined for heaven, and some are destined for hell. This is called predestination. God makes the choice.

It wasn't the first time we'd heard this. One Calvinette, Brenda, raised her hand to ask the question I'd never dared to frame: "But doesn't God love everybody the same?"

"It's true that God loves everybody," the teacher said. "But it's also true that not everyone is saved."

"That doesn't seem fair." Brenda wrinkled her nose in distaste.

"Remember that God's ways are greater than our ways." The teacher leaned forward in her folding chair, her body straining to fold in the right places. "Imagine that God is sitting on His throne, just like I'm sitting on this chair. Around His feet are all the people of the world." She let her hands drop toward the floor and swished them around.

"All the people who ever lived anywhere?" Lauren asked. She was always the teacher's pet.

"Exactly. At God's feet are all the people who have ever lived anywhere." The teacher's hands swooped about, stirring the people pot. "All the people in Europe and Africa and even China. People with every skin color. They are all spread at God's feet, and they are all lost."

"You mean lost from God," Lauren said.

"Yes. And isn't that a sad thing?" The teacher's down-turned mouth invited us to mimic her expression. Then her eyebrows lifted. "But God doesn't leave them there. He reaches down into the sea of people"—she swooped one hand into the masses at her feet—"and He scoops up a precious few." She carefully pulled her cupped palm to her lap, then held it out to us, like an offering. "This is where you and I are, girls. Safe in God's hand. Safe in the covenant."

That's when I surprised myself by asking a question. "What about Davey DelGaudio?" Davey's family lived next door to us. They were the only non-Dutch family I spent much time with. Davey was friends with my younger sister Beth. "Is Davey in God's hand too?"

"Does Davey love the Lord?" the teacher asked.

"I don't know," I said. "He's Catholic."

"Does he go to church?"

"Not much," I said truthfully. "Not nearly as often as we do."

"Then probably not," the teacher said. She used the same matter-of-fact tone she might have used if she were passing back a test with red-ink corrections.

Brenda asked straight out, "Do you mean he's going to hell?"

"I'm afraid so."

I'd always suspected as much, but nobody had ever said it aloud before. Tears sprang to my eyes. The truth was, I didn't care much about Davey, but he had an older brother, Victor, who was the most handsome boy I'd ever seen, with black hair and piercing dark eyes. I could sometimes glimpse a necklace in his open collar. I had a secret plan to convert Victor and marry him when we grew up.

"It doesn't seem fair," I managed to say.

"We are not to question God," the teacher said. "But if you feel bad, you can always invite him to church."

Lauren said, "You can save him, Ruth! Think of it! You can save the whole family." Her eyes were shining.

"Oh, forget it," said Brenda. "If God wants him saved, somebody else can do it, right?"

"No," said Lauren, "that's not right."

"The teacher just said it's all figured out ahead of time! If God wants him saved, he'll get saved."

All eyes turned to the teacher, awaiting her verdict.

"Well, it never hurts to invite someone to church," she said weakly.

I imagined Davey and Victor and their family walking through the door of our church. Their mother had black hair that she teased into a bouffant whenever she left the house. She wore tight-fitting skirts and sequined tops, even to the grocery store. She had an entire wardrobe of false eyelashes. Davey showed them to me once, a drawerful of little packages holding spidery bits. I tried to imagine

Mrs. DelGaudio walking down the center aisle of our concrete-block church, her heels clicking on the linoleum floors, her blouse all sparkly and her hair all poofed out. I couldn't imagine it.

There was no hope for them.

PART 2

THE AFTERMATH

November 1978–August 1979

*My God, I cry out by day, but you do
not answer, by night, but I find no rest.*

PSALM 22:2, NIV

Remember that you own what happened to you.

ANNE LAMOTT

9

On Monday night—twenty-four hours after the intruders broke into our home—I was finally able to get some rest, at least for a few fitful hours. I slept in a single bed in Mary Lynn's tiny spare room, while Teresa had a mattress tucked under the eave in Danny's nursery.

The next morning when I came down to the kitchen, Mary Lynn was gone, but I found a cheery note and twin lunches all packed, complete with little bags of carrot sticks. Teresa and I drove to the Calvin campus in her battered car. We had arranged to meet Marty and Cheryl in the coffee shop at lunchtime. Even though we hadn't slept at all on Sunday night and had slept in strange beds on Monday night, we were determined to make it to class on Tuesday morning, as if we were indomitable.

"We'll show the bastards!"

"They can't stop us!"

The day was cold and windy and wet and gray, the worst of late fall in Michigan. At least the discomfort made me notice that I was a body moving through space. Otherwise I might have been a ghost passing across someone else's campus, a character in someone else's dream. As it was, the wind forced me to put lead in my feet. Misery as an anchor.

Teresa and I had classes in adjoining buildings, so we walked to class together and then made elaborate plans to pick each other up afterward. People whispered behind their hands when we passed them in the hall, a reaction that made me feel exposed and invisible at the same time.

Did they somehow know what happened to us?

I sat in class as if it were any other day. This was my Tuesday-Thursday class, so I hadn't missed anything. There was no reason to talk to the professor. I simply occupied my seat until the time was up and then went to meet Teresa. We put our heads down and walked through the wind to the coffee shop.

As we ate our sack lunches, Teresa told me something shocking. She knew some victims of a similar crime. That was why she had asked the detectives about other crimes. Their evasive reply had only confirmed her suspicions. The other victims Teresa knew were a family unit. They had reported their crime to the police but otherwise kept it quiet.

"But when you talk to them, you can't say anything to anyone, ever," Teresa told me. "Imagine a guy lying next to a loved one who's getting raped. They went through that. So they get it. But you can't breathe a word."

I didn't question the need for secrecy. I understood the stigma they were under. The stigma *we* were now under. Victims must accept the mark of disgrace. What other choice was there?

When the two male students approached us in the coffee shop, I knew them by sight. They were dudes, tall and lean and tough looking, but their faces melted like wax when they saw us. Without saying a word, one reached out his arms to me. Even though I barely knew him, I slid my arms inside his open army jacket, around his flannel-shirted waist, and pressed my cheek against his shirtfront. His strong arms crushed me against his chest. I could have stayed that way all afternoon. I maybe could even have rested.

⌒

For the next week there was no hour, no moment, that wasn't about this new course of study: rape. It was a crash course. I ate rape. I drank rape. I talked it. I didn't talk it. I slept it. I didn't sleep it. Rape was my only reality, my only world. There was no thought other than this. I was being indoctrinated in the rape worldview.

This fact made me furious. I hadn't asked to study this. Eventually my fury made me exhausted. But my exhaustion made me furious again. Why should I be so consumed by a subject I hadn't sought out? In this way, the fury and the exhaustion chased each other ceaselessly, like small, furry animals—first this one on top, then the other. So the first lesson the rape worldview taught me was simple but brutal: fury functions like caffeine.

I spent every waking moment with Marty and Teresa, who had their own reservoirs of fury. We borrowed freely from one another, refueling with bitter conversation. Feeling such constant fury was jangling and overwhelming. I couldn't contain the emotion. I needed to expel it, like menstrual blood. To spray it, like vomit. The anger sought a target. The rapists, of course. But also the professionals who were supposed to fix things but didn't—nurses, doctors, cops, detectives.

And as each day crawled by—each day its own lifetime—the college authorities provided another bull's-eye. After all, they did nothing to help us. Individual professors offered platitudes about "moving on." The clichés were maddening. Most egregious of all was the office of the dean of students. When Marty talked to them about our housing situation, they simply said that as seniors, we were on our own.

By the time my mother visited the weekend of November 11–12, less than a week had passed, yet my life had changed completely. I could no longer quite remember who I used to be. Had I been cheerful and optimistic? Whoever I had been before, I doubted there could be much of a connection between that person and this one. My mother loved the old Ruth, the Ruth who no longer existed.

Still, I appreciated that my mother had made the trip. It was an unprecedented expense for her to fly out. I was the third of my siblings to attend Calvin, and no one had ever made the trip between New Jersey and Michigan by air. We always drove the thirteen hours. I didn't even know how a person went about buying a plane ticket.

That year I was working as a waitress at a breakfast restaurant on the weekends, but that first weekend after the break-in, I arranged to have someone cover my shifts.

On Saturday my mother and I had a meeting with the college chaplain, a meeting that was not helpful. Maybe we didn't know exactly what we had hoped to get, but whatever that might have been, we were disappointed. The chaplain offered no words of spiritual counsel and no particular help with logistical problems such as housing and classes. "Talk to your professors about extensions, if you need them," he said.

Afterward, my mother and I went to the Alexander house to pack up my belongings. For the time being, anyway, I was moving everything to my sister's house. The other housemates were packing that day too, and a few of us had relatives there to help. The house hummed with determined activity.

I hated stepping into the dining room but couldn't avoid it. There was no other way to reach my bedroom. The dining room was the damned room, heavy with ghosts. Its windows had let the rapists in. Its floor had been our prison. But it was the hub of the house, and at some point on that Saturday, all of us happened to converge in that cursed room. Teresa's mother reached for her, Karen's mother reached for her, and my mother reached for me.

For me it's a capsulized memory, like dancing at a wedding or holding the widow's arm at a graveside—a small sensory moment that captures the emotions of a much larger experience. I remember the brashness of the Saturday light coming through those godforsaken windows and the disorder of the room, still filthy with residue from fingerprint powder. I remember the feel of my mother's shoulders, rounded and shaking. The sound of weeping.

Perhaps it sounds like a touching memory. But I was dry eyed after a week of tears. I just wanted to finish packing, get out of that house, and never come back. I recall that I rubbed my mother's back and, over her shoulder, saw Teresa rubbing *her* mother's back. Our eyes met. We were both stone faced. I had the urge to make a silly expression, to make Teresa laugh, but how can you explain that to your weeping mother? Still, there was something fantastical about the wretched scene.

My mother was in her own state of shock. She whispered to me through her tears, "This is the worst thing that has ever happened to me."

I continued to rub her back, but I felt my new companion, fury, rising up in me. Was I supposed to attend to my mother's feelings too? Didn't I have enough to deal with?

As I comforted my mother, something else occurred to me. This was the worst thing that ever happened to *her*? My mother was almost fifty years old! And this hadn't even happened to her; it had happened to *me*! How was I supposed to survive such a horrific event if just being associated with it was *the worst thing*?

My life must be beyond salvaging.

I have often wished I'd said something at that moment—that I'd protested or asked for clarification. But instead I tried to be a "good girl." I swallowed my protest, swallowed my anger, swallowed my desire to argue.

Nearly a decade would pass before I became a mother myself and glimpsed this scene from a mother's point of view. It's a different sort of pain to watch a daughter struggle. A mother would rather bear her daughter's pain than look on helplessly. So she attempts to shoulder her daughter's pain, and so her own load is doubled. But the daughter cannot know this. The daughter is lost in her own world of pain. Because if anything at all is true about pain, it's this: pain is isolating.

But I knew none of that at the time. I knew only what I interpreted my mother's words to mean: that my suffering quotient had overflowed and my life was over before I had even turned twenty-one.

My mother went home, and on Monday we all went back to class. Without a shared house, the campus coffee shop became our gathering place. As I'd always done, I carried an unbreakable mug and a small jar of instant coffee in my backpack, along with a stash of quarters in a pill bottle. A few times every day, I paid a quarter to the lady behind the register and drew hot water from a giant urn. The spoon stirring in the plastic cup made a *clackety-clack* as the coffee powder dissolved. The ritual was a source of comfort. So was the brew, which was bitter but gave me the jolt of energy that I craved.

Karen wasn't part of the coffee-shop dynamic. Before the crime, Karen's on-campus world had rarely overlapped with mine, and after the house broke apart, our worlds didn't coincide at all. I heard she had moved in with her sister.

Cheryl was immersed in her language studies, preparing to leave Grand Rapids at the end of January to spend her final semester in Spain. I once overheard her explain to a friend, "I just kept reciting the Twenty-third Psalm over and over, and I guess God heard me."

Did she really not know that we'd all been saying that psalm while our noses were smashed into the nap of the carpet?

I kept my distance from Cheryl after that. She'd had her own experience of the crime and her own reaction. Her belief that God had intentionally spared her obviously gave her comfort. Who knows? Perhaps in her shoes, I would have felt the same. But Cheryl seemed unaware of the back side of her belief. What did it mean for the rest of us, who had not been spared? I knew this dynamic was painful for Marty and Teresa, too—unspeakably so, because we didn't speak of it. What could we say? Cheryl was our friend.

Lisa, the housemate who hadn't been home that night, remained at the periphery of our group. She was occupied with her boyfriend, who was tall and handsome and headed to graduate school. Together they were the perfect couple, attractive and brilliant, with a shiny future. The sight of them was unbearable to me. I mean that literally. I couldn't help but turn my head when I saw them.

Marty and Teresa and I continued to find refuge in our shared anger. We were furious for slightly different reasons and in slightly different ways, but fury was our common ground. In time we became ever more practiced at fury, more expert at its rhythms. At class time we trudged across campus, occupied our seats in class, and then regrouped in the coffee shop. We talked about finding a place to live together again. This wasn't the senior year we'd pictured for ourselves.

"We can't give those scumbags our senior year," Marty said. "We'll show them."

When our fury spun itself out, we discovered the hidey-hole that exhaustion leads to—a territory I hadn't even known existed but one we now entered together. This is the place where tears continue to flow even after tear ducts run dry. This is where despair continues to shout even after words give out. We entered this world of waterless tears and wordless despair right there in the coffee shop, folding our arms on a tabletop and pillowing our heads, letting one another stand guard at the entrance of our fury while we each found a moment of respite. These moments felt sacred. I thought of Moses, hidden in a cleft of rock, or the Israelites, hidden from God's vengeance. Marty and Teresa were my cleft of rock, sheltering me from truths that would have overwhelmed me if I were alone.

When Marty and Teresa began searching for a new place to rent, I let them sort it out while I created a castle in my mind. While they found us an actual place to live, I needed a refuge I could escape to, right now.

⌒

The crime spree finally hit the media. The criminals were given a name: the Heritage Hill Rape-Robbers.

"I don't get it," I said to Marty. "We lived in Eastown, not Heritage Hill."

"Apparently our rapists aren't great map readers," she replied dryly.

I was glad that people were being warned. But reading the news made me feel exposed, even though we were never named. I figured the Dutch grapevine had filled in those tidbits of information. To be safe, I avoided almost everyone. I particularly avoided people who seemed happy—especially my fellow seniors who were moving steadily toward graduation in a cloud of confidence. They were naive. They were ignorant.

And oh, I wanted to be one of them again.

In hindsight, I'm sure that many people tried to say the right thing. But what would that have been? We victims had such strong emotions, and there were so many of us. We built barricades out of the things we learned that awful night—things other people didn't know, couldn't know. The men on campus, in particular, had a fine line to navigate. They needed to express outrage at the atrocity we'd endured, but they couldn't suggest we were destroyed by it. They needed to direct vehement anger at the criminals but couldn't spout violent rhetoric ("I'll kill the bastards!"). If they crossed that line, they were simply perpetuating the culture of brutality that led to rape.

Or so we said. The whole subject became politicized immediately. It stuns me to recall how quickly Marty and Teresa and I—students of philosophy, history, religion—shaped a particular interpretation of what happened to us. This crime was not personal, nor was it entirely random. Instead, this crime was one violent act in the long history of violent acts that men heap upon women. This is how the world works. This is how men treat women. Our blinders had been torn away, and we had been enlightened. We took a strange comfort in this perspective. We had joined a club we never wanted to join, a club that women from around the world joined against their will. At least we were in it together.

10

It was Cheryl who found us a place to live, at least in the short term. A family she babysat for in East Grand Rapids had a garage apartment they were willing to rent out. Geographically the apartment was about two miles from our Alexander house, but it was in a different world. The apartment was built over their four-car detached garage and accessible via an outdoor staircase. The family used the rooms infrequently—usually to house members of the symphony who came to town.

The apartment was as clean and impersonal as a hotel room. We moved very few belongings up that staircase, only our clothing and kitchen essentials. We said aloud that this would be a place of healing. The white-walled rooms echoed our words back at us. Underneath us, the garage housed a Maserati, a BMW Roadster, and two luxury sedans.

Every morning I caught a ride to campus in one of my housemates' cars. Cheryl's car was a beater like Teresa's, but Marty had an almost-new, baby-blue Volkswagen bug, a gift from her parents. After classes I would catch a ride home with one of them.

I was aware of what a load I was, but I didn't know what to do about it.

Jim showed up at the garage apartment in the early evenings. He'd spent a lot of time at the house on Alexander, and we were all grateful he resumed his visits. He would call out cheerily as he clomped up the outdoor stairs. When we opened the door, he'd have a game tucked under his arm or a magazine or a bag of snacks. The four of us would give him a hero's welcome. He was our brother. He was our babysitter. Our distraction. Our confidant. We could say anything to him, but he never probed. He'd grown up with three sisters, so he wasn't afraid of us and our messy emotions.

Instead of studying, we'd play Boggle or Tiddlywinks or fill in Mad Libs. One day he brought a *People* magazine that had a life-sized picture of John Travolta's face. He punched a hole between the lips, slapped the picture onto his face, and started singing "You're the One That I Want" from *Grease*. We joined in, squeaking falsetto through the "oo-oo-oo" part. We laughed until we snorted and then rolled on the floor, clutching our sides.

Jim was free with his hugs. He hugged me like he hugged the others, like a brother. Marty, Teresa, and Cheryl felt free to cling to him, but I was afraid of being too forward. Still, I was jealous for the comfort of his arms.

One day Jim appeared with a big box addressed to me. It had been delivered to the Alexander house, and our landlord had asked him to give it to me. The package was from L.L. Bean. I'd forgotten that I'd placed the order, which was surprising since I'd deliberated over the purchase all summer, intent on finding the perfect coat for a Michigan winter. I'd finally settled on a combination of two pieces: an unlined water-repellent jacket in slate blue and a down vest in burnt orange. To economize, I'd decided to sew the vest myself, so I ordered the kit version, which was a brand-new option.

That package was better than any Christmas gift I'd ever received. I was full of gratitude, and Jim grinned at my happiness. I felt like

God's hand had mysteriously intervened at last. I kept saying how blessed I felt and how fine the coat was and how wonderful it was that Jim had brought the package for me. And how had the landlord even known? What a blessing!

Eventually both Teresa and Marty told me exactly where I could stuff it, my coat and my blessing.

Marty or Teresa or Cheryl frequently asked Jim if he'd mind spending the night on our couch. We all liked having him there. I was happy to wait an extra turn for the shower in the morning, especially if it meant Jim would be the one to give me a ride to campus. That gave us a few precious minutes alone in the car, even if those conversations were the same as the ones we had with the rest of the group.

It was obvious why we wanted Jim there at night. That's when the terrors came. Like the others, I lay in bed and craved the sensation of safety. I thought about Jim, sleeping so close by on the couch, and wished I could lie in his arms. I felt so vulnerable. Were we safe here? I thought about the fleet of cars stored beneath us, all so solid, so valuable, with so much heft. But they couldn't protect us. I tried not to replay the events of the night of the crime or to worry about whether it could happen again. But I did. I replayed and I worried.

When I fell asleep at last, I had terrifying, confusing dreams. Sometimes I dreamed about microphones, black and phallic with men's lips pressed against them, saying garbled words that brought applause from everyone listening. Sometimes I dreamed about megaphones held by men in uniform, broadcasting across the campus, which was now a prison yard, while we women stood shivering in our inadequate striped garb.

Before the crime I'd been a good sleeper. My mother used to tease me about having the "gift of sleep," a gift I inherited from my father. I didn't know how lucky I'd been—that not everyone can crawl into bed and become oblivious until morning. After the crime I discovered that the rapists had stolen my gift of sleep. It had vanished along with our grocery money and Marty's beanbag chairs and my heart-shaped locket that I didn't realize was missing until several days later. Now I could see that they'd taken more valuable things too: my ability to focus, to plan, to hope.

Two weeks after the crime, Marty, Teresa, Cheryl, and I decided to go to church together. As the four of us filed into a long, curved pew in the center of the sanctuary, the congregation grew silent. Every eye followed us.

Of course, that may have been my imagination. But certainly the experience of filing into a pew, which I'd done more times than I could count, had never felt like this before. This felt like a conspicuous act, a display of vulnerability. It may have been the first time in my life when I was in church not because of duty but because of need.

What I needed most, perhaps, was permission to ask the terrifying question: *God, what did I do that You would let this happen to me?* That question had overtaken me, yet I didn't dare lay the words end to end in my mind, much less allow the words on my tongue.

There was nothing unusual about the worship service that Sunday—I don't recall the sermon. But after the sermon came the pastoral prayer (which children called the "long prayer" and for which mothers passed peppermints as fortification). On this day the long prayer lived up to its name. A few minutes in, the pastor prayed for us. He didn't mention us by name, but he prayed for the household of young women who had recently been the victims of a break-in. I couldn't hear anything he said after that because of the blood pounding through my head. Tears leaked through my closed eyes, through the cracks I couldn't seal shut. My shoulders shook with the futile effort of clamping down.

I was grateful to be prayed for, to be on the hearts and minds of all those people. But I was also appalled that I had become a nameless victim and that the crime had been reduced to a "break-in," as if the violation were no more grievous than theft. The theft meant nothing to me. Besides that heart-shaped locket, which had been a gift from Cheryl in junior high, I hadn't missed any other items. This crime wasn't about property damage; it was about bodily damage—which apparently couldn't be named in church. *Rape* was an unspeakable word that reverberated in silence.

During the fellowship time after the service, I was self-conscious about my blotchy face. At the same time, I wanted my tears to be seen as evidence, as testimony to what I'd endured. In the end, my face and my tears didn't matter. Everyone was busy with their own thoughts, affairs, and conversations. Life really does go on.

Over Styrofoam coffee cups, people talked about their plans for the Thanksgiving holiday, which would begin in just a few days. I watched with detachment until I noticed a couple I didn't see often, both of whom were from New Jersey. Don and his wife, Debbie, were three years older than I was. I knew them in the awestruck way that a freshman knows a pair of really cool seniors. I'd heard that Don was in seminary now, which was no surprise. Back in high school, Don had given me rides to early morning prayer meetings. This group consisted of a bunch of students who were experimenting with being charismatic and using Spirit-filled language. It had been a delightful way to worry our parents, being holier than they were. I felt a pang of nostalgia as I remembered those days. We had all been so young and innocent, so certain God was smiling on us!

I noticed how beautiful Debbie looked. She was radiant and wearing a seasonally mismatched outfit—a turtleneck under a smocked summer dress. The outfit said she had more love than money. But she was going to be a minister's wife. In other words, she had love and hope and a future. She had everything I wanted and now knew I'd never have. The sight of her filled me with despair.

Looking back, I see the wall I had so quickly built. I was angry at every person I encountered simply because they hadn't been a victim that night. I craved compassion, even while I spurned whatever portion of tenderness I received. I wanted someone to recognize that I was no longer the same person I'd been, even while I wanted to believe that I *was* still the same person. I wanted someone to acknowledge that my life was over, even while I wanted to believe that my life was *not* over.

—————

Day after day, we kept going to class. Marty, Teresa, Cheryl, and I agreed we would all graduate on time. It was the fixed point we moved toward. From time to time we pumped ourselves with anger.

"We won't let the slimeballs win!"

"I'm not giving them one more minute of my life!"

Sometimes our brash words echoed through my mind as I dragged myself across campus. Was it simple Dutch stubbornness that kept us going? I stumbled into classrooms and occupied a seat. I listened, by which I mean that sound floated through space and I didn't attempt to block that sound from entering my ears. Sometimes I even wrote words in a notebook. But I felt curiously out of body, as if I were perched high on a wall, observing from a great distance. This was not always unpleasant. These were high-level classes in my favorite subject areas, after all. My professors lectured about the morphology of linguistics or the five pillars of Islam or how an author might handle an unreliable narrator. These were topics I could concentrate on for a few minutes each day.

Time in class was actually easier than the time between. I hated walking across campus. If I was alone, I spooked easily. If I spied a lone figure wearing a dark jacket and close-fitting hat pulled low, my heart would pound in my chest. I knew it was just a student on his way to class—someone trying to stay warm, someone with white skin.

Which meant that I battled one of the tenets I'd held on to for so long: that skin color shouldn't matter. *Red and yellow, black and white, all are precious in God's sight.* Yes. But white skin meant that this person could not be my rapist.

The irony wasn't lost on me. How many times had my friends and I decried the tidy safety of the Christian bubble? We derisively called Calvin a white womb. White skin filled the classrooms. White snow blanketed the campus. But now that very whiteness had an upside. It offered a sliver of comfort, a sense of protection.

Walking across campus with my friends was less frightening than being alone, but it was uncomfortable in a different way. I felt conspicuous in our little clutch. As we passed other students, I caught—or imagined I caught—pitying looks. My feet became leaden with disgrace. I believed that if I was pitied, that meant I was pitiful. I could only imagine what they whispered to each other after we passed. How happy they must be, not being us. Did they speculate about what we had done to deserve our fate?

The truth was that I didn't need anyone else to blame me. I already blamed myself. My conscience was heavy over something I'd done the previous summer—something I didn't confess to my sister that day in the car. Maybe it's why I told her about the sleeping-bag rape in the first place. Maybe I was connecting the dots. That attack by a fellow hiker had been the first punishment for something I'd done—something sexual. Now I was being punished again.

Are you recoiling against this theology? Are you saying, "Surely she knows that's not how God works"?

But think about it. Good Christian people say, "There but for the grace of God go I." They say it with an exhale of piety, and everyone nods. But doesn't the expression itself imply a flip side? The existence of a place on the other side of grace?

That's where I found myself living—on that shadow side. How had I gotten to such an awful place except by my sexual misdeeds? After all, I'd gotten the message from both church and school: a girl was as good as her sexual purity. If she wasn't pure, she was damaged. That damage was different from other types of sin. It was less redeemable. Let's call the message sexual shame. It's not a refined message, but it's insidious. It's as common as a tick bite, with as much destructive potential.

Like a tick-borne illness, shame spreads in hidden ways and damages a person. It's similarly hard to treat.

So the metaphor works. But I won't leave you with only a metaphor.

Here's the story I felt so guilty about. When I got to Yellowstone the previous summer, away from my church bubble, I luxuriated in my newfound freedom. I did things I'd never done before, had never even considered doing. I smoked a cigarette. I shot pool in the smoky employee bar. I hitchhiked with friends to a trailhead. I soaked up attention from guys.

And when one guy continued to pursue me, I stopped saying no. His name was Dange, short for Dangerous, and that pretty much sums up his appeal. I didn't love him, and I didn't pretend that I did, not even to myself. I just wanted to have the experience. I wanted to feel wanted. Afterward I was filled with shock . . . but also a heady rush. I wasn't such a good girl after all. Or put it this way: I wasn't *just* a good girl. There was more to me than that. I was also adventurous. Fun. Desirable. Maybe even carefree. But I felt guilty, and when, shortly afterward, I went hiking alone and was attacked, I felt like I was receiving the punishment I was due.

When I got back to college in September, I confessed everything to Marty and Teresa. They teased me about my overactive conscience. But since they themselves were more virtuous, I couldn't help but contrast my own behavior and continue to believe that I had fallen from grace. Meanwhile, another school year was beginning. I shoved the summer aside and resolved to become a good girl again. But just two months later came the break-in.

Is God punishing me? Is God simply vindictive?

11

THANKSGIVING VACATION OFFERED A REPRIEVE—a few days off from class and a change of pace. I also looked forward to a little time away from the other victims, though I wouldn't have admitted such a thing aloud.

I'd spent my previous Thanksgiving breaks in Chicago with my brother and his wife, and I planned to make the trip again. We always ate the holiday meal with the Huizenga side of the family, gathered in a church basement. My parents couldn't make it most years, but there were usually sixty to eighty of our relatives there. The number had been known to surpass one hundred.

As he had in other years, Jim offered to give me a ride to Tim and Annette's house. Jim's parents lived in the western suburbs, and it was easy for him to drop me off. In the past, I'd loved those long rides with Jim. We talked intimately, telling family stories and laughing. I loved the way he loved his parents and sisters. As darkness fell, we'd lower our voices and talk about the kind of family each of us wanted to have. Our headlight-swept conversations stirred my hopes for a future together. This time Jim said he wanted to check out the campus of Northwestern University. Did I want to go with him? He was trying to decide if he wanted to apply to their graduate program in theater.

I looked forward to the car ride and was thrilled at the chance to explore a campus together, picturing possibilities. But was I going along as a friend or as a girlfriend? Was he babysitting me or courting me?

Driving down Highway 196 that Tuesday before Thanksgiving, I loved having Jim all to myself within the confines of the car. I asked him about his hopes for Northwestern and where he saw his career going. We talked with our old energy. Approaching St. Joseph, Highway 196 merges onto Interstate 94, and just beyond that the road bends. As we sped along, another car bumped ours in that grazing way that's bound to at least leave a scratch. The other car was full of young black men. When I saw them, I screamed at Jim, "Don't stop! Keep going!"

I knew that the black men had followed me. They were pursuing me as easy prey. I was furious at God for targeting me in this way. Why would He spoil these few hours with Jim? Would He never stop punishing me?

Jim didn't stop the car and kept up a stream of lighthearted chatter.

At last we arrived on Northwestern's campus, just off Lake Michigan. Jim drove around for a long time looking for a parking space. Finally we found one and put coins in a meter. The wind came off the lake, tunneled between the buildings, and blasted across concrete courtyards. We ran to some bulletin boards listing on-campus events and stood there, shivering. With our hands in our pockets, we read notices about upcoming performances. I imagined us as a couple, seeing shows. Perhaps Jim would have roles in some of them. Perhaps there would be parties afterward.

In an attempt to direct the conversation toward something hopeful, I said, "I'd love to see how they do Shakespeare."

"I'm thinking more commedia dell'arte," Jim said.

I didn't care—I just wanted him to take my hand, to put his arm around me, to pull me over the threshold of romance. But I understood that he might not want me anymore.

We didn't spend long on that windblown campus—probably less time than it took to find the parking space. Then Jim drove me to my brother's brownstone, unloaded my bag from the trunk, hugged me, and said something cheerful about picking me up for the return trip. Watching him drive away, I knew I was losing something by inches, but I didn't know how to stop it.

The Huizenga Thanksgiving gathering could be a rather overwhelming experience under the best of circumstances. My father was one of eight children, each of whom had married and produced between three and six offspring. I believe there are thirty-two Huizenga cousins in that generation. Most of my cousins had married, and another generation was underway. The place literally crawled with Huizengas. Not everyone could travel to the Chicago area every year, but many did. It was a sight to behold—so many fair-skinned people who shared my name and DNA. The church itself brought back memories. It was the same one I'd attended as a young child, decked out in a poofy-skirted dress and patent-leather Mary Janes.

The Thanksgiving meal was a traditional feast: turkey and stuffing, mashed potatoes and gravy, yams in syrup, canned corn and green beans, homemade rolls. After the meal but before the pie, a cousin would play the piano, and one of my musical uncles would lead everyone in singing hymns while we "younger folk" did the dishes. Then came board games and visiting. After a few hours, we'd fortify ourselves for departure with a turkey sandwich and Jell-O—and, of course, another piece of pie.

Tim and Annette and I arrived at the church around noon,

dressed in corduroys and sweaters. Annette had fulfilled her assignments and was carrying a home-baked pie and a Jell-O salad. Tim had no assignments. He simply had his pipe in hand and went outside to smoke with some of the male cousins.

Since I saw these relatives only once a year, I usually felt awkward. This year the crime was just three weeks old, and I could only assume that the news had traveled. But I didn't know who knew what.

I hugged the aunts who approached me but otherwise hung back. When one uncle glanced at me, his face contorted before he could turn his head away. That glimpse of emotion prompted my eyes to fill with tears. I did the only thing I could think to do: escape to the ladies' room.

The small room was as I remembered, with two pink-painted toilet stalls and a wreath of plastic flowers over the mirror. A wooden chair was tucked between the stalls and the sink. I supplied myself with toilet paper and perched on the chair to cry.

Eventually the door opened, and one of my older cousins came in. I'd been in awe of her since I was a little girl. She was so beautiful and poised. She walked past me to the mirror and brushed her shining hair, which flipped at her shoulders. She applied lipstick. Smiled at herself. Checked her teeth. Straightened her collar. Left, the door banging behind her.

Did she really not see me here, crying? Hadn't she heard what happened? Did she simply not care?

Suddenly I knew I couldn't be there when the next person came in. I couldn't bear to be invisible, not when this mountain of pain already threatened to obliterate me. I splashed cold water on my hot face and slipped out of the room, ducking up a flight of stairs to the sanctuary. The cavernous space was unchanged from my childhood. The plush carpet was still baby blue, the pews were still a medium-toned wood. I trailed my hand along the pew backs, the way I had done as a child, so lovingly. I looked to the rear of the sanctuary, above the balcony. There, high up, was the stained-glass window shaped like a rosette. I used to love the way the glass colored the light that poured into the space on Sunday mornings.

I found the pew my family had occupied, about two-thirds of the way back, on the right-hand side. I sank onto the cushion and tried to recapture how I'd felt as a child, so safe and secure. Once upon a time, going to church had proved that everything was right with the world, that God loved everyone, but me especially. That feeling seemed laughable now. Quaint, at least. The knowledge that I would never again feel that way skewered me with grief.

At the front of the sanctuary was the baptismal font. I suddenly remembered my sister Susan's baptism day. I'd been six years old and thought the whole family should go up front with the baby, but they said there wasn't room for a family of seven. So Mom and Dad had carried baby Susan up front while we siblings stayed in the pew under Mary Lynn's watchful eye. My father held the baby, and my mother stood beside him wearing a pretty dress and a hat. Despite my disappointment at not being up front, I felt the pure delight of the day. Was anything better than belonging to God and to my church and to my family?

I could picture the other sacrament too, which we practiced only quarterly. On those special Communion Sundays, the church elders—all men—filed into the front row and sat shoulder to shoulder. When I was a child, that solemn line had made me feel safe and protected. Now the memory of those dark-suited shoulders reared up like a barricade, an entirely masculine wall between me and the baptism font. I no longer had a place in church. Maybe I never would again. I lay down on that cushioned pew and sobbed myself to sleep.

After Thanksgiving break, Marty, Teresa, and I met with two volunteer counselors from the local Rape Crisis Team. About a month had passed since the crime. Teresa arranged the meeting at a friend's house, and I rode there with her. The counselors brought a box of crackers and a hunk of cheese, which they plunked, still wrapped in plastic, onto a coffee table. Teresa made some tea. We sat in a circle, and no one suggested beginning with a prayer.

At the counselors' prompting, we described what had happened. They reacted strongly to our story. Did we know Susan Brownmiller's book? It was called *Against Our Will*, an absolute must-read. Maybe we'd read it in a class? No, but, Marty and Teresa had both picked up the book.

The counselors rehearsed the book's main tenets. How culture is stacked against women and has been since the beginning of time. How men rape women as an act of violence rather than an act of sex. How men use the threat of rape to control and intimidate women. How rape is virtually unknown in the animal world. How simple and ugly the truth is: that every man is a potential rapist.

I wasn't ready for such an intense escalation of the subject. So I unwrapped the cheese and crackers and busied myself eating more than my share. Toward the end of our meeting, one of the counselors asked if any of us planned to buy a gun. If so, she had some suggestions. Her offer shocked me. The memory of the guns' physical presence still made me feel ill. What comfort would that metal be, cold and heavy in my hand? Could I ever bring myself to pull the trigger?

On the drive back to our apartment, Teresa and I agreed that we didn't want to end up jaded and angry and old. Although I didn't know how we could avoid it.

"I don't want to spend my whole life being mad at all men," Teresa said. "I still want to believe there can be love."

"Do you think it could be Sam?" I asked.

"It might be," she said.

I was glad she had Sam.

I can't say I was mad at men in general. I was mad at the ultimate Man—I was mad at God. My indoctrination into sexual shame had connected the dots between rape and punishment. As mad as I was about that connection, it did serve one important purpose: it let God off the hook. Because if getting raped was punishment for being sexually active, then I'd simply gotten what I deserved. At least that was fair. Straightforward. It might have been distasteful, but it made sense. And that paradigm—correct or not—had worked as a logical way for me to understand the attack when I went hiking. But it didn't work for a break-in by armed strangers in the middle of the night. It didn't work to explain the level of terror we experienced, the hours when we believed our lives might come to an end. We didn't deserve that, not by any stretch. None of us did.

So what did that mean? Were my friends and I the innocent victims of a random act of violence? That may seem simple enough, unless you believe that God is sovereign, so nothing that happens is truly random. If everything happens according to God's will, then God must have willed the rapes to happen. Maybe "rape as punishment" was distasteful, but "rape as God's will" was absolutely unpalatable.

At the very least, God could have prevented the crime but chose not to. Why should I forgive God for that? Put it this way: if I, a mere human being, am aware of random violence about to be committed against someone I love and have the power to stop it, am I not morally obligated to do so?

So why should I expect less of God?

Now if someone had said to me, "Ruth, somebody has to be the victim. Why should you be exempt?" I would have agreed. I would be willing to take my turn. But the idea that everything is preordained meant something different from turn taking. It meant that God's finger had hovered over the map of greater Grand Rapids, passing over the neighborhoods of Eastown and Heritage Hill in ever-narrowing circles until it landed on our roof. Alexander Street.

Tap tap. This house. These sleeping women. These are the ones who will get raped tonight.

Despite all my indoctrination in God's sovereignty, I couldn't make my heart line up with that. God singled us out for this crime? I couldn't stomach it. I preferred randomness. At least then I could stay on speaking terms with God. I could stomach being faceless in the sea of humanity, a victim of random misfortune. Even random evil.

But there was a problem with the random theory.

Rape doesn't feel random. Rape feels the opposite of random. It feels personal. There's nothing arms-length about this crime. Your body is not some pocket that can be deftly picked by an opportunist while you're looking the other way. Anyone's wallet will do!

No, rape isn't a crime against property, despite the fact that women are so often treated as chattel. Rape is a crime against your person. Rape targets the most private, most hidden part of your person. Your softest center. Your singular self. To suffer this sort of attack feels anything but random.

And at the same time, I didn't mean to overstate the situation. We victims were still alive, weren't we? We had survived. We hadn't suffered permanent physical damage. Perhaps in the eyes of others, we *had* been spared. In my eyes, Cheryl had been spared, but in truth, she had suffered her own trauma.

I had been so shielded growing up, and now all the pain in the world lay exposed before me. I could hardly bear it. Dear Jesus. Was all of life a valley of shadows? I fell largely mute in the face of what I saw.

⌒

After spending two decades in ministry, I can imagine the kind of pastoral care that might have been helpful to my college self that winter. Most important, someone needed to ask the right questions, to help me express what I believed. Our most powerful and shaping beliefs are the ones we don't articulate—which is why theology matters.

Someone might have asked, "Ruth, why do you think you deserved to be raped? Why would anyone deserve that? And why you in particular?"

If I had told someone my Yellowstone stories, my secret sexual shame would have been exposed. Treatment would then have been obvious. After all, the tools were at hand. I had been schooled in redemption and forgiveness, at least in the abstract. I knew that God could take something damaged and make it whole, restored, beautiful again—that, in fact, this is what forgiveness is and that it happens all the time, after many kinds of failings. I just hadn't applied these ideas to my sexual self. Instead, I'd learned to hide my sexual being. I had overlearned an overemphasized and oversimplified lesson. No wonder the shame latched onto me like a tick, injecting me with its poison.

Someone might even have asked if the sexual-shame paradigm was indeed sacrosanct. Did Jesus treat sexual sin as somehow more grievous than other sins? No one helped me question the bedrock beliefs about sexuality that shaped my response to being raped.

Still, there were things that did help. For one, I clung to my childhood sense of being beloved by God. I hadn't given up on God. I had only given up on certain understandings of God.

For another, I had my friends' experiences as a counterpoint to my own. I knew that they were pure of heart and body, even if I wasn't, so the rapes couldn't simply be God's punishment for sexual sin. And our conversations helped me see that this crime wasn't just an event between myself and God. This crime involved actual criminals. Perpetrators. "Clowns," as the doctor had called them. Let's name them for what they were: rapists. Men who chose to do wrong.

The rapists, not God, had victimized us.

Maybe the rape crisis counselors were right. Maybe our guilt was less complicated than I made it out to be. Maybe we were simply guilty of being born female in a man's world.

12

We moved again in mid-December, into a small house on Ardmore Street. Karen and Lisa had moved in with their parents, so it was just Marty, Teresa, Cheryl, and me, plus Dianne, a high school friend from New Jersey. I was surprised Dianne agreed to Marty's invitation to live with us, but that was fine with me. Cheryl would be moving out in a matter of weeks, and even though this house was smaller, it cost substantially more than the previous one had. Besides being in a better neighborhood, this place was newer and nicer, with an immaculate kitchen, decent wallpaper, and a hanging light fixture over the dining room table. The dining table and chairs even came with the house, as did the beds. Since we didn't have living room furniture, we made do without it. We just sat on the soft, clean carpet.

Jim came over to the Ardmore place as frequently as he had the garage apartment and the Alexander house before that. He teased us that we would never be rid of him. Sometimes he brought a friend or two. As before, we laughed so much and so hard over so little that anyone watching might have thought we were deranged. Quite often the laughter would dissolve into tears, but by then we'd be exhausted enough to sleep.

None of us could sleep the way we used to—that was a given. In the past, I would fall asleep with the expectation that when I woke, I'd feel refreshed and clean, like a kitchen sink after someone took scouring powder to it. But sleep was no longer a cleansing agent or a sweet-smelling disinfectant. Sleep was something dark and fearful, a stretch of time when consciousness dropped away and danger entered through dreams. Nearly every night I woke to screams, either my own or those of my housemates.

Still, the days and nights passed.

One day we found something unexpected on a high shelf in the front hall closet: one of those fake logs designed to go in a fireplace, with a red lightbulb, a revolving fan, and a few strips of red filament to blow in the breeze, like flames. We set the log in the center of the empty living room, and after supper we'd plug it in and sit around it like a campfire.

I liked the shadows it cast. I liked the way it gave us license to act like children, making shadow puppets with our hands. I liked the sense of impermanence, as if we could pick up and leave as soon as the fire burned just a little lower. I liked the tribal feel of it, as if our history were merely a story we could tell—and perhaps make up a new ending.

Sometime in December, Marty got a dog, a young Doberman she named Gypsy. Marty said the dog would keep us safe, but Gypsy was hard to restrain and barked at everything. It was a problem. I tried to ignore the problem.

I had other problems, like transportation. We were now living farther from campus, and our schedules had become unpredictable and complicated. Sometimes one of us had to find a professor during office hours to plead for an extension or an Incomplete. Sometimes one of us ended up weeping in a corner of the campus without any way to communicate with the others. The only option was to physically find the others, which wasn't always possible.

On the weekends, I had trouble getting to my waitressing job. The breakfast restaurant was close to the old house on Alexander but not our new place on Ardmore. I had requested day shifts only, but that didn't solve my transportation dilemma. Plus, I was spending more time at my sister Mary Lynn's house. I liked the domesticity there. Good smells came out of the kitchen, and she was making progress sewing my down-vest kit. I would do my laundry and help take care of Danny, who still wasn't walking. His needs were simple enough that I could meet them: carry him, feed him, change him. When I tried, I could always elicit one of his wide grins. His grins made me feel seen and loved.

I decided it was time to buy my own car. I'd been planning to buy one after graduation, but why wait? I had about $350 in savings. Mary Lynn suggested that Roger could help me find something in the classified ads, so he and I spread out the newspaper. We found an old Plymouth with low mileage, and Roger arranged for us to look at it the next day, before it got dark. He said he'd take off work a bit early and pick me up right after class.

The next day the weather was cold and windy, with blowing snow. As usual, I was wearing my new slate-blue jacket. Roger had on his olive-green hunting jacket. The white-haired gentleman who was selling the car wore a beautiful overcoat, along with gorgeous leather gloves. We stood there looking at the car, which was squarish and light blue, with minimal rust.

"I wonder if this baby has a push-button transmission," Roger said, shooting me a sidelong glance. "It looks almost that old."

"This was my wife's car," the gentleman said, "but she can't get out anymore. She only drove it twice a week—on Wednesdays, to buy groceries, and on Sundays, to go to church."

I had my doubts about whether that was true, but I wanted it to be. I studied the gentleman and his overcoat and constructed a mental picture of his white-haired wife, a matched set. I wanted a car that had safely ferried a vulnerable woman from one kind of nutrition to the next: groceries to God and back again. Then I noticed the silver letters spelling the model name: Valiant.

Of course I wanted to own a Valiant. I wanted to slip into the driver's seat and become valiant. Would that quality rise up through the steering wheel? Emanate from the dashboard? Seep into me through the sensible cloth seats? In the end, I gave the man $325 in cash and drove away.

Once I had the car, I realized how desperately I needed this independence. Inside my protective Valiant shell, I was free to drive anywhere I wanted to go. Some of those places surprised me.

Lake Michigan, for instance. One day I skipped class and drove to Holland State Park, where I could look across the beach to the water. I sat in the warm car sipping coffee from my thermos and watching the wind whip across the freezing water. I had intended to get out and walk along the beach, but I contemplated the wind and waves and thought, *Aren't I miserable enough?*

The day's dreariness cheered me immeasurably.

One night when I was driving home after dark, I purposely drove the Valiant through our old neighborhood and stopped by the Alexander house. Nearby, in Martin Luther King Jr. Park, streetlights illuminated the basketball court, which had been shoveled clear of snow. Young black men spilled everywhere; the whole place seemed to be moving.

Watching them, my body started shaking, but inside my car, I felt free to let it shake. They couldn't see me, and the Valiant provided a refuge, as well as an escape route. I watched the players the way someone might watch tigers at the zoo, dangerous but out of reach. The men shouted at each other, their voices booming. They strode toward each other, their legs stretching impossibly far. They greeted each other with raised arms, their hands slapping easily. Every motion they made was mesmerizing to me. As I sat braked at the corner, I felt the familiar terror rise inside me. Normally I spent my energy keeping this terror at bay, so there was a sort of exhilaration in letting it rise. My foot hovered over the accelerator.

I studied the men. These were neighborhood men. One of them might be the very man who had raped me—or the other one, the leader, who made me strip. Spontaneously I cried, "Oh God!" But the men outside didn't hear. If they had, they probably would have laughed. I felt sure my anger would amuse them.

The pure injustice of the situation roiled inside me. I yelled at God with everything I had. "Oh God, why did you let this happen? Why did You do this to me? Why? Why? Why?" I pounded the steering wheel in punctuation. "You worthless Old Man!"

I don't know which aspect of that moment was most electrifying: the sight of the black men, the sound of my own full-throttle voice, or the sour taste of anger in my mouth. Panicked, I pumped my foot on the accelerator and the Valiant lurched away, leaving a trail of exhaust. The blue smoke was satisfying, a marker that I had been there with my rage. And that I had escaped.

After that first visit, I went back quite frequently. You might say I courted the terror. Maybe I wanted to wear it out, to see if I could get to the other side. I just know the idea took hold of me. Like most addictions, these drives were something I had to do alone. I felt virtuous, almost, that I could be so daring. The visits filled me with something I couldn't name at the time. Looking back, I understand that it was a sense of agency, of personal power. I was taking what little action I could to regain a feeling of control.

Somewhere during this time, my beliefs about God began to

change, to disappear, to trail away. My old faith, which had once been so rock solid, now felt as insubstantial as car exhaust. Evening after evening, I drove away from everything I'd once known for sure.

———

At Christmas break I went home to New Jersey. At some point during the two-week holiday, I took a bus into New York City—a common enough outing for me to take when I had the chance.

For reasons that I have long since forgotten, I ended up taking a return bus into Paterson alone. Perhaps when my parents and I made the arrangements, I forgot how early it gets dark on the eastern side of the time zone in the winter.

When my bus arrived in Paterson, it was already dusk, and my father's Galaxie 500 wasn't there waiting. The street was lined with businesses, but the lighting was dim. A long row of windows advertised a "White Sale." I had never seen such a sign before. What exactly was on sale?

I was the only white person around. Older black women wearing thin cloth coats hurried by with shopping bags, their heads wrapped in scarves. Their maternal presence gave me a moment of calm. Then I noticed a group of young black men loitering across the street. I ran to a nearby phone booth. I was almost too frantic to get my coin into the slot, to dial the numbers. My mother told me that Dad was on the way; it would be just a minute.

By the time my father's car pulled up, I was furious as well as terrified. I yelled at my father, which I couldn't remember ever doing before. "How could you keep me waiting? There were men!"

"Nobody was going to hurt you," he said.

No? And you know that how?

I stared out the side window as the dark streets of downtown Paterson slipped by. As the emotion ebbed, I felt altogether alone. Why couldn't my father even try to understand? Was he unwilling to come into this place of terror? This was my life now, whether I wanted it to be or not. This was my new reality. I couldn't rewind time and reenter his world—a world where black men never meant any harm. I hated my father's innocence and his liberal world, even as I longed to rejoin it.

13

JANUARY WAS INTERIM TERM AT CALVIN, which meant that we took one class all month. Back in September, I'd signed up to study Frisian, the language spoken in Friesland, a province in the northern part of the Netherlands. When I signed up for the class, I was fascinated that such a small land area was split by two different languages: Dutch (a Germanic offshoot) and Frisian (which is closely related to Old English).

I had preregistered for the class on the off chance that I might decide to become a linguist. Late in the previous year, one of my English professors, Dr. Stanley Wiersma, had approached me about pursuing a career with Wycliffe Bible Translators.

"You have an aptitude for linguistics," he told me. "A real gift for language. People like you are exactly what Wycliffe needs."

I was flattered. "I do love words."

"You could live in Madagascar—wouldn't that be something!" His enthusiasm was contagious.

"But isn't it a three-year commitment?" To me, three years seemed like a lifetime.

"It's a lifetime commitment," he said. "But what a life—think about it!"

I didn't especially want to go to Madagascar—not for a lifetime, not without a husband. But I was intrigued enough to think about studying linguistics. So I decided to learn Frisian.

It's astounding how much can change in four months. The class that had sounded intellectually exciting now had the opposite appeal: since the course was pass/fail, I'd have zero homework and could get away with sparse attendance. I could take a break from thinking. Maybe I'd waitress a few extra shifts. I needed the money, especially after buying the Valiant.

I had started waitressing the year before, as a junior, at an IHOP on the East Beltline. I enjoyed the tidy rhythm of the work: pouring coffee, writing orders on a pocket pad, serving hot plates. The big negative, of course, was the syrup. Life at a pancake house is unendingly sticky.

My senior year I got a better job in Eastown, at Breakfast Just Breakfast, a trendy spot that opened at 11:00 p.m. and was completely full by midnight. I loved the late shift. The tips were good, and I needed them to cover my living expenses and make my tuition payments. Every two weeks I plunked three rolls of quarters and one roll of dimes onto the counter in the financial aid office. Carrying the weight of those coins in my backpack was both a nuisance and a pleasure.

But the late shift was also fun because it had a very particular rhythm. The first few hours typically flew by. The night crowd came in all at once, booming and restless, clamoring for cheesy omelets and syrup-soaked pancakes. After those folks cleared out, a lull descended until the morning people arrived, one person at a time, all tidy and tucked in.

For me, the between time—the hours between three and

five—had their own magnetism. These were the hours of suspension, no longer night and not yet day. Nothing much happened, but it felt like anything might. I would stare out the plate glass windows as I refilled my saltshakers and sugar packet holders, wondering what was coming next. The windows themselves intrigued me with their two sides. On this side they were black and opaque, but on the other side they were bright and well defined, rectangles revealing a clean, well-lit place. People driving by knew they could find cheer here, and fresh coffee and a plate of eggs with sunny yellow yolks.

Traffic was sparse that time of night. I followed each set of headlights as they passed, piercing the darkness. I mused that headlights always illuminate what's just out of reach. A college senior can become obsessed with such an idea, especially when the future seems both frighteningly close and impossibly distant.

After the break-in, I had asked to be put on day shifts only. The tips weren't as good, but that was a trade-off I needed to make. Life was complicated as we moved from place to place. Besides, the night hours no longer seemed like my friend. In early January, I asked to work nights again. I needed to rebuild my bank account. But I also missed the hours of suspension in the middle of the night. I was often awake then anyway. Why shouldn't I stare out plate glass windows at passing headlights? Maybe I wanted to peer into the unreachable future.

What happened during that first night shift was inevitable, I suppose.

It was the midnight rush. I was making a pot of coffee when the hostess sat four young black men in my section. I glimpsed them as they walked to my table. They looked like any group of young black men, with Jheri curls and Afros and tight jeans. They were swaggering like they owned the world. I should be fair and say that it seemed to me, from the brief glance I got, that they were swaggering. At the very least they had some swank going on.

In the middle of making that series of familiar movements—dumping out the used coffee grounds and slipping in a new filter—I went blank. My hands stopped. All my energy went into my ears, into listening to the men pull out their chairs.

Then I looked down at my hands, which seemed separate from the rest of my body. I was clutching the brown plastic filter basket against my chest as if it were armor. With an effort, I loosened my grip and finished the motions to begin a new pot of coffee. Then I watched the bitter brew drip. I tried to think.

I needed to carry the coffeepot and coffee cups to their table. What I had to do was pick up the coffeepot with my right hand and the handles of four cups with my left and then cross the room. I had done this hundreds of times. I could do this. A full coffeepot was ready to go. I needed to pick it up. My body did as instructed. My right hand opened and closed around the handle of the coffeepot. My left hand collected the handles of four ceramic mugs.

As I approached their table, one of the young men made a gesture, the dark back of his hand flipping to show the lighter-colored palm. I began to tremble. I halted, involuntarily. My mouth went dry. Even the single word, "Coffee?" was beyond me.

My hands still clutching their props, I bolted. Past the bus cart, through the swinging door into the refuge of the kitchen, behind an enormous stack of eggs in gray cardboard flats. I took a gulping breath.

The short-order cook looked up, spatula in hand. "What's wrong?"

I set the coffeepot on the counter. Then I looked at my other hand and told it to release. The four mugs dropped onto one of the empty gray cardboard egg trays—a muffled, harmless descent. The cook looked at me, then at the fallen mugs. He leaned over his grill to peer through the slot of the pass window.

"Sally's got your table," he said. "See for yourself."

I came from behind the tower of cupped eggs—such a fragile shelter—and looked through the window of the swinging door.

Sally, a waitress in her thirties, was always kind to me. On my first shift back, I'd told her about the break-in to explain my absence. She had been solicitous. I suspected she had informed the cook, who was the owner's son-in-law.

Now Sally was standing beside their table with her back to the kitchen. I could see long legs and arms sprawled around the booth. They were tall, all four of them—like basketball players.

Cheryl was taller than both of our assailants. Cheryl was five foot eleven and a half. Those were facts. I repeated them in my head. Facts. Which meant that these men were too tall to have been our rapists.

I felt grateful that I wasn't out there taking their orders, but I was also ashamed of myself. Was this me? Fearful and suspicious because someone had black skin? But I was. My muscles were clenched. The hair on the back of my hands stood at attention. My armpits were suddenly damp. My breathing was shallow.

"Number four, your order's up," the cook said, matter-of-factly.

I was number four. I went through the swinging door and pulled the platters from the pass window. Two orders of pancakes. I stacked the hot plates along my arm, imagining them as a barricade that would get me safely to the couple who'd ordered them. I served the platters, refilled coffee cups, fetched hot syrup. Then I escaped behind the safety of the counter.

Sally passed me to slide the order ticket into the pass window. "You okay?" she asked. "I can cover your other tables too."

"I'm all right."

Sally studied me for a moment. "Take my next four top." She was offering me her table of four as if staying even on tips was the main thing at play here. I was so aware of her kindness, this subterfuge dressed up as the waitresses' code, that I could have sobbed in gratitude.

"Sure," I managed to say.

I tried to keep my eyes from straying in the direction of that table but failed. Easier to keep a tongue from probing the spot where a tooth was just pulled. The body is fascinated with this unaccustomed source of pain. It didn't hurt there before. Why does it hurt now? Will it hurt if I try again? This time? You want to believe you can wear out the hurt with probing. But you can't.

I heard one low rumble of laughter from their table. When the cook put their order up, it took Sally two trips. I didn't offer to help. I scanned the dishes as they went by: omelets, sides of sausages, short stacks with blueberries. The blueberries cost extra. So they had money.

From my spot behind the counter, I watched them eat. They lifted forkfuls of pancakes dripping with syrup, shoveled in eggs blanketed with cheese. I couldn't keep my eyes away from their chewing mouths. Those full lips. Those full black lips. They were young black men—that's what they were. They were young black men eating breakfast. They were not rapists.

Just allowing my mind to frame the word *rapist* spurted adrenaline into my body. Panic can cycle endlessly, it seems, pulsing its poison. I told myself to breathe. To pour coffee. To do something different, to *be* something different. Anything but this. I didn't want to be this person who was jangled with adrenaline. I wanted to be the old Ruth, the waitress who chatted but not too much, who did her tasks with the rhythm of experience, who enjoyed the darkness of window glass at night.

The tension in my muscles reminded me that the old Ruth was gone, perhaps forever. This was me now. Better get used to it.

The table left a good tip, and Sally offered it to me. Breaking the waitresses' code like that revealed her act of charity for what it was. I shook my head, and Sally didn't press it.

A few weeks later, Sally invited me over for supper. She was the only person who extended such an invitation that year. She fixed a soufflé with chili peppers and said, "You'd think I'd get sick of eggs, but I don't." Then she told me about a guy she'd dated once, who had forced himself on her. "So I know what it's like to want to kill somebody," she said. "It's the only reason I believe in God. So the bastards will rot in hell."

14

MIDWAY THROUGH THAT SNOWY JANUARY, Jim suggested we skip class and go cross-country skiing, just the two of us. The next day was going to be a sunny, cold day—perfect for skiing. He would teach me how. I would love it. We shouldn't waste all this great snow.

I tried to hide my feelings, but I was terribly excited. Jim and I hadn't been alone since Thanksgiving. We spent time together every day, but always with others: Teresa and Sam and Marty and Cheryl, and now Marty's rambunctious Doberman, Gypsy. Since I tended to hold back in the group, I was eager to have Jim's full attention. I wanted to ratchet down the emotion and have some fun.

The next morning Jim picked me up with a car full of skis. I was touched that he had gone to the trouble of borrowing his sister's equipment for me to use. The two sets of skis formed a wall down the center of his small car. The skis' tulip-shaped tips jutted between us, a hard-edged bouquet that I lifted out of the way every time Jim needed to move the gearshift. We drove northeast to a church camp that had hundreds of acres of untrodden woods.

When we turned off the main road, my already high spirits

soared. The bright sun poured through the forest, silhouetting each tree branch and illuminating sparkles in the snow. It was like we were driving through a snow globe that had just settled. This enclosed world felt fresh and untouched and harmless. I barely registered the signs that the snow was quite deep and therefore deceptive—that the cushiony white mounds made smooth covers over tangles of underbrush. I noticed only that everything looked pristine, as if anything were possible.

We parked on the side of the road, hugging a gravel-streaked snowbank that a plow had scraped up. I had to get out on the driver's side of the car after Jim extracted the skis. The long skis were awkward to clamp on with my gloved hands, and I handled the poles clumsily. But the cold air was invigorating, and Jim showed me how to move my arms and legs in rhythm. I practiced on the plow-packed road, laughing self-consciously, but Jim was encouraging. Once I had the four limb movements down, we clambered over the snowbank and into the woods. Our skis immediately sank into the soft drift.

"I'll go first," Jim said. "If you stay in my tracks, it'll be a lot easier—I promise."

This was exactly what I wanted: to follow a strong man who laid down a reliable track. It didn't even matter which direction we went. I felt my spirit relax while my limbs went to work.

Jim headed across an expanse of snow while I followed, trying to imitate his stride. Occasionally I found the rhythm: push-slide, push-slide. Invariably, after a stroke or two, my ski would leave the track and sink. I'd pull my ski out of the snow and back onto the track Jim had made. The vigorous exercise filled my muscles with blood and my lungs with air.

After a while Jim stopped. I caught up with him, panting. "There should be some trees here," he said. "Three big pine trees, in a triangle. You'd love them. But where'd they go?"

I didn't really care. I was happy to follow wherever he led. At the same time, I wanted him to find what he was looking for. As he considered which way to head, I leaned on my poles and listened to the muted sounds of the winter woods: the chittering of birds, the scramble of squirrels, the occasional plop as a snow clump fell from a branch. I almost didn't dare to acknowledge how lighthearted I felt. Or to think that Jim and I could have other happy days together. That we could leave all the trauma behind.

He decided on a route and headed across a field. I followed him. Sometimes I managed the rhythm of skiing; other times I simply trudged. Eventually he paused by some clumps of evergreens.

When I caught up to him, I noticed his strange expression. "What's wrong?"

"I think these are the trees," he said. "But just the tops. That's how deep the snow is."

I laughed in surprise, but I could tell he was disappointed. The unveiling wasn't as glorious as he'd anticipated. In his mind the triangle trees were magnificent. But in the snow they were reduced to three clumps.

We went on, but my clumsiness made the effort exhausting. I fell farther behind, out of breath.

After Jim waited for me yet again, he said, "I have an idea. You just rest."

Ahead of us stood a lone pine tree. Only about five feet of it was visible, but it was probably enormous underneath the snow. Jim skied straight toward it. When he was a couple of yards away, he paused and carefully lifted his left leg from the snow, the ski flailing. Then he placed the tail of his left ski in front of the tip of his right ski to create one continuous track. Arms windmilling, he shifted his weight forward and lifted his right ski to repeat the maneuver. He did this a number of times, laboriously laying a single track that curved around the right side of the tree. Once he reached the other side, he brought his other ski down and skied across the clearing in a normal double track, some thirty feet. Then he turned around and skied back to the spot where the single track began. He repeated his gymnastics in the other direction, creating a second single track that curved around the opposite side of the tree.

He rejoined me, panting from exertion and looking pleased with himself. The two halves of track created the illusion that someone had skied up to the tree, then split their legs twelve feet apart to ski right over it. He said, "Do you think someone will come along and think a giant left ski tracks?"

His goofy sense of humor could be endearing. I said what I thought he wanted to hear: "It's like a track made by a superhero."

Jim's face fell. "I don't want to be anybody's hero," he said. "I'm just a guy."

As the light began to diminish, we headed back, trying without success to follow the happy track we had laid down a few hours earlier.

I'll admit that I skipped my Frisian class quite frequently, but the hours off weren't much of a reprieve. January still seemed endless— a loop of bitterly cold weather, early darkness, and exhausting emotions.

As I grew weary of my own pain, my friends' pain became another sort of snare. On the rare occasions when the old Ruth would resurface—caught up in a book or feeling rested after a few hours of sleep—one of my friends would be angry or crying or waking from a nightmare. High alert would take over. My transient good mood would be replaced by guilt. Who was I to take a break from trauma? I needed to be there for them. We were in this together. Who else could understand?

But I couldn't carry the burden. I could barely cope with my own emotions, much less theirs. It was an issue of surfeit: when something is full, it's full. My trauma cup was full. *My cup runneth over.*

Although I was less aware of it at the time, I'm sure the same held true in reverse. I've come to realize what a passionate person I am, but I didn't know that then. During this traumatic time, I coped by trying to tamp down my emotions, which no doubt made them bleed onto my friends in unhelpful ways.

We did have fun sometimes. There were moments of gaiety—an almost ferocious gaiety—when Marty wrestled with Gypsy or we sat around our plastic campfire. Even so, the center of our friendship couldn't seem to hold. Our energies began to go in different directions. Perhaps that's the way of things during the final year of college, even without trauma. The long-awaited future gradually becomes the present.

Teresa was forging a relationship with Sam. I admired the two of them, that they would stake a claim on something as tenuous as love, even now. Life would surely unseat something so precarious. In truth, I was jealous that Teresa had someone who loved her. It was a petty jealousy. *Be happy for them,* I told myself. But I didn't know what was going on—or wasn't going on—between Jim and me. He said he didn't want to be a hero, but he constantly swooped in to cheer us up, which I found disheartening. I wanted something more real from him. Of course I agreed when Teresa and Marty marveled at what a great guy Jim was, how steady and solid, how funny. But I doubted that he and I would ever share another tender moment.

Was that my fault?

And Marty. She always seemed to be angry—not just at the rapists, but at every authority figure. Not that I blamed her. My coping method was to turn a blind eye, but that didn't work for Marty. Not only was she processing our violent experience and its aftermath; she was also dealing with a dilemma she was no longer willing to keep stuffed: her attraction to women, which was a huge taboo in our conservative culture. I tried to be there for her, but I was weary. And really, I had no idea how to help.

"I'm sick of being angry all the time," I told her once. "Weren't we taught that women are supposed to be sweet and submissive?"

"Right," Marty said. "And how did that work out?" We both laughed without humor. "All I know is, I'm sick of backing down. If that means I've got to be angry, I'll be angry. Is that so bad? Look at Gypsy. She's ferocious. That's it, Ruth! You need to get a dog!"

"I don't want a dog," I said.

"Then get a gun. Something. A woman has to even the field somehow."

I felt a bit desperate. "Maybe I can just walk away."

"From what?"

"The Christian Reformed world," I said. "Could I just leave it altogether?"

"It's a church," Marty replied. "We're not exactly prisoners."

"Maybe not. But I never thought I could leave."

"Do you *want* to leave?" she asked.

"Maybe. How would I know? I don't know anything else. I've spent my whole life in the church's bowels."

"You mean *womb*." A rough laugh bubbled from her throat. "People say they come from a tradition's womb, not its bowels."

I laughed along with her, but I thought, *Maybe I do mean bowels. Maybe this is something that should be vacated. Not something that can give birth.*

—

But if I left, where would I go? Who would I be? I was Dutch and Calvinist in the same way I was female—to the bone. How could I walk away? Yet, increasingly, I knew I had lost my place.

The world, which had once seemed safe and God created, was revealed to be full of danger. The church, which had once told me where I belonged in the world, was blind and oblivious and unhelpful. My very body was a liability, a source of pain and vulnerability, a target.

I wanted to love myself, to love my life in a woman's skin, but that no longer seemed obvious or easy. In fact, what I saw was not only more complicated, it was maddening. For when God created me as a woman, God set me up as a target. *Set me up.* What a bald statement! I resisted it. Avoided it. But there it was. A hard truth.

The best I could do was hedge it all around with softer truths. There were upsides to being female, surely. And God had given me other gifts. Loving parents. A good mind. Wavy hair. But these felt like obfuscations—lines you'd tell children to distract them from their temporary unhappiness. This was different, more serious. When the distraction was gone, the hard truth would remain. To be created a woman is, on some level, to be set up as a target. Think historically. Think sociologically.

And thinking theologically didn't make things better. The doctrine of God's sovereignty continued to weigh heavily on me. My question was never "Did God will this to happen to me?" My question was "*Why* did God will this to happen to me?"

Internally I roared against the question. I suppose you could call that internal roaring *prayer*, though it gave me little comfort. Theology was supposed to be a comfort, a bulwark in times of trial. Wasn't that why we studied the catechism and learned doctrine? I had done those things. I had been a good girl. Now I wanted my comfort.

In fourth grade, I had dutifully memorized the first question and answer of the Heidelberg Catechism, as was expected. That catechism was written in 1563, the year John Calvin died, and is still a central teaching tool for Reformed churches, especially those of Dutch background. It frames theology in terms of comfort:

Q: What is your only comfort in life and in death?

A: That I am not my own, but belong with body and soul, both in life and in death, to my faithful Savior Jesus Christ. He has fully paid for all my sins with His precious blood, and has set me free from all the power of the devil. He also preserves me in such a way that without the will of my heavenly Father not a hair can fall from my head; indeed, all things must work together for my salvation. . . .

Remember, the question asks about comfort. Not just the comfort of a hot bath or a nice cup of tea, but existential comfort, comfort in the face of death. And right there, square in the middle of the answer, it says, "He also preserves me in such a way that without the will of my heavenly Father not a hair can fall from my head."

Let's take that answer in two parts: preservation and hair-fall.

Had God preserved me? Well, yes, my physical life had been preserved. I still had breath in my body. I no longer knew where and how I was supposed to live my life. But I had this precious thing. I had my life.

So, hair-fall. Had a hair fallen from my head according to God's holy will? Yes, it had. Actually, many hairs had fallen! Though not from my head. From a place more private. From the place at the center of my femaleness. I still closed my eyes against the memory. Three heads bending low over my pelvis. The nurses whispering. The comb. The exhausted doctor scraping hairs into an envelope.

Such heat rose in my belly that I could hardly breathe. So God had willed those hairs to fall, had He? Hair was evidence, all right. First, it was evidence that a man had raped me. And according to the catechism, it was evidence that my heavenly Father had willed such a thing to happen.

I didn't know what to do with this knowledge. I didn't want it. It made me furious at God, and I couldn't stand to be furious at God. So I chose other targets. I didn't realize that's what I was doing, but I see it in hindsight. My anger had to go somewhere. I became furious at men in authority: the college officials, the denominational bureaucracy, the church patriarchy. Really, I became angry at men in general. All that oozing anger joined forces with my fear of black men until I hardly recognized myself and my behavior.

I recoiled at the glimpse of a young man with dark skin, especially if he walked with a particular slouching swagger. For the first time I understood what people meant by the expression "My skin crawled." I didn't like being in this skin, but what could I do about it? This was me now. No wonder people avoided my eyes.

In class I sometimes noticed a person looking at me, then glancing away quickly. I felt like a shadow, a phantom. I sometimes retreated to the coffee shop simply to see acquaintances who would greet me. I needed to be reminded that I wasn't disembodied after all. I still existed. I still occupied space.

Over my years in pastoral ministry, I've learned that the most fundamental thing anyone can do for a person in pain is to simply look at them. Make eye contact. *See* them. But so many people looked right through me.

Maybe I'm remembering incorrectly. Maybe people tried to look me in the eye and I didn't raise my head. Or maybe they glanced away out of good motives—to protect me, to hide their tears of sympathy. But I interpreted those glance-aways to mean that it was painful to look at me. That I was ruined. What's more, that my ruination was irreversible. Rape could never be undone.

15

The police arrested a suspect on January 25, 1979. Surprisingly, I don't remember exactly where I was when I heard the news—maybe on the sidewalk leading to the library. It was Teresa who told me. Marty joined us a few minutes later, and she had already heard. I remember a sense of happy surprise, the feeling you get when a hoped-for thing becomes real, like getting an A on a term paper.

Maybe God knows He owes us this much.

Teresa explained the plan. As always, I admired her ability to think ahead. We had to go to the jail together to identify the suspect in a lineup. She had identified a day we could all go in the early afternoon, following our morning classes. I could ride with her if I wanted to.

All five of us victims converged at the Kent County jail at the appointed hour. The detectives met us there. They were pumped up and kept repeating themselves, reminding us how crucial this step was and how we had to be absolutely sure of our identification.

As they talked, it became clear which of the assailants had been arrested: the one we called the leader. Not the one who raped me. Something they said made me realize that my rapist had been quite young, maybe even a minor. Would they decide not to arrest him because of that? I wanted to ask, but I knew they wouldn't give me a straight answer. And I didn't want to sound unappreciative. They were happy with their catch. I was too. They had caught the leader!

But I couldn't help but wonder about the other rapist. Were they hunting for the man who raped me?

The detectives gathered us for some instructions before we went into the lineup. The air sparked with emotion. They told us, "The room is small, so we'll need to divide you up."

"There's a window, isn't there?" Karen asked. "With one-way glass?"

"Yes," the detectives reassured us. "Don't worry—he can't get at you."

It hadn't occurred to me that perhaps he could. I looked at the holstered guns worn by every man in the room. I thought maybe they should unholster them, just to be safe. But they didn't.

The detectives divided us into two groups, three in one and two in the other. They gave us each a blank card. The men on the other side of the glass would be holding numbers. When we were sure which one was our assailant, we were to write down that number on our blank card.

"One more thing," the detectives said. "We'll ask each of them to say something, so you need to decide what you want to hear. Maybe a sentence you remember him saying."

It was Marty who volunteered the phrase. "In case you're wondering, it's for real." She smacked the heel of her hand against her temple as she said it, simulating the gun.

We chimed our agreement.

"I'll never forget that."

"I'll know that voice as soon as I hear it."

Would I ever forget that voice? I could only hope so, although it didn't seem likely. Could the voice that had once caused my hope to vanish, itself vanish from my memory?

Marty, Teresa, and I were the first group to view the lineup. The detectives brought us into a small, darkened room, barely large enough to hold the five of us plus a uniformed cop. Just a few feet away, on the other side of a window, with lights overhead, stood a row of men. They were all young and black. They wore light blue work shirts and jeans and held cardboard signs with numbers in front of their chests. Their faces were impassive, or perhaps impatient. Behind them were height markers. The experience didn't seem real. Maybe it was those height markers, or maybe it was the window framing the men, who were only a few feet away—as close as a TV camera. I almost expected someone to yell, "Cut!"

A host of emotions churned through me: glee and jubilation, but also the familiar fear and anger. Plus a stab of terror at their nearness. Perhaps most surprising, and most unwelcome, was a sickening sense of sadness. One of the young men in front of us was the monster who had destroyed my life and my friends' lives. And also his own. Why?

In a movie, a scene like this would pass without all this distracting internal dialogue. The soundtrack would be triumphant yet poignant. The viewer would know that this experience represented a culmination, a victory. But there was no soundtrack, and I did not feel victorious. Instead I sobbed as warring feelings tumbled through me.

Still, we had a job to do, and we had to do it carefully. Our identification needed to be ironclad. I examined the line of men. They were the embodiment of the stereotype that terrified me: young black men with surly expressions. Which one of these men had broken into our house? There was so much at stake. The detectives had made that abundantly clear. We needed to be absolutely sure before we wrote a number on our card.

Two of the men were about the right size. Looking at them, I felt the hair rise on the back of my neck. Did that mean anything? Their facial features didn't seem familiar. But the intruders had never removed their masks. Their faces meant little. What I remembered was an overall sense of size and shape and, most of all, their voices. Looking at them, I remembered the weight of the rapist's body on top of mine. But no. That was the other one. Don't think about him now. Breathe.

The detectives had each man step forward and speak the sentence: "In case you're wondering, it's for real." When number three opened his mouth, I had no doubt. He was the one. I wrote the number on my card. We were ushered from the room.

As soon as we were out of the tiny room, the detectives asked us whether we were sure. Which trait had stood out to us? For me it was his voice. I said as much. Immediately, I second-guessed myself. Shouldn't I have been able to identify him by sight alone? The stakes seemed enormous. The only thing that could make this ordeal worse would be to point a finger at an innocent man. I could hardly draw a breath when I thought of that possibility. Really, I wasn't 100 percent sure, not on sight alone. Gulping, I crossed out my number and asked if I could go back in.

When I went in a second time, with Cheryl and Karen, I recognized the same men, who were now in a different order. Going through the procedure again, I felt steadier, simply because it was less foreign. The experience moved from the surreal to the real. I was really here, identifying one of the rapists. One of the criminals who ruined my life. This time I was sure, absolutely sure. I aimed all my rage at him through the glass.

When the lineup was done, the five of us victims sat down with the detectives. They had a tableful of guns they wanted to show us. Which was the kind the criminals had used? I wasn't very helpful. I had been too good at taking myself out of my body that night. Teresa seemed to have the best handle on the guns. I was shocked at the forthright way she touched them. She even picked one up and put it against her temple. "Yeah, this one feels the same," she said.

The detectives were circumspect about what they told us, but they would confirm facts if we asked direct questions. Yes, the perpetrators had entered through the dining room window. Yes, the same criminals were suspected of hitting a series of houses. Yes, they had raped some or all of the women present in those houses, but not the men.

We asked if there were commonalities between the houses that were hit. How did they choose their victims? What we were really asking, of course, was the question between the lines: Had we done anything to make ourselves a target?

"All I can tell you is that each of the houses had a Volkswagen bug," one detective said. "And each one had an out-of-state license plate. Maybe that's how they found college students. That's as much as we know."

So Marty's baby-blue bug—the beautiful new vehicle I had so often envied—had made us a target.

So much for the rape being totally random.

My mind spun. Did that mean it was the rapists' will to choose the Volkswagen? Or was it God's will that the rapists chose the Volkswagen? I couldn't even frame the question. It was ludicrous. But wasn't it valid?

Meanwhile, the detectives were talking again. Now they were more forthcoming. They said that yes, we had identified the right guy. They even told us his name: Philip Ricardo "Ricky" Hayes. One of us asked about his astrological sign. They answered readily. Hayes was a Virgo. Same as Cheryl. Apparently he thought too much of himself to rape a fellow Virgo.

So much for Cheryl's theory that her recitation of Psalm 23 had preserved her from harm. Maybe the psalm needed to be amended: *Yea, though I walk through the valley of the shadow of death, I will fear no evil, for my astrological sign is Virgo.*

In February Cheryl flew to Spain while the rest of us prepared for our last semester. Objectively speaking, my classes sounded interesting: Shakespeare, John Milton, Creative Writing, Religious

Studies. Even so, the semester stretched before me like a four-month sentence. I became less functional than I'd been in November during those first weeks after the crime. I was exhausted, and my reserves were entirely gone. My fuel of anger was no longer novel and therefore not as potent. Perhaps this was the first sign of addiction, but I couldn't increase the dosage. My anger was already at full throttle.

With Hayes in custody, Marty, Teresa, and I had a new topic of conversation: keeping tabs on Hayes as he progressed through the criminal justice system. This was another bureaucracy that would undoubtedly fail us. We also tried to pay attention to news about the other rapist, the one they called the accomplice. This was difficult, because apparently Hayes had used multiple accomplices.

At the same time, our denomination was generating news that concerned us. They were ramping up for the synod meeting the next summer. There they would ratify—or not ratify—the previous summer's ruling that allowed women to be ordained as deacons. Imagining those doors opening made me giddy with hopefulness. Church offices were different in function rather than esteem, so after women became deacons, it would be just a matter of time before the door would open to women elders and ministers. No wonder rhetoric about "slippery slopes" abounded. Male voices thundered: "Women in church office? Surely that wasn't what God willed!"

I couldn't stop paying attention as the debates raged in publications and pulpits. What *was* God's will? And why were these men so sure they knew?

I was a daughter of the denomination and wanted to find a way to stay, a way to serve. But as I listened to the pious-sounding arguments, I began to realize that my denomination had no idea what to do with women. The problem seemed to lie in our bodies themselves, our female bodies. Our wombs.

In the coffee shop, I mimicked the condescending tone of the arguments. "Sorry, ladies, we're just following the Scriptures. It's not up to us. The Bible clearly says that women have their place. And an important place it is! Don't you worry now."

"It's hopeless," Teresa agreed. "Don't forget that the proceedings will be conducted by men."

"Because what good are women?" Marty added, her tone bitter.

I didn't dare to admit that I was considering applying to seminary. Fuller Seminary in Pasadena offered a master's degree in pastoral counseling, which would allow me to study theology but skirt the ordination issue. Counselors didn't need to be ordained. I didn't talk about my plans much, for fear they somehow made me part of the system of oppression. Besides, I couldn't say why I wanted to go to seminary. I just did.

———

Week by week, news from the justice system dribbled in, tidbits fed from the prosecuting attorney to the detectives to Teresa. Hayes had been given a court-appointed defense attorney. Out of the fifteen or so crimes in the spree—and fifteen possible cases that could be brought against Hayes—the state's attorney would most likely prosecute ours. Our case had five positive identifications plus solid physical evidence, especially in recovered stolen goods. If our case did go to trial, the court date would be in early summer. We received fewer updates on the other suspect, the one who raped me. I tried to put that out of my mind.

I marked the date of Hayes's trial on my appointment calendar in red ink, imagining it as the gateway to a new version of my future. After graduation, I would testify and be set free. I would take the GRE and apply to seminary. I daydreamed about the sunny skies of California.

More news came down the chain from the prosecuting attorney. Hayes's public defender had been dismissed—something about a conflict of interest. The detectives couldn't say more than that; it was all confidential. But not to worry—Hayes would be assigned a new attorney and a new court date. I crossed out the dates in my calendar and wondered about the application deadline for seminary.

"Now the lowlife has another month to marshal his defense."

"On taxpayer money, don't forget."

Our conversations boomeranged from the criminal justice system in general, to the vile scum who had raped us, to specific fools in the Calvin bureaucracy, to the flaws of our denomination, to the misogyny rampant at Calvin and the larger culture, back to the criminal justice system.

Not one of these conversations was theoretical or esoteric. These individuals, these bureaucracies were the structures that created the confines of our lives. So we bounced around within those borders, like balls sprung by the levers of a pinball machine.

Our conversations were often angry and laced with profanity, but when we talked about God, we were entirely academic. Our tradition treated faith questions as purely cerebral, so we did the same. We debated: Where had God been that night?

At one point Teresa arranged a meeting with two pastors from a local church. We squeezed into their office and asked flat out, "Why did God let this happen?"

The pastors spoke at length, but their words felt empty and abstract. I suppose they felt they needed to provide an answer. But the question is unanswerable. Better to have engaged us in conversation. Asked about our specific struggles. Affirmed to us, gently, that we weren't the first people to have experienced terror. Reminded us that Scripture is full of lament. Perhaps we would have been comforted to know that we would manage to survive the way others had before us, day by day, with the help of God, until someday we would find ourselves in a new future. They could have reminded us that we were beloved children of God and that it was healthy to be angry at the injustices of human existence.

16

DURING OUR FINAL SEMESTER, classes themselves became a sort of haven for me. At least I knew how to be a student, how to sit still and look like I was listening, how to scratch things down on paper from time to time. Fortunately, my professors were understanding. They knew my previous work and made allowances. I was willing to reap some small benefit from the fact that every single person on campus seemed to know what had happened to us. If I had to live with a blinking red light over my head, one that said "toxic," then it could at least grant certain concessions. Still, I was amazed how few people said anything to me directly.

My Shakespeare professor, Dr. Charlotte Otten, was an exception. She wanted the class to watch a number of film adaptions of Shakespeare's work. One of these was Roman Polanski's 1971 version of *Macbeth*. Professor Otten warned us that this was a bloody interpretation of one of Shakespeare's bloodiest plays. On the day of the showing, she pulled me aside and gave me explicit permission to skip the film, which I declined. We all walked over to the seminary auditorium, the same place I'd listened to Marchiene Rienstra give her enlightening talk about the role of women about two years previously. Professor Otten and I sat side by side in the back row of the lower section.

The film *was* violent. I was fine until the fourth act, when Macbeth goes on a murderous rampage in the Macduff castle. This scene is the apex of depravity, as Macbeth is intent on killing the children who are the rightful heirs to the throne. As truly awful events so often do, the scene begins sweetly. A mother is tending to her laundry as her prepubescent son bathes, standing in a basin. The boy prattles about traitors and honest men and the difference between the two. There's a commotion in the courtyard below. Intruders enter the room and dagger the boy from the back. As the son staggers against his mother's skirt, he says, "He has kill'd me, Mother!"

As if this piercing line is not tragic enough, the camera follows as the mother escapes down a hall to a doorway, where three soldiers are holding a woman down and raping her. The camera lingers so there can be no doubt as to what's happening. While the woman screams, the men are laughing—the full-throated laugh of men enjoying themselves.

I sat frozen, hardly able to register the fact that I'd been listening to the woman scream for some moments. My whole body began to shake. I felt complicit in the violence. I stood up, letting my wooden seat flip up with a crash. Professor Otten touched my arm as I walked out.

I was quite sure that Shakespeare's text didn't include a rape scene, so Polanski had chosen to add it. As if he wanted to do Shakespeare one better. As if killing an innocent child isn't violence enough. As if the only way people comprehend depravity is to be titillated at the same time.

I'd never walked out of a class before, and it was oddly energizing. For the rest of the day I felt powerful.

That semester included other moments that underlined the ways

I was changing. One day I arrived at my creative writing class a little late. It was a workshop with fewer than a dozen students around a table. The professor, Dr. John Timmerman, said, "Miss Huizenga, we were just sharing what it is we hope to write in the future. What would you say?"

I thought for a moment. "I'll write about loneliness."

There was scattered laughter.

"I meant genre," the professor said gently. "What genre will you write in?"

Afterward one of my classmates told me she appreciated my willingness to be vulnerable. I remember watching her lips move as she said those words. I didn't feel vulnerable. I felt like a stone. Impenetrable. I was unable to respond to her kind words in the moment, but I held on to them as a sign of hope.

In my Milton class, we were assigned the full texts of both *Paradise Lost* and *Paradise Regained*. That's more than ten thousand lines of iambic pentameter. My resolve, even my Dutch stubbornness, faltered. I decided that I didn't need to read every line. Instead I read bits here and there, plus section summaries. *Paradise Lost* was not easy, but it made sense. *I know what it means to fall from grace,* I thought. The sequel, *Paradise Regained*, had less traction for me. I wasn't surprised to discover that it's less often studied. Our class debated why this was so, but I knew. The fall is a more universal theme than restoration.

———

As the semester progressed, Teresa, Marty, and I spent less time together, and the time we did spend became more painful. Our shared trauma had united us, but it also tore us apart.

The experts say that trauma creates universal feelings—grief and anger and sorrow—but each person experiences and expresses these feelings in particular ways and on their own timetables. I've read that this is why couples who lose a child so often end up divorcing. Grief has a ripping quality. Our group experienced a similar dynamic. On the one hand, we had shared a devastating experience, which for a while collapsed the boundaries between us. We had endured the same four hours on the floor. We had borne violent acts by the same two criminals. We had been trussed up by the same bonds, those lengths of speaker wire. But for all that, we hadn't shared the same experience. No two people ever do. There is shared trauma, but there is also an end to what can be shared. At the end of that end, one discovers a private trauma.

And there was also the matter of our naiveté and embarrassment. We never discussed the details of what we'd endured. We knew we hadn't been treated identically, but that knowledge didn't open the door for us to talk freely about the most personal details. Perhaps we didn't have the language. Perhaps we were too self-conscious, too saturated with modesty. Perhaps we were trying to shelter one another from certain kinds of knowledge that, once spoken aloud, we could never again un-know. Perhaps we were just ashamed.

The upshot was that—loss upon loss—each of us had to navigate this terrible time alone. Our friendship was one more thing the rapists had stolen from us, perhaps the most valuable thing. Gradually our evening conversations became less frequent. Our hilarity around the electric log in the living room died down. I suppose every flame eventually sputters, even a campfire made of red lightbulbs and rotating plastic.

———

About five weeks into the semester, our Ardmore house broke up. Marty, Teresa, and I all moved in with our older siblings. I don't remember what Dianne did. I didn't care at that point. For me, the separation of the three of us victims stung like failure. These were my best friends, and we'd been through so much together.

Along with the sting, however, our separation brought relief. Now that we weren't living in the same place, I could shed my own tears without having to deal with theirs as well. I could have a good day without feeling guilty. I could think about my future a bit more freely without being reminded of the traumatic past.

It was my sister Mary Lynn's idea to have me move in with her family. She presented the possibility as a win-win: I needed a safe place to live, and she needed help with Danny. Mary Lynn was eight months pregnant, and Danny, at nearly two years old, still couldn't walk. He was a solid block of a kid, and it was too much for her to carry him, especially up and down the stairs of their little house.

In many ways our living arrangement worked as Mary Lynn had envisioned. Danny was always in a good mood when he woke up. I changed his diaper, dressed him, and carried him down the stairs. His breakfast was the same hot cereal every morning, and I soon began eating with him.

I would put a pan of water on the stove and, when it boiled, stir in the tablespoons of Malt-O-Meal. Then I would pour the smooth, hot cereal into two bowls, take two spoons—Danny's was small and tipped with white rubber—and alternate feeding us bites.

By the time Mary Lynn came downstairs, her big belly leading the way, the dining room would be fragrant with coffee and Danny ready for the day. He'd sit between us on the floor, playing with blocks while we chatted over a cup of coffee. Our talk was usually pleasant, about logistics or supper menus. Mary Lynn was a good cook, and I appreciated having regular family meals.

On the days I had a later class schedule, we'd sometimes watch *The Phil Donahue Show* together. Donahue turned the microphone over to the audience, and the conversations could go anywhere. Mary Lynn and I enjoyed tuning in to see what the topic would be. During the commercial breaks we talked in animated tones.

The one topic we learned to avoid, however, was doctrine. Mary Lynn and I both called ourselves Calvinists, but we meant different things by that term. To Mary Lynn, God's sovereignty meant that God wills everything that happens. Our role as humans is to submit our wills to the divine will and to live with gratitude for whatever happens, always praising and glorifying God for His providence. She took the Old Testament figure of Job as her model. Job lost everything and still confessed his absolute faith in God.

I had been taught the same things and believed in God's sovereignty too, in the sense that there is nothing above, or equal to, God. But increasingly, I wasn't so sure about the matter of will. Yes, God has a will, and He exercises it in mysterious ways. We pray, "Thy will be done." But aren't humans made in the image of God, also with will? I had to believe we made choices that mattered. Without that ability, humans would be puppets. What joy could God derive from watching us dance if He was pulling the strings?

Even in high school, in Ref Doc class, I had wrestled with this interplay between divine will and human free will. But the matter was no longer academic. Two criminals had invaded our house and robbed us and raped us. Who willed that, exactly? I was unwilling to say that God had orchestrated those actions. And how meaningful was our response?

At some point, Mary Lynn and I discussed this directly. The conversation began with her situation. Did God will for Danny to be disabled? Had God, in effect, caused his disability?

Mary Lynn spoke soberly. "Yes, God made Daniel just the way he is. There's no accident about it. I find comfort in knowing that God will work all things together for good, as He promises in His Word. That's the source of my comfort."

She described Danny's condition as a test sent by God, not as a punishment but as a message, to teach her deeper reliance on Him.

"God sends trials to draw us closer to him, as difficult as that sounds," she told me. "After all, we are not exempt from the curse of sin in the world. God chastises those whom He loves."

The comparison to my situation seemed obvious, so I named it. "So you're saying that God sent those rapists to our house to teach us a lesson?"

"All believers have their valley of the shadow of death," she said. "That's what earthly life is. That's why heaven is our real home."

"And back here on earth?" I pressed.

"God will fulfill His purposes in ways we don't understand. So yes, whatever God gives us on earth is a blessing. Even if it's not what we want."

That's what we'd been taught in catechism class. I had believed it too. Until now. I spat back with vehemence, "Then you and I have different Gods, because this is no blessing. My God never wanted this to happen to me."

As I said it, I realized how fundamentally I was changing. The doctrine I had been steeped in all my life was no longer adequate. To believe that an all-powerful God willed evil things on unsuspecting people seemed wrong, even sadistic. And for God to expect us to respond with gratitude? Wasn't that like an abuser who demands that his victims express thanks for the hardships he inflicts? To me, the thought provoked outrage.

My sister said I was willful. Maybe she was right.

The truth was that I couldn't replace the carefully constructed doctrines of Calvinism with some kind of alternative perfection. If I debated doctrine with my sister, she would win. Her Calvinism was more pure than mine. It was perhaps even more pure than John Calvin intended, with all the inherent doctrinal tensions sanded away. To me, the predicament of will—divine will and human will—was an insoluble puzzle, a result of our being made in the image of God.

I used my will to cling to what I knew of God. I clung to God as a sparring partner does. To stay on my feet. To stay in the game.

During this time, the memory of my childhood dream became my companion again. I couldn't actually enter the experience and rise from my bed, but I would call the memory to mind, detail by detail, searching for hope and guidance. I lingered over each image. What would prompt a child to gaze on rooftops with such compassion, unless she was surrounded by love? Who sat at that long table with a ledger and wrote such a mild accounting? Where was the place of soft carpet that felt completely safe? I clung, not to doctrine, but to what I had experienced of God. I had to believe that I could be lifted beyond my own skin, beyond divine judgment, and find a sanctuary.

———

It turned out that there were other victims of the Heritage Hill Rape-Robbers on campus. The criminals had been active for eighteen months, our house being one of the last targets of their spree. Two of Hayes's accomplices were now in custody. That probably included my rapist, but it was impossible to be sure. I tried not to think about it.

Sometime that spring, a staff member in the college's Student Life office created a support group for us victims. There were almost a dozen of us, fewer at any one meeting. We sat in a circle in an office with the blinds turned for privacy. We didn't know each other. Our connection—having been raped by some of the same men—made a strange foundation for friendship. The other women were as traumatized as we were and seemed brittle and angry. I realized I probably seemed the same to them. No wonder people avoided me.

I was grateful for the group and never missed a session. But I also felt self-conscious about belonging to the group. Membership here confirmed my new identity, an identity I had not sought. I would prefer to be on the other side of those turned blinds, where carefree students were blithely chatting about reading assignments or upcoming parties. But I was on this side, where we talked in tense sentences about our new lives as rape victims. Sometimes that label itself caused arguments.

"Don't say *victim*; say *survivor*."

"Face it. Once a victim, always a victim. No matter what you call it."

"*Survivor* means we could have died. And we could have."

"Sometimes I wish I had."

"Not me. I'll show the bastard. I'll have a great life!"

We spit our words into the great void that had opened around us when we became rape victims. We were like chained people whose blindfolds had been removed, who could now clearly see our captors. It was true that every man was a potential rapist. It was true that culture favored the patriarchy. I didn't disagree, but even daring to say these truths out loud made the world feel off-kilter, with me spun out and careening from side to side. I felt like the robot in *Lost in Space*, flailing and tilting as red lights flashed and a mechanical voice warned: "Danger, Will Robinson!"

⸻

Sometimes our support group shared other people's reactions to our stories. Marty said that her mother overheard church women gossiping about what happened to us, not realizing that they were talking about her daughter. The gossips had blamed us for what happened. "Those girls chose to live in that unsafe neighborhood."

We all worked up a good froth over that. We elaborated on their words, mimicking the imagined voices: "Those girls didn't have the sense to close the blinds. They pranced around in their underwear with the lights on." How could they blame the victim? It was outrageous. Yes, it fueled our outrage.

Years passed before I understood why people do it—why they blame the victims. It's a simple defense mechanism. Random violence is hard on the psyche. It's bad enough when terrible things happen. But when terrible things happen randomly, it's quite threatening. What's to keep that random bad thing from happening to *me*? So the brain looks for a reason. An explanation—any explanation at all—proves that the terrible thing wasn't random after all. If it was a deserved consequence, then there's a wall between me and the victim, because I will never deserve that same consequence. I am still safe in my world, my little walled world.

Good luck with that.

Occasionally our group had visitors who offered resources: a Rape Crisis Team member, who talked about the Take Back the Night march, or an attorney, who went over the logistics of the judicial procedure. The attorney knew how things worked generally, but he didn't know the specifics of our cases. This series of crimes was especially confusing, because there were more than a dozen break-ins, at least two dozen rapes, and three or four criminals. The officials were still deciding which crimes would go to trial. Even the simplest facts of court dates and charges seemed shrouded in mystery. I decided to ignore what was going on as much as possible. I let Teresa and Marty filter the information for me.

Our leader always wore a button that read *biblical feminist*. I pondered the two words together. They appeared to be an oxymoron, if you believed in a biblical mandate for female submission. But maybe they were something else, an elusive third way. I wanted to believe that women were equal to men in God's eyes. I was beginning to realize that I couldn't simply sob and rage for some allotment of time and then return to the old me. I had to think differently. I had to become something new.

The weeks passed. I looked in the mirror and saw little change. Maybe I didn't smile as frequently, but I still brushed the same mane of hair, still dressed in the same clothes, still slung the same backpack of books over my shoulder. I thought I still wanted the same things I'd always wanted: meaningful work to do, someone to love, someone to love me. But these goals seemed ever further out of reach. Graduate school lay on the other side of our court date, which was still unspecified, still impossible to think beyond.

And Jim. What was going on between us? I didn't see him much anymore, now that the Ardmore house had broken up. He was busy with student teaching, so he was rarely on campus. I heard he was dating someone. He was still a great guy. I didn't deserve him.

In late March, my sister went into labor, a bit ahead of schedule. That morning I stayed home with Danny until a family friend arrived. Then I had to get to class. The pains that sent Mary Lynn to the hospital turned out to be false labor, but she was admitted anyway. Danny's disability wasn't due to a problem during labor and delivery, but the doctors wanted to keep an especially watchful eye on the process.

My sister must have been nervous about the birth, but I was oblivious. I had no frame of reference for childbirth. More correctly, I wanted to have no frame of reference for childbirth. I was quite sure I would never be a mother myself. Motherhood seemed fraught with pain. I'd had enough of that. I built a wall around my heart.

Mary Lynn's baby was born on March 26, which happened to be our mother's fiftieth birthday. A few days later our mother came to visit, and there was much rejoicing over this new baby girl, so healthy and perfect. I looked on the scene as if from a great distance.

In April the leader who ran our support group suggested I meet with a counselor at Pine Rest, a Christian mental health facility. I don't recall requesting the visit or knowing who paid for it. I do remember that my brain stalled out at the words *Pine Rest*, which to me meant "loony bin." Being sent there only confirmed what I suspected: that there was something seriously wrong with me.

April might sound like springtime, but it's not—at least not in Michigan. I went straight from class, so I was wearing my usual jeans and a plaid flannel shirt. My hair was on my shoulders, long and thick and wavy. I had given up wearing mascara months ago. Why bother when tears would inevitably smear it away?

The meeting was with Chaplain K., who wasn't just any counselor but the head chaplain. His office had plump chairs facing each other and a Kleenex box on the table between them. We sat down, and I told him the story of the crime. I'd told it a number of times by now and could disengage for a few minutes while I rattled off the facts. To my surprise, he asked no questions about the event or how I felt about it. Instead he asked about my plans for the future.

"I don't really have a plan anymore," I said. "My plan is ruined."

I liked the word *ruined*, a perfect descriptor of my life. To my ears it had the ring of truth. *My name is Ruth, and I'm ruined.*

Chaplain K. said, "I see that you're reacting against societal expectations." His gaze took me in from head to foot, resting on my clunky boots. "You're obviously downplaying your femininity. Was that true before, or is this a result of what happened to you?"

I felt surprised at his words but tried to comply. Pine Rest was the premier mental health facility in my world. Certainly the head chaplain knew what he was talking about.

"This is how college students dress, pretty much," I said.

"Well, I see other students, and they don't all dress like this. You shouldn't be afraid to be feminine. Don't let that be taken from you. Femininity is a God-given gift."

As his words sunk in, the emotions came over me like waves, one at a time. First was shock that he would make such insulting comments. Then came hopelessness, since I would obviously never measure up to his standards. And finally, blessedly, anger. Anger, because I was a plaid-shirt-wearing woman before some creep raped me.

Femininity is a God-given gift? Well, so is anger.

He didn't seem to notice how stunned I was by his words. "This is why my wife sells Mary Kay cosmetics," he said. "She sees it as a form of ministry. It's natural for a woman to want to feel attractive. When a woman feels pretty, she feels like the woman God created her to be."

17

I graduated from Calvin in mid-May. My parents and two younger sisters, Beth and Susan, drove out from New Jersey for the weekend. My brother, Tim, and his wife, Annette, drove up from Chicago. Mary Lynn and Roger were there too, of course, ready to host a party at their house afterward. They brought their two-month-old daughter and Danny, who had recently celebrated his second birthday and taken his first steps.

I'd attended my brother's Calvin graduation four years before, so I knew what to expect of the day: a ceremony in the fieldhouse followed by a punch-and-cookies reception on the lawn. The month of May can be quite cool in Michigan, but my graduation day was sunny and lovely. Before the ceremony, we graduates gathered in the labyrinth of rooms surrounding the main gym. I could hardly believe that Marty and Teresa and Cheryl and I had actually made it to this day. I was thrilled to imagine the empty folding chairs waiting for us on the gym floor and the friends and family all around, filling the bleachers.

At last the band began to play. The faculty strode in first, passing us. As they went by, I whispered to Marty, "Look at all those hoods and funny hats."

"Vestiges of academia," she whispered back. "To make our parents feel better about the beaucoup bucks they shelled out to this place."

My parents?

On the salaries paid by the Christian school system? Did Marty think I waitressed for the fun of it?

The band began playing "Pomp and Circumstance," and we graduates, eight hundred strong, marched in wearing our black caps and gowns. Everyone in the bleachers rose and clapped. They were wearing spring finery, which painted the bleachers with a pastel palette. The gym was like a great bowlful of flowers rippling with applause. As we graduates filled in the chairs, we created a black bottom to the bowl.

I was seated toward the front of the English majors, near Marty and Lisa, who were the only two female philosophy majors in our class. While I waited for the rest of the student procession, I searched the bleachers until I spotted my family. I waved madly at them. I was happy and proud. I was really here, an almost-graduate. I just had to finish one Incomplete in Religious Studies; I would officially get my degree in August.

Nothing about this year had happened as I'd imagined. But my friends and I had prevailed. We had not been cowed. I was bursting with pride and didn't tamp it down. For once I wasn't going to allow any notion of piety or false humility to prick my happiness. Today I would feel triumphant until I exploded. This year was over at last!

There were prayers and speeches. When those were done, the degrees were conferred in groups, by major, with the president announcing each group. When he said, "The candidates for the degree of bachelor of arts with a major in English," we English majors rose as one body and the applause thundered out. For a moment, I pretended that the applause was for me alone. After all, I had done the undoable. I had survived. I had graduated. I would go on with my life now, and it would be as if this year had never happened.

After the ceremony, everyone spilled onto the campus lawn, where tables were set with cookies and lemonade. The sea of people seemed to part for me. The robe didn't trip my feet. The grass didn't stain my shoes. I floated from one "Congratulations!" to the next.

We went to Mary Lynn's house and celebrated the Dutch way, with ham buns and fruit salad and a homemade cake. My sister had made a lovely spread in my honor, and now she beamed at me across the buffet. Beth and Susan had fussed over the details of crepe paper and cake decorations. Usually I was the one who did such things for them. I enjoyed being the center of attention.

Over paper plates full of food, my parents said they were proud of me. My mother said she hoped I was ready to move back home.

"You mean to New Jersey?" I said, surprised.

Had New Jersey ever felt like home? I had never really fit in there, with my inability to say "caw-fee" and "wood-er" for coffee and water. Now New Jersey seemed lifetimes away. The bubble my parents inhabited there felt like another bundle of problems altogether. What would I do if I moved there—become a teller at the local bank? Whom would I hang out with? My only New Jersey friends were Marty and Cheryl, and they wouldn't be there. After graduation Marty was staying in Grand Rapids for a new job, and Cheryl was planning to travel.

"Think about it, Ruth," my mother said. "Come home."

I was glad they wanted me to live with them, but how long would that last? If they knew who I really was—who I'd become lately, so angry and bitter and foulmouthed—they'd be shocked. And I couldn't stand the thought of living with their disappointment.

"I'll think about it, Mom," I said. "But remember I have a job here."

I was still working at the restaurant. It wasn't a career, but I liked it and made good money.

People were passing around my empty diploma cover, which was inscribed with the college seal. My sister Beth brandished it and spoke in a teasing voice: "Look, you got this—do you even need what goes inside? Maybe the cover's good enough. I mean, who wants to spend the summer finishing an Incomplete?" Everyone laughed as she played to the crowd. "What's your paper supposed to be about anyway?"

"Radical Christian community," I said.

"Oh, brother," she said, in her best comedic tone.

We all laughed some more.

"Are you applying to any seminaries?" my brother asked. His wife, Annette, had a seminary degree, and he thought I should get one too.

"I don't know. I'm waiting to decide until after the trial."

"When's that?" someone asked.

"We won't know until after the preliminary hearing," I said. "And that isn't even scheduled yet."

"Why don't you go back to Yellowstone this summer?" Tim asked.

I wasn't surprised that he asked. My brother was fond of Yellowstone. In fact, my spending the previous summer there had been following in his footsteps. He had introduced me to an ecumenical organization called A Christian Ministry in the National Parks. ACMNP helped college students find jobs in lodging and food services, and on the weekends the students conducted worship services. Tim had worked at Yellowstone during the summer of 1974—that was how he and Annette had met.

"I can't schedule anything right now," I told him. "My life is on hold. That's just the way it is."

"So you're going to waste your summer serving breakfast?" he said.

Beth rushed to my rescue. "What waste? She'll make loads of money!"

"Plus, I'm going to apply for a proofreading job," I added. I had recently spotted the job posting and thought it sounded grown up. But I wished people would quit asking me about the future. As if I could control anything at all.

A friend who was leaving town for the summer said, "Maybe I'll see you when I visit in August."

I was glad for the change of subject. "What's happening in August?"

"The wedding."

I must have looked blank.

"Jim's wedding," my friend said.

I looked down at the half-eaten piece of cake in my lap.

The friend sounded embarrassed. "I assumed you knew."

"But—" My voice came out as a squeak. I couldn't quite catch my breath.

"Hey!" Beth said brightly, "Did you check out this diploma cover?" She thrust it at someone and then snatched the plate from my lap. Grabbing my elbow, she guided me to the refuge of the kitchen, where I could lean against my sister's counter and try to breathe.

"What a jerk-face," she said. "You're better off without him, Ruth. Believe me."

———

Shortly after graduation I moved in with two acquaintances, Anne and Cindy. They were a few years older than I was, and I admired them. They were renting a two-bedroom apartment on the second floor of a house not far from the restaurant. They suggested I move in with them. They had space enough for my mattress on their enclosed porch, which had a sturdy door with double locks. The sleeping arrangement would do for the summer, at least.

In June I applied for the proofreading job and got it. I was assigned a cubbyhole and given two stacks of papers to read against each other: typed manuscript on the left, typeset galleys on the right. I read syllable by syllable, my fingers moving slowly down the dueling documents.

I thought about quitting my waitressing job, but why? I didn't mind having two jobs. Waitressing was an antidote to proofreading. All that movement and talking after sitting in silence all day. Besides, it cheered me to don my red-and-white checked smock and hobnob with the other waitresses and customers. Each shift had its own rhythm and was a world unto itself.

Finishing the Incomplete was easy. I wrote the most mediocre paper of my life and turned it in. Check that box! Internally I dared the professor to fail me. To my mind, the college owed me a diploma and then some.

In July the church's synod held its long-awaited vote about the ordination of women as deacons. Someone came into the restaurant and told me the news. I set down a stack of dirty plates and cried. I wasn't just angry and disappointed. I felt foolish for having had hope. Of course they hadn't ratified their previous decision. Of course they were going back in time. I should have known that the cracked-open door would slam shut. Why had I dared to envision myself in any sort of ministry?

I didn't see much of either Marty or Teresa that summer. Marty was busy with her new job. Teresa had gotten engaged to Sam and was busy planning their wedding, which was scheduled for Thanksgiving weekend. I said I didn't know if I could attend because of the holiday. I felt a trace of compunction over my words. Shouldn't I be able to arrange my life to attend their wedding? The truth was that their happy life seemed more and more remote from my own.

That summer I spent quite a bit of time with Anne and Cindy. The three of us cooked vegetarian feasts, which we consumed with gusto. Our conversations were interesting because both women were facing big decisions. Cindy was agonizing over whether or not to become a nun. Anne was debating whether or not to marry a tall Texan man she'd been dating. Both Cindy and Anne created pro-and-con lists to help them make up their minds. We edited and reviewed the lists endlessly—sometimes with great seriousness, sometimes with hilarity. I enjoyed the conversations but found the lists confounding. Wasn't becoming a nun or a wife a heart decision, not a head decision?

The Texan didn't seem perturbed by Anne's list. He encouraged her to weigh the options and see how much sense marriage would make. Privately he told me, "The bigger they are, the harder they fall."

I wondered if I wanted a man to say such a thing about me. I decided I did. I decided I wanted to be very big. And I wanted to fall very hard.

———

I did end up receiving an invitation to Jim's wedding. I attended, with Teresa and Sam. It was a foolish thing to do. I was able to remain composed during the ceremony, but the reception was another matter. That celebration was held at the newlyweds' home, an older house they'd been fixing up with paint and wallpaper. The happy couple opened gifts as people milled around, eating cake and making jokes. The bride and groom both looked at ease, surrounded by friends.

I hung back from the crowd and escaped to the staircase, where I sat down and wept. I told myself I didn't want any of this. Not the wedding. Not this house. Not this husband. But I was lying to myself, and my shoulders shook with the force of held-back truth. This was exactly what I wanted. This was exactly what I had lost. Married life in a house like this, beside a good man like Jim. Was there a moment when that future was taken from me, or was it my fault? Had I somehow let it slip away? Elbows on knees, I hunched on Jim's newly carpeted steps, weeping into my closed fists. People stepped around me to get to the upstairs bathroom, but I didn't look up. I was almost, but not quite, beyond embarrassment.

Eventually I was able to make a dash out the front door and into the sanctuary of my car. Once I was alone, the grief and hopelessness opened me like a faucet. The heart wants what the heart wants. Why would I never have those things? I drove to Anne and Cindy's apartment through a curtain of tears, then clomped up the stairs in my wedding heels. I kicked off the shoes with sudden fury and dropped onto my mattress on the sleeping porch. In a dehydrated haze, I wondered how my life had come to this. Exactly how had I become a college graduate who slept on her friends' floor? Who spent all day bent over other people's manuscripts and all weekend serving eggs? Who had absolutely no plans for the future?

Jim and I never did talk about why things fizzled between us. Maybe I didn't want to know. I could think of only two possibilities, and both were devastating: either he had never loved me, which meant my feelings were unrequited, or he *had* loved me, and the rape had ruined me. Either possibility left me desolate, so what was the point of asking?

On a rare evening off, I decided to drive to Lake Michigan alone, to one of the beaches that had dune grass and quiet. I looked forward to the drive, to the wind rushing in the windows of my trusty Valiant. The car was running well, but the bottom had begun to rust out. The floor on the driver's side had developed an actual hole, meaning there was only a thin layer of carpet between me and the road. I was aware of this, and I solved the problem by getting in and out of the car quite gingerly. Once in, I rested my feet on some stationary rods below the carpet. I assumed the rods were the driveshaft or something.

Driving up Highway 96 toward the lake, I smelled smoke. I looked all around the countryside to locate the fire but saw nothing. The smell was acrid. It seemed to be coming from my feet. Glancing down, I saw small orange flames licking the carpet near my feet.

The flames were moving toward the gas pedal. I don't think I even screamed, because there was no one to hear. I happened to be going downhill, so I simply lifted my foot from the gas pedal.

An exit appeared before me like magic, and I coasted onto it. A gas station appeared, like more magic, and I maneuvered to the entrance. I jammed the car into park, hopped out, and began yanking at the carpet. By this time the flames and smoke were quite visible. A man who was at a gas pump noticed my problem and sprinted to my car. He helped me wrench the carpet loose and pull it free of the car in an awkward, heavy, smoking mass. When the still-burning carpet was lying harmless on the asphalt, we stomped it out and laughed. What an unexpected thing to happen!

I asked the man, who was a fatherly sort, where my gas lines ran. I was mainly concerned about whether or not I could finish my drive to the beach. I checked the brake pedal and the gas pedal, and then the man double-checked them. Both seemed to be operating just fine. We worked together to heave the mangled carpet into the gas station's Dumpster. Then I thanked the man, shook his dirty hand, and drove away in my Valiant.

As I drove down the highway, I could feel the breeze coming up from below my feet. Every now and then a pebble shot up from the road and hit my calves. My heart was buoyant. Once again God had preserved me from greater harm. I felt a sense of gratitude and peace. I sang folk tunes in the sanctuary of my Valiant.

The answer, my friend, is blowin' in the wind
The answer is blowin' in the wind

At the beach I sat on a dune cliff and watched the waves roll in. The western sky was streaked with clouds, which turned pink and gold as the sun dropped low. I absorbed the horizon's expansive sense of possibility. On the way home I treated myself to a soft-serve ice-cream cone at the Whippi Dip.

A few days later, my brother-in-law, Roger, patched the Valiant's floor with a round disk of Formica he'd salvaged from someone's kitchen remodel. The round piece had been cut out to make a hole for the sink.

"That oughta get you through until it gets cold, anyway," Roger told me.

I was happy to have the problem solved. The arrival of cold weather seemed impossibly far away.

———

Summer ended, and I was still waiting to hear a court date. Over the Labor Day weekend, I waitressed during a particularly slow overnight shift. As I moved around, I kept glimpsing my reflection in the darkness of the plate-glass window. My image quavered, ghostlike, as if it held a message. At last I stopped and studied myself: the pinkish smear of my checked smock, the pale round blob of my face, the smudge of my unrecognizable features. It looked like I was disappearing.

A line from a T. S. Eliot poem ran through my head: "I have measured out my life with coffee spoons." Was that what I was doing? Measuring out my life, coffee spoon by coffee spoon? Was I waitressing, or was I waiting?

At that moment, I told my reflection I would get on with my life. I would take the GRE in December. I would apply to seminary. And as soon as the trial ended, I would move on.

PART 3

THE COURTS

September 1979–January 1980

Grant me justice against my opponent.

LUKE 18:3

Life must be understood backward.

But . . . it must be lived forward.

SØREN KIERKEGAARD

18

Soon after Labor Day, I was informed that the trial date had been set for September 17. After more than seven months of waiting, the big event was less than two weeks away. I scrambled. I didn't want to feel unprepared. Not this time. Not in court. This time I would be ready to face evil.

My conversation with Chaplain K. that past spring had been maddening but had taught me one helpful thing: people would make judgments about me based on my clothing. So I needed to wear just the right outfit when I testified. Anne, Cindy, and I discussed how an ideal rape victim should appear. We tossed out words. Feminine. Appealing. Not the least bit provocative. We settled on the adjective *demure*. Anne consulted the dictionary and read the definition aloud with a theatrical flair: "Demure: modest, unassuming, meek, mild, reserved, retiring, quiet, coy; decorous, decent, seemly, ladylike, respectable, proper, virtuous, pure, innocent, chaste; sober, sedate, staid, prim, goody-goody, straitlaced."

An upscale women's clothing store was going out of business, so Anne and I combed the racks of clearance items. We found a long skirt in blue corduroy, pieced in three tiers. I loved that it fell below my knees and would meet the tops of my boots. No leg at all would show. We also found a salmon-colored sweater jacket that was the perfect cross between serious and soft. Anne lent me a white peasant blouse with a high neckline. I tried on every piece of jewelry the three of us owned and settled on a small cross necklace.

I was armed and ready.

A few days before September 17, we got word about another delay. Some legal rigmarole had pushed the trial date well into October. That changed things. My mother hadn't been planning to come, because the start of the school year was such a busy time for her. But she felt it would be possible to take a few days off in October, so she arranged to fly out.

On October 23, the group of us assembled downtown at the Hall of Justice. Our case had been assigned to Judge Stuart Hoffius. Before proceedings even began, we were all dismissed. The prosecuting attorney, Joel Hoekstra, explained that Hayes was going to plead guilty. There would be no trial after all. We could all go home.

After all the months of anticipation, it was a shock to be done waiting, especially when nothing had happened. We would need to return in a week or so to hear how the case pled out. Meanwhile, we were done. We all had an awkward lunch together, and then my mother flew back to New Jersey. I felt chagrined that my parents had borne the expense of another flight for nothing.

A few days later, we were informed that the plea deal had fallen through. There would be a trial after all. We were given a new trial date, this one just a few days away. This time when we appeared at the courthouse, a jury was selected. It took hours. Then the attorneys and judge disappeared to meet in the judge's chambers. When they returned, we were told that the proceedings had ended again. We weren't told why. Judge Hoffius simply said we'd have to set a new date and suggested mid-November. However, that date conflicted with Teresa and Sam's wedding over Thanksgiving weekend.

Judge Hoffius smiled, wished them well, and scheduled the trial for just after the wedding, on December 10.

I consulted my pocket calendar. December 10 was just two days after I was supposed to take the GRE, my first big step toward applying to a counseling program. I wondered if I should take the exam or wait until the trial was over. I wondered what other dominoes I might be forgetting about.

The whirlwind of schedule changes gave me emotional whiplash, but the court transcript sums up the situation rather neatly, as if all of it were quite normal:

> The matter was set for October 23, 1979. And the Court was ready to proceed but was informed that the defendant was ready to plead to the charge. And that did not result in a plea. And as a result, the Court adjourned it for just one week to October 29, 1979, which is still in the September–October term. At that time the Court undertook to select a jury. We spent almost a day at it. Defendant refused to stay in the courtroom. And accordingly, he requested and demanded he have new counsel. The Court then granted his request for new counsel. New counsel was assigned in the first week of November 1979. The Court immediately asked that the case be reset for trial.

Over Thanksgiving I didn't attend Teresa and Sam's wedding. Instead, I went to New Jersey to spend the holiday with my parents and younger sisters.

On December 3, I turned 22. I have no memory or record of how, or even if, I celebrated.

On December 8, I went to a classroom on the Calvin campus and took the GRE without studying for it. I had decided I was tired of delaying my life.

On December 10, I put on my testifying outfit again—the long blue skirt and the salmon-colored sweater—and went back to the Hall of Justice. Hayes's new attorney, a public defender, tried once again to delay the proceedings but was denied. The trial began.

In his opening statement, prosecuting attorney Joel Hoekstra spoke for the People of the State of Michigan:

> So then what is it that Mr. Hayes is charged with? . . . Essentially, with respect to the crime of armed robbery, it is going to be the allegation of the People of the State of Michigan, and I believe the testimony that you will hear from the witnesses, that Mr. Hayes, accompanied by another man, broke into these young women's home, and that this occurred on the evening of November the 5ᵗʰ, 1978, a little bit over a year ago at this time. Actually, I believe by the time the assailants actually got into the house, it was past the twelve o'clock midnight hour, so it would actually have been into an early Monday morning. But it was, for common parlance, common way of speaking, a Sunday evening.

Perhaps it's no wonder that to this day I need to consult a calendar to figure out which date was which. The two periods of time seared into my brain—Sunday night and November 5, 1978—are not the same day. Not that it matters. The discrepancy is insignificant. But my persisting confusion speaks to the way time shifted and scrambled and then congealed in a jumble.

Prosecuting attorney Hoekstra went on to preview the testimony the jurors were going to hear:

> The girls—I believe the testimony will show that they had retired for the evening and that one of them, Marty, had gotten up and was getting something to drink from the

kitchen area, or something like that, when she suddenly was confronted by a person wearing a mask. She screamed and fled to the upstairs portion of the home; and that subsequently, a man—the same man, presumably, came upstairs, [and] got her and the other two of her roommates that had bedrooms in the upstairs portion of the home. Those two are, if I'm not mistaken, Teresa and Karen. Ruth had a bedroom on the main level of the home. And I believe that Cheryl had a bedroom in the basement of the home.

Hoekstra referred to a diagram of the house, which made me feel curiously detached from the crime he was describing. What part of this was mine? The exhibit belonged to the court. It concerned a house that did not belong to me.

Ultimately, all five of the girls were rounded up, so to speak, and congregated in the dining room portion of the home. And at that time they realized there were two assailants that had entered their home, two masked Negro male individuals, and that both of these individuals were carrying guns with them at that time.

From that point on, the tale essentially goes along these lines. Initially, they were led one at a time out of the dining room area of the home into a portion of the home that was pretty much their own, either the bedroom or the area where their valuables were kept. While one of them went with them to this portion of the home, the other one stayed in the dining room area and stood guard over the four remaining girls. And it was during this first session that they were taken out that they were individually robbed. I hesitate to say that this happened to each and every one of the five, but at least a great majority of them were individually led out of the dining room to the bedroom area and robbed by one of the assailants while the other one remained guard with the other remaining four.

After this process was completed, then the assailants, for lack of a better word, at this point in time began systematically leading one of the girls out at a time, forcing them to engage in sexual intercourse with them, again, while the other one remained behind and stood guard over the other four. And then that girl would be returned to the dining room. Then the other one, presumably, would take out one of the other girls, take them to another bedroom portion of the home, would sexually assault that one. And this process was repeated a number of times. The testimony will indicate that four of the girls were all attacked, two of them by both assailants and two of them by just one of the assailants. This process, as you can understand by now, was repeated a number of different times over and over during the course of the evening.

At one point in time toward the end of the episode, they were, for some reason or another, led down into the basement portion of the home. They remained down there for some brief period of time, and then were escorted back up to the main portion of the home. And ultimately, the assailants fled the home.

Hearing the night's events laid out with dispassion was like hearing a familiar story but told by echo. This night sounded similar to ours, but less sharply edged. Our events had been chaotic; these seemed systematic. Our hours had been endless and confusing; these were well ordered and logical. Listening to the attorney lay out the night of the crime for the members of the jury, I suddenly realized—how had I not seen this before?—that there had been nothing haphazard about that night. The criminals had moved from invasion to robbery to rape, exactly according to plan. They were practiced at their craft. How had I not seen it? This was not some impulsive action but the calculated, willful execution of a crime.

I tried to control my breathing so I wouldn't miss any of Hoekstra's words.

Based on these facts, ladies and gentlemen—and this, I submit to you, I believe would be essentially what the testimony of the five girls will be. And it will be in considerable more detail and in considerable more length than what I just outlined to you. But as I indicated, this is just a statement and attempt to acquaint you briefly with the facts of the case as I believe the testimony will come from the lips of the witnesses.

From this testimony, ladies and gentlemen, it will be the contention of the People of the State of Michigan that all five of these women were the victims of an armed robbery, that the men were armed with guns, that their property was taken, or the common property of the household was taken and removed from their home against their will at gunpoint, and the gun obviously being a dangerous weapon within the context of this statute. I submit to you that based on their testimony, you will find there was an armed robbery that took place of them during the course of this early morning hour of November the 6th.

Further, it will be the contention of the People of the State of Michigan that the crime of criminal sexual conduct in the first degree was committed against four of the five girls. The testimony will be that Cheryl was not sexually attacked, but that the other four were all sexually attacked. Mr. Hayes sexually attacked . . . personally two of those girls and had sexual penetration with them, and that his partner, his accomplice, his co-assailant, what have you, was responsible for attacking sexually all four of the girls during the course of this evening; and that as a consequence, either as a perpetrator or as an aider-and-abettor, . . . that he is guilty of committing the crime of criminal sexual conduct in the first degree.

———

Once the opening argument was finished, we victims were dismissed. We weren't allowed to hear each other's testimonies until after we had testified. We sat in a room in the Hall of Justice with police officers who were also waiting for their turns on the stand. They had a deck of cards and seemed happy to be earning overtime.

As the day progressed, the detectives stopped by to fill us in. We asked about the other cases too. The women in our support group had also identified Hayes, and some of their stolen property had been recovered. We were eager to know when all that evidence would be introduced. The detectives explained that none of those other crimes were being prosecuted, so none of that evidence would apply. This was our case only.

Somehow I was shocked. I was used to thinking of Hayes's crimes as related since they were a continuous string. I hadn't fully comprehended that Hayes would be tried on a mere fraction of the evidence against him. It was worrying. What if we didn't have enough evidence? I was still trying to wrap my head around the fact that only Hayes was being prosecuted and not his accomplice—the man who raped me.

We had no choice but to fully trust the detectives and prosecutors, yet I wondered how they could stand to obey all the rules. I supposed they were used to it. I watched the police officers play cards and wondered how much they were earning in overtime. Mainly I wondered if I could keep wearing the same outfit every day until it was my turn to testify—and how many days that would be.

As it went, Marty testified first, to lay out the events. Then it was Cheryl's turn, and then mine. The prosecuting attorney, Joel Hoekstra, had us tell the events of the night, going forward chronologically.

Here is my testimony, picking up after I'd been robbed by the accomplice and taken upstairs by Hayes:

RUTH: . . . And then he ordered me to strip.

HOEKSTRA: What were you wearing that night, Ruth?

RUTH: A flannel nightgown.

HOEKSTRA: Anything else?

RUTH: And underpants.

HOEKSTRA: You took those off?

RUTH: Yes, took off the nightgown. And he fondled my body all over. And I was shaking very badly. I mean so my whole body shook, and I was crying. And he told me if I didn't stop shaking, he was going to blow my brains out, which didn't help me stop shaking. Then he seemed to be very upset that I was upset and got mad at me because I kept crying. Finally, very irritated, he said, "Well, just forget it. Put your clothes back on."

Much of the testimony had to do with our ability to see, or not see, the two assailants, due to the lack of lighting and the ski masks. There were also many questions about who was where at what time. The crime had happened over the course of four hours, more than a year earlier. Things had been confusing at the time. Now the interrogation made every answer sound muddled. But the questions I worried about most concerned the sexual assaults. We began with the accomplice groping me in the basement.

RUTH: He [the accomplice] kicked me in the feet, told me he wanted me to come. And then I had to stand next to him. And he put his hand under my nightgown and tried to make me kiss him. He kept kissing me.

HOEKSTRA: Did you allow him to do that?

RUTH: Well, I just stood there. He had an arm around me with a gun here, and then he was kissing me. And I felt the gun against my head. If I squirmed, he just hit it against my head so I wouldn't forget it was there. And then the other guy, the leader, came downstairs with Teresa. And he was very angry that we were down in the basement . . . [When we were back in the dining room,] we [housemates] had been holding hands on the floor, touching each other, reassurance. He made us lay so they could see our hands, getting very strict. And then—

HOEKSTRA: Why were you holding each other's hands?

RUTH: We were scared out of our pants.

HOEKSTRA: Okay. This was a comfort?

RUTH: It was comforting to know they were there, and we were all very close friends.

About halfway through my testimony came the moment I'd been dreading: the explicit questions about the rape by Hayes's accomplice.

RUTH: And then he kicked me in the feet—the one who wasn't the leader, the other one—kicked me in the feet, and told me to go upstairs again. We went upstairs to Marty's room. And he told me to strip.

HOEKSTRA: Is that his words?

RUTH: Yes, that was his word. He said, "Strip." I took off my nightgown. He said, "The rest." I took off my underwear. He said, "Drop it," because I was holding them against me. And then he made me turn around and parade up and down in front of him. And then he said, "Lay down on the bed." And then he got on the bed and raped me.

HOEKSTRA: What kind of act did he have with you? Was it normal sex?

RUTH: Yes, he was on top. It was my period and I had two tampons in and it was extremely painful, but he didn't notice. And he just told me to shut up and quit crying. He was very upset I was crying and made me wipe all the tears off my face. He asked me a lot of questions. Before he actually got done, actually having sex, he asked if I had a boyfriend, or what my name was, or why I didn't have a boyfriend. Then he told me I was very pretty, and if I was good to him, he would not let the other guy get me. And he asked me who our neighbors were and asked me what my horoscope sign was. And then afterwards too he asked me a lot of questions, you know, small talk. And he seemed—he seemed angry that I wasn't responding wholeheartedly. If I cried or anything, he got angry. And he wanted me to talk to him as if we were friends. And he asked me if I liked it. He kissed me and said, "Do you like it when I kiss your breasts?" I said, "No." And he was very upset.

HOEKSTRA: Was he holding anything during this time?

RUTH: Yes, the gun was either in his hand or for a while he put it on the pillow right next to my head. He would pick it up if I squirmed or moved around.

HOEKSTRA: Just for clarification, Ruth, you did not willingly consent to this act of sexual intercourse?

RUTH: Not at all.

19

At first, testifying was excruciating. It took all my courage to use intimate words like *tampons* in front of strangers. But I prayed silently for strength and purposely turned my head to look at the members of the jury. This was not about my embarrassment. This was about justice. This was the time to speak. Maybe I needed to look demure, but I didn't need to feel demure. I didn't need to act demure. I was in the witness seat now, and he was not. Now *he* had to listen to *me*.

Maybe he would remember my voice a fraction as often as I remembered his. I could only hope so. Maybe he would hate the sound of my voice as much as I hated the sound of his! This surge of feeling was like electricity, like voltage, like power. I felt like I had the ability to change the way the world worked, at least for today, at least for one criminal.

After the direct testimony, I was cross-examined by Hayes's attorney, the public defender who had been appointed late in the game. He was a young African American man who seemed inexperienced. His questions weren't skillful, and I almost felt sorry for him. Almost. Much of his cross-examination simply opened the door for me to elaborate on details that hurt his client's case.

This is an excerpt from my cross-examination:

PUBLIC DEFENDER: Now when did you, during the course of these events, start to distinguish between the two individuals?

RUTH: When the one who seemed to be in control hit me with a gun.

PUBLIC DEFENDER: Well, okay. How many times were you hit with the gun?

RUTH: Repeatedly. I don't remember how many times.

PUBLIC DEFENDER: And where were you?

RUTH: Well, it was during the course of the evening.

PUBLIC DEFENDER: And the other one did not hit you with a gun?

RUTH: Yes, he did. They both did with their own guns hit me repeatedly.

—⁓—

We had another matter to testify about: the lineup to identify Hayes. The procedure had been complicated. Not only had I crossed out a number at the first lineup and gone back in for a second lineup, but when the cop recorded my number the second time, he made an error. This caused much confusion.

Prosecuting attorney Hoekstra addressed the matter of identification in his closing argument.

What is the evidence that says that Mr. Hayes, the man that is in the courtroom today, was one of the two men, and not only that but was the leader, the man that was in charge? That evidence comes from three different sources, ladies and gentlemen, essentially, and the first is the identification that each one of the five girls has made at the time of the lineup on January 29th.

What did they say? What did they testify to? I had them talk about what they remembered about the leader from the night that this happened. . . . Remember, ladies and gentlemen, that this isn't something—the ordinary armed robbery or the ordinary criminal sexual conduct in the first degree thing that is over very quickly. These women were with these men for over four hours at a time. For four hours these men were in their home. To a greater or lesser degree over that period of time, they heard them speak, they saw them, they observed them. Now, you can qualify that by the lighting conditions and the circumstances, their fear and their fright, but that's four of the longest hours that you can imagine, I submit, and that was time when they had to listen and to be fearful and to think.

What did they tell you about the leader? They said a number of things. First and foremost and primary in this case is the voice, the voice of Philip Ricardo Hayes, the defendant in this case. To a woman, they all said that the man that was in charge had a distinctive voice, a voice that they remember. I recall the words of Cheryl, who said that night, as she was lying there, she was saying to herself, "If I ever hear that voice, I'm going to be able to identify him. If I ever hear that voice again, I'm going to remember it, and

I'm going to remember him." And that may have been the most succinct phrasing of it that any of the girls was able to come up with, but I submit that that speaks for all five of them in this case. A very distinctive voice; a low voice; a monotone voice; a raspy, gravelly voice; a unique voice; a voice that each one of them said to a person was distinct and a voice that they all remember.

I trembled physically as I listened to this part of the closing. To know that someone understood the impact of that voice was enormously moving. I looked toward the jury box and saw many jurors with tissues in hand, dabbing at their eyes.

Several of them recalled his lips—and we start right now—we get into the physical. You remember you're lying on the floor, you are face down, your belly is to the ground, you're commanded not to move, you're commanded not to look around. You can't stop somebody from hearing. You can stop somebody from . . . looking—but you cannot stop somebody from listening by putting them on the ground, like Mr. Hayes and his accomplice did in this case. Well, some of the girls said that they got an opportunity to see his face through the mask, but, nevertheless, see his face.

"Your belly is to the ground." Hoekstra understood how it had been! Belly to the ground. But not anymore. Now we were sitting tall in court.

On the day of January 29th, they were asked to appear at a lineup. That lineup took place at the Kent County jail. The incident was November the 6th. November the 6th, December the 6th, January the 6th, January the 29th, not quite three months later, these women are asked to come out and anticipate the possibility of being confronted again by the men—one of the men possibly that terrorized them for four hours. Put yourself in their positions. Think about it. How would you feel? The anxiety, nervousness, the apprehension. Put yourself in the fact that these are five young women who are college students. They are seniors in college.

I don't know how many of you have been to college or how many have a chance to know what a college atmosphere is like. I suggest to you that college is a place where you are required to test and probe and think and discern, that you are not allowed the luxury of black and white but everything is in gray areas, and then you are impressed before you go into that lineup that you must be positive, you must be absolutely certain, the concept that has been foreign to you for some four years during the course of your college experience. You are asked to go in there under these nervous, anxious times, and you know when you go into that lineup room the thing that you are going to do. You're going to be able to identify anybody at all, but you are going to remember that voice, and you will remember that voice.

What happens, ladies and gentlemen? Out of those kind of circumstances, those kind of possibilities—look at those pictures—every single one of them, at one point or another, identifies the defendant in this case, Philip Ricardo Hayes, as being the leader, the man that was in their house that night. . . .

Do you doubt Ruth Huizenga when she says she was in a lineup, that when she heard that voice, she started to cry? Do you doubt her when she became so anxious and upset, she crossed that number out, that number three, which was the defendant, put down a zero, and asked if she could take the opportunity to view a second lineup? Do you doubt her identification? Do you doubt that what happened because [the sergeant's] notes that he wrote up the next day say she didn't identify anybody? Do you believe that there's some kind of great conspiracy here to subvert or tangle or falsify the results of that lineup by these young women?

When Hoekstra called out my bungled identification in front of the jury, I winced. Hearing him describe me as anxious and upset made me want to shrink into my seat. But hearing the empathy he conveyed made me dare to sit up straight again. Ever since the lineup, I had regretted my emotionality and lack of calm during that experience. Not to mention my indecision! For months I had worried that doing the lineup twice had somehow contaminated my identification and would imperil the whole case. That worry had intensified since the trial began, as I more fully understood the mechanics of the case. In a sense, our case against Hayes represented a dozen others. That raised the stakes in terms of my flub. Would the jury understand my hesitation, or would it cast doubt? I was grateful that Hoekstra had put my moment of indecision into a larger context. So many futures hung in the balance! I dared to glance at the jurors. No one was looking at me with irritation. No one condemned me.

In that moment, I knew what grace is. Grace is more than simple forgiveness; grace says that it's all right to need forgiveness in the first place.

But Hoekstra was still talking. He was bringing up the matter of Hayes's distinctive voice, reminding the jury that they'd heard it themselves. Hayes hadn't testified or uttered a word in court, but a cassette tape had been played. On that tape, Hayes rambled about the meanings of various astrological signs.

Then we have the voice, and you've heard that voice, ladies and gentlemen, you heard that voice. Ask yourself if you heard that voice on and off for four hours in your home, would you forget it? Even if you tried, could you forget it?

Again, Hoekstra's empathy pierced me. I had spent more than a year feeling like people didn't understand, that they secretly thought I was making too much of this event. But here was a prosecuting attorney, acknowledging the power of that criminal's voice. The feeling that flooded me was validation.

Ladies and gentlemen, this is the Christmas season, and this is a truth-seeking process that we are about here. I ask you to give justice and truth a Christmas present. I ask you to return a verdict of guilty. Thank you.

The jury deliberated for barely half an hour. We victims and our family members had been brought into another room to relax but were hurried back into the courtroom. Once we were settled, the members of the jury filed in, looking sober. My heart was thumping wildly. I expected this part to proceed like a TV drama, with one word ringing out: "Guilty" or "Innocent" before the gavel fell.

But it was more complicated than that. There were many counts, and the clerk of the court read each count individually, then issued each verdict. At the first "Guilty!" my friends and I whimpered in relief, clutching each other's hands. My eyes filled and spilled as I strained to hear every word. Surely every verdict would be the same. The clerk read count after count. Each time the verdict rang through the courtroom: "Guilty!"

The court transcript captured the final ruling:

THE CLERK: Members of the jury, I have your verdict form on People of the State of Michigan versus Philip Ricardo Hayes.

In reference to Count I, armed robbery, [Teresa], guilty.

In reference to Count II, armed robbery, [Cheryl], guilty.

In reference to Count III, armed robbery, [Marty], guilty.

Count IV, armed robbery, [Karen], guilty.

Count V, armed robbery, Ruth Huizenga, guilty.

Count VI, criminal sexual conduct in the first degree, [Teresa], guilty.

Count VII, criminal sexual conduct in the first degree, [Marty], guilty.

Count VIII, criminal sexual conduct in the first degree, [Karen], guilty.

Count IX, criminal sexual conduct in the first degree, Ruth Huizenga, guilty.

And in reference to the felony firearm violation, guilty.

Ladies and gentlemen of the jury, listen to your verdict as recorded. You say upon your oaths that this is the verdict agreed to unanimously in the manner and form as the People have in the Information in this cause charged. So say you, Mr. Foreman? So say you all ladies and gentlemen of the jury?

THE JURY (in unison): Yes.

THE CLERK: Thank you.

The sentence would not be pronounced for some weeks. I went home to New Jersey for Christmas, the second Christmas I would spend treading time. But this was much better than the previous year. This year I had something concrete to wait for. I was awaiting the sentence of justice.

Meanwhile, both Anne and Cindy made their decisions and moved on. Anne decided to marry the tall Texan. Cindy decided to move west to join a group of novitiates. When I returned home from the Christmas holiday, I found myself alone in an echoing apartment. I wondered why I had bothered returning to Michigan at all. The trial was over. My friends had dispersed. Other than my mundane jobs, what was there left for me? Maybe it was time for me to make some bold decisions too. Soon I would know how I scored on the GRE.

The sentencing took place six weeks after the trial, on January 30, 1980. Before we entered the courtroom, the detectives met with all of us victims. They told us that everything was going well, that the sentencing would be routine, that we should relax. But their body language was tight. I knew they were highly invested in the outcome of this trial. They'd been after Hayes since his first crime, nearly three years before.

The detectives had a bag of evidence to return to us. Each item bore a tag for identification, although we recognized our own possessions. When I held up my prized flannel nightgown, I gasped. The fabric had been punched with holes and littered with *X*s in permanent black marker. I squashed the garment back into the bag. Why hadn't I realized that my nightgown would be ruined along with everything else?

We asked again about the other rapist. There were articles in the newspaper, but it was hard to be sure which criminal was which. Were the detectives absolutely sure they had our rapist in custody? And had he been on trial yet?

The detectives confirmed that the criminal we'd read about was our rapist. He had been sixteen years old when he broke in through our dining room window. He had been tried for a separate crime and was awaiting sentencing. But they were sure he was the one who had been at our house. We didn't need to testify against him. We had done our civic duty.

Good, I thought. *Maybe this is really over.*

We victims filed into the front row of Judge Hoffius's courtroom—all of us except Cheryl, who was out of the country. Our family members sat in the row behind us. We each had somebody there. I had my sister Mary Lynn, Marty had her brother, Teresa had Sam, Karen had her sister. We turned around to scan the room to see if Hayes had family members too. There was a scattering of people in the courtroom, but I couldn't bear to keep my head craned or to speculate. I clutched a Kleenex, my hands in my lap. I wondered how I was supposed to feel. I felt cold. I was glad that the corduroy skirt of my court outfit was long and warm.

Hayes was brought in through a side door. He was shackled. He held his head up. At the trial he hadn't glanced at us victims; he had been entirely focused on the jury. He didn't glance at us now either. He was looking at the judge.

Act as if we're not worth your attention, I told him silently. *You might be done with us, but this court isn't done with you.*

There were preliminaries, such as entering into the record the dates Hayes had already spent in jail. At last Judge Hoffius said to Hayes, "Now you may make any statement you wish."

When Hayes spoke, his voice sounded as I remembered, rough and low and ominous. A prickle went down my spine. Fifteen months had elapsed, but I had not misremembered the timbre or cadence of that voice, which was too deliberate, too calculated.

HAYES: First of all, your Honor, I don't feel I was entitled to a fair trial due to the fact Miss E— P— that was on the jury was on my last jury. And she sat on my trial until the last day. Then she was pulled off by some coincidence. Miss E— P—, she was on my last jury that found me guilty. And she was on this one too.

The judge and the attorneys and Hayes went back and forth regarding this point, consulting endless piles of paperwork. There was talk about another trial under Judge Snow and court terms and witness lists. I didn't know anything about a second trial and a second judge. I felt like I'd been accused of daydreaming in math class when I'd been diligently doing the work all along.

HAYES: You know, I told my lawyer, but you know, he asked me was I sure. I told him I was sure. Did nothing get did about it . . .

JUDGE HOFFIUS: I'm sure I will find it is not the same person.

HAYES: The way I recognize her, she was heavyset. She had the red curly hair with the tinted glasses to match her hair. And she wore pantsuits all the time. And from time to time, she wore pantsuits which she wore back then. And she wore brown earth shoes, like structure shoes. I remember it was the same person.

What was going on? Had somebody flubbed up? Could the verdict be overturned on some technicality? I felt a frisson of fear. Up and down the row we looked at each other, eyes widening. For some twenty minutes there was more consultation and more flipping of pages. Then the matter was dismissed. All of us victims took a deep breath.

JUDGE HOFFIUS: Mr. Hayes, I sat through this jury trial. And to me it was one of the most offensive, horrible offenses I think I have ever heard. I cannot disagree with the jury's verdict. They found you guilty on a number of separate and independent charges. The criminal sexual conduct in the first degree charge is a very, very serious charge. There are four young women who were college students who were held for a period of almost four hours under most unusual circumstances. And the jury found you guilty of criminal sexual conduct in the first degree on each of the four women. It is therefore the sentence of the Court that you be taken from here to Jackson, Michigan, there delivered to the Corrections Commission to serve a term of not less than 40 years nor more than 60 years, sentence to start upon completion of your felony firearm statute violation as consecutive to that sentence. The armed robbery charges and the criminal sexual conduct charges may run concurrently.

I think what has happened to these young ladies has probably marred and scarred their personal relationship with men and their personal outlook on life to such an extent that I feel it is one of the most serious charges that has ever come before me.

"Marred and scarred." Judge Hoffius spoke the truth. Amen. I sniffled into my tissue but sat up straight. Not only had the prosecuting attorney understood the impact of our ordeal, but so had the judge. I felt seen and heard by the justice system. Avenged, even. The full weight of justice had been rendered against our opponent.

From the moment we heard the sentence, my friends and I had some sense of how unusual this outcome was.

More than a year before, we had entered a club we hadn't sought membership to: women who have been raped at gunpoint by a stranger. Now we entered a smaller club: women who have seen their rapist convicted and sentenced.

I wished I could feel triumphant. I felt something, but it wasn't exactly triumph. It was a sort of sickness in the pit of my stomach. I wondered how much prison time Hayes would actually serve. I wondered about the other one, the one who raped me. Would he ever be free again? I wondered what had brought the two criminals together and why they had chosen to ruin their lives. And *my* life. *All* of our lives. And I wondered if Judge Hoffius was right. Were my friends and I marred and scarred beyond repair?

PART 4

THE FALLOUT

January 1980–May 1981

Work out your own salvation
with fear and trembling.

PHILIPPIANS 2:12

Got to kick at the darkness 'til it bleeds daylight.

BRUCE COCKBURN

20

On January 30, 1980, with Judge Hoffius's words "marred and scarred" still reverberating in the spaces between us, Marty, Teresa, Sam, and I went to a local dive to celebrate. The White Rabbit was the sort of place you entered from the back, from a gravel parking lot with potholes deep enough to bottom out your car. The jukebox was famous for playing whole album sides instead of singles, so the place would be saturated for half an hour with the Rolling Stones or Bob Dylan or the Grateful Dead. From the back room came the crack and clatter of pool balls, forever careening.

As usual, the place was full of Calvin students, whose parkas and hats and backpacks littered the ripped booths. The interim term had just finished, so there was a post-finals gaiety in the air. Jim was sitting at some pushed-together tables with his wife. I hadn't seen him since his wedding almost six months before. I wondered if Teresa or Marty had asked him to meet us there.

He stood up to give us each a hug. The brief press of his chest against mine was a reminder of what I could never have. I sat down quickly and pretended it was too noisy to converse. I hummed along with Bob Dylan.

How does it feel
To be without a home
Like a complete unknown, like a rolling stone

People I hadn't seen in a long time came by. The men slapped me on the back and said "Congratulations!" in overly hearty voices. The women were quickly tearful, speaking in voices so low and quavering that I could catch only single words like *God* or *justice*. I thanked them and began humming again.

What *about* God? What *about* justice?

At one time, the two words had seemed to mean the same thing. In the Kingdom of God there would be perfect justice. But now we'd found justice quite apart from God, in a building with linoleum floors and too few benches, in nondescript rooms where men we didn't know exerted themselves on behalf of the state of Michigan. Was God responsible for that justice? Be careful. Because if He was, then wasn't He also responsible for the injustice—the crime that brought us to court?

It had been more than a year, and I still couldn't live with the implication of the doctrine I'd been taught: that everything happens according to the will of God. The God I loved simply wasn't that monstrous. Even though justice had now been dispensed, which was statistically unusual and for which I was grateful, justice didn't erase the theological conundrum. In fact, it sharpened it. Could I thank God for justice but not credit Him with injustice? That wasn't how it worked. But how *did* it work? I didn't know anymore.

I felt bereft. I missed knowing who God was.

I wanted to put Him back in my hip pocket where He used to fit.

Still, that night at the White Rabbit, I tried to soak in the sense of absolution. After all, in bringing a guilty verdict and imposing a long sentence, the justice system had laid down at least one moral certainty. That in itself was a comfort. By finding the rapists guilty, we victims were vindicated. Held blameless. At last I was no longer to blame—not in anyone's eyes, including my own. Fifteen months after the crime, I knew it for a certainty: I was not to blame for what happened to me. That in itself was something to hold on to.

Who exactly *was* to blame? The rapists, of course. But only them? What did it mean that God was sovereign? Did God will the rapists to act, or did He simply allow them to act out of their own will?

Across the table, Marty talked in animated tones with Jim. People stopped to congratulate Teresa and Sam on their recent wedding. As the word about the verdict spread, more people came by, as if we were in a receiving line. Their comments bounced off me, and I felt bad for having a heart of stone. But years later I understand that I had to harden myself that night. Their words might have been well meaning, but they smacked of gossip, and I would have none of it. Where had these people been the past year? Why did they get to lick their lips now over the juicy bits, the verdict and sentencing? Horror can be such a delicacy in sample size. These folks knew nothing about what we'd endured. They had chosen to keep their distance from it until this happy ending.

I tried to be a good sport, to sit and smile and nod at all the right times. I tried to feel victorious. But I quickly grew tired of people who wanted to ride the coattails of my terror. Had we gone, in a few months' time, from being the object of gossip to being the cause for public celebration? Maybe that was the same target with slightly different arrows.

This was a significant night, yes, but after all the waiting, was I supposed to be able to pick up where I left off? I was filled with fury and grief at the thought. Sitting at that table, I was reminded of everything that had been stolen from me, everything I would never get back. A circle of best friends. A boyfriend. A future. Those things would never be pulled from an evidence bag and returned to me, not even in tatters.

I knew I was supposed to feel victorious, but I felt bitter. And I didn't want to be that person—the one whose life would be forever shaped by what she'd lost.

But something can never be unmarred or unscarred, can it? I felt a familiar throb of desperation.

Someone raised a glass: "You nailed the bastards!"

"They'll rot in jail the rest of their lives!" someone shouted.

It seemed that everyone was eager to raise a glass in triumph, even if they had the facts wrong.

Someone waved at me from a booth along the back wall. It was Don, the seminarian from New Jersey. Seeing him and his wife in church shortly after the break-in had once swamped me with despair. The two of them had reminded me of all the things I would never have. Now I pretended I hadn't noticed his wave.

But I was tired of sitting at that boisterous table. And my emotional stew wasn't Don's fault. He was a nice guy, easy to talk to. Those high school prayer meetings had been fun, once upon a time. All that charismatic praying and singing with our hands in the air.

I headed over to Don's booth. He greeted me warmly and introduced me to his friend Ed, a fellow seminarian. Both men were clean shaven, with longish hair, but Ed's was straight and dark blond, and he had prominent, widely spaced cheekbones and a square jaw.

Don said to Ed, "Remember I told you about my Holy Roller phase in high school? Well, Ruth here was part of that."

"You don't say." Even in the dim light, I noticed Ed's laughing blue eyes. He patted the bench beside him. "Sit right down and talk to me," he said. "I'd love to get some dirt on this guy."

"I've told you all there is to tell!" Don protested.

After I slid into the booth beside Ed, Don turned serious. "Ruth, I heard your case went to trial. I'm so sorry you had to go through that."

"We just heard the sentence," I said.

"You mean that Heritage Hill case? That was you?" Ed asked. "That's heavy."

I couldn't help but smile. "People have said a lot of things. But *heavy*?"

"Ed here is a child of the sixties." Don laughed. "A Vietnam vet. But tell us the sentence. Was it life in prison?"

"Right, life. Forty years. Plus a year for possession of a firearm during the commission of a felony." I tacked that on the way the prosecutor had. It made the sentence sound real.

"That son of a b— will never get out!" Ed said. "Are you celebrating?"

"I guess so," I said. I didn't really know what we were doing.

"We need another pitcher," Don said.

I watched the two guys josh about whose turn it was to pay and then pool their money, spilling dollar bills and quarters onto the table. I liked their easy camaraderie.

While Don left to refill the pitcher, Ed lit a cigarette. "That Heritage Hill crime spree? I was out of town at the time, on internship. I hear it was all over the news."

"I guess it was, toward the end." I watched him smoke, which he did as if it were his natural state. I noticed his wedding band.

"And it's been what, a year?" He exhaled smoothly while regarding me. "What have you been doing all that time?"

"Waiting," I said. "Waitressing."

"That takes courage."

I pretended not to understand. "Does waitressing take courage?"

"You know what I mean. Waiting."

It was the most real thing anyone had said to me in weeks, maybe months. "Thanks."

"Look, I understand. Something like that happens—it affects everything. I mean, even me. When I heard, I went out and bought a knife."

I wanted to roll my eyes. First he said *courage*, which sent a tremor of understanding through me. Then this stupid, canned response: a knife. Right, a knife would have solved everything. We could have taken on two armed assailants if only we'd had a knife. I studied him—the relaxed posture, the worn sleeves of his work shirt, the easy motions of his smoking. He was older than I was and more at ease in the world. But was he suggesting, like so many religious men, that virtue was paramount? Should we have fought back? Was it better to be armed and resistant and dead rather than unarmed and raped and alive?

"Did having a knife make you feel better?" I said at last, sarcasm lacing my words.

Ed was inhaling as I spoke, but he laughed, which made him cough. "It made my *wife* feel better. She wanted me to get a gun. But I told her I'm never gonna carry a gun again. So I got the knife instead. It was stupid."

I liked that he could laugh at himself. "Right!" I said. "As if sleeping with a weapon under my pillow would have solved everything. As if I could whip it out and just kill somebody—"

I stopped, remembering that he'd been in the war.

"You don't want to kill," Ed agreed. He rolled up his chambray sleeves, flashing a fuzzy blue tattoo on the underside of his forearm. A vestige of Vietnam, no doubt. So I wasn't the only person who'd been through something awful. What did I know about that war? Only that it was a mess. That the guys who came back were wrecked.

Ed was looking at me intently.

Emboldened, I asked, "Did you get wounded in 'Nam?"

"Everybody gets wounded there. So yeah, I was a pretty f—ed-up mess."

I was startled, surprised that a seminarian would talk that way. He laughed. "I landed stateside. Got married. Got divorced. All in a few weeks. And let me tell you, that'll bring you right up against Jesus!"

He laughed, and I did too. His face was so expressive that I couldn't keep my eyes off it. I tried to calculate the age difference between us. But why should I? He was married. What a pity. We would make a good match, both of us wrecked and hanging on to Jesus by our fingernails.

"Sounds interesting," I said. "What else have you done?"

"Me? I've had every kind of job. I sold cars. Drove trucks. For a while there I was running drugs."

"Really?" I wondered what that meant exactly.

"That was before I got saved, so don't hold it against me," Ed said. "Still, I don't usually tell people. Don't know why I just told you." He shook his head and his hair rippled under the light. "But look at you. A survivor. A beautiful survivor. You know what it's like to bear the unbearable. Not many people do."

Don returned with the pitcher and poured a round. We lifted our full glasses and clinked. Ed said, "To the crap that happens, and to the love of God."

21

THE NEXT EVENING I went back to the White Rabbit alone. Ed was in the back room, bent over a pool table. When he looked up and saw me, an enormous smile spread over his face. He didn't even take his next shot—he just handed his cue stick to his partner. "Take this, you idiot. Some sunshine just walked into my life." It was an outlandish thing to say, but I was thrilled. Did Ed know I'd come here to find him?

I suppose I had some idea what would happen next, even though I tried not to know. To say I was lonely doesn't capture it. I was alone in an existential sense. I wasn't sure who I was, or even *if* I was. I'd been birthed into a certain role and groomed for it all my life—good girl—and now that had been rubbed out by the rape. So did Ruth still exist?

I saw the answer I wanted in Ed's eyes. I existed, most definitely.

That second night we settled into a booth with a pitcher and two glasses, and the world sealed off around us, just as it had the night before. Ed plied me with questions, and I told him all sorts of things about myself—things I'd almost forgotten.

He was curious about my job in Yellowstone two summers before, so I described the geyser basin that I remembered so fondly. How the boardwalks passed through drifting steam. How the hot pools were so intensely blue that they looked cold. How I listened with one ear for Old Faithful to erupt.

"You can tell the geysers apart by the way they sound?" he asked.

"No, but the crowd roars for Old Faithful. And a thousand cameras go *click-click-click*. Kodachrome!"

Making Ed laugh was a tonic. It reminded me that my life had once been colored by adventure and humor rather than trauma. Perhaps it could be again. Ed repaid with stories of his own. His father had been a truck driver, and as a child, Ed sometimes rode along with his dad. One time they were at a truck stop and the waitress said it was an anniversary—her son had committed suicide exactly one year ago that day. Her shift was ending, and she had no idea what to do. Ed's dad told her to take off her apron and sit down. Then he went behind the counter. He poured her a cup of coffee and served her a piece of coconut cream pie.

I loved that story. I wanted to live in a world where people didn't have to hide their pain. Where they could set it on a counter, pick up a fork, and dig in.

When Ed asked about my plans for the future, I told him my old cover story—that I was thinking about becoming an English teacher. People usually took this at face value, but Ed could tell I didn't actually want to teach English. He pressed and I admitted my secret: that if my GRE scores were good enough, I was going to apply to seminary to get a counseling degree.

"But I might have tanked the test," I said. "Taking the GRE when I did was stupid. I was distracted. But I just couldn't wait anymore."

"You're a mover," Ed said. "You're going to *do* something with your life."

"You don't think seminary is a crazy idea?"

"You'll love it," he said. "There's nothing better."

The evening ended, only to be continued the next and the next. We were having a continuous conversation, interrupted only by daylight when we were forced to be apart.

Ed loved to talk about his seminary readings and lectures—tenets he was still working out in his mind. He was especially enamored of Kierkegaard and explained the "leap of faith" to me, his hands gesticulating above the tabletop. "Faith and doubt aren't opposites, Ruth. They're twins! Faith is like love—beyond rationality. Reason comes to an end, and on the other side of the chasm is God. You just have to leap!"

His views were intoxicating. My ministers had always talked about God as if He were a distant, unknowable figure lurking behind the clouds, manipulating us in complex ways. To Ed, God was a passion, a force, something as close and throbbing as a person's own blood supply. To Ed, God was love.

What if Ed is right? My head pounded with the implications. *Maybe God didn't set me up like a puppet after all.*

Ed liked to smoke cigarettes and drink beer while he told stories, the three activities merging into one. Sometimes he talked about Vietnam, shutting his eyes as he spoke, as if closing out the memories. When his voice dwindled to nothing, I didn't urge him on. I knew there were things a person couldn't tell.

His voice turned velvety when he talked about his seminary internships. "I preached God's love—that's all I did. And you wouldn't believe how those churches changed. People don't want to hear judgment. People need God's love."

I loved to hear Ed say "God's love," as if he knew firsthand what it was, as if he were directly connected to the supply. I wanted to believe that God's love could siphon from him to me, that it could put to rest my existential loneliness.

"Tell me more about your family," I said. I always felt I understood people better when I knew how they grew up.

Ed had been an only child; his parents had divorced. They were both dead now. "My mother liked to sit in the dark, smoking and drinking. I could hear the ice clinking in the glass. I watched the red tip of her cigarette." His mother was so different from mine that I cataloged each detail like a translator working among a foreign tribe.

He had more to say about his truck-driving father, who worked hard and saved up for years to buy his own rig. Then he bought another truck and another—a small fleet. One night he went gambling. He lost everything in his wallet. Then his savings. The story spiraled down even further. He put the title to a truck on the table. And when that was gone, the second title. And then the third. By morning it was all gone—a lifetime lost in one night. Ed cried, wiping his tears with the back of his hand.

He knows there are things worth crying over, I thought. *There are nights that change everything—nights you lose things and never get them back.*

It didn't matter that Ed told these stories in the White Rabbit in Grand Rapids, home of Calvin College, center of the Christian Reformed world. His stories were not tidy tales, neatly categorized into boxes labeled "God's will" or "man's sin." With him I stepped out of that well-ordered world and went down a rabbit hole into a different sort of place—a place where unspeakable things were spoken of, where chaotic experiences weren't shoved into neat packages but sprawled into their own shape and story, where life ended but then picked itself up and went on. Ed's life had been as ruined as mine, but he was still walking, still talking, still loving God. What he gave me was hope.

At the time I only thought, *What a shame he's married.*

He was the one to bring it up, finally. "Let me tell you why I got married."

I thought he meant his current marriage, but he was referring to an earlier marriage—the one he'd mentioned so casually in our first conversation. "I came home from 'Nam. And, well . . . who expects that? Who comes home from 'Nam alive? When I sobered up, a week had passed, and I was wearing a wedding ring. That's how that happened."

I wouldn't judge him for that, though I knew others would. Say something should have killed you, but it didn't. People expect you to be glad you survived. But you're living outside of time now. You ought to be dead, right? Who can you be? *Where* can you be? It's like being trapped in a room without a door. At some point you just bang on the walls, the floor, looking for something to give. People see you banging, and they think they can judge. They say, "That's good" or "That's bad." But you don't care about that. You just bang and hope that something will open. Maybe that's what happened to Ed. And when he stopped banging, he was married.

"So you made a mistake," I said. "Don't we believe in grace?" Offering him forgiveness made me feel powerful.

I met Ed a couple of times a week for the whole month of February. One night I told him what happened in the house on Alexander. I backed into the story, first describing what it had been like to go back to campus, how everything had slipped away that semester. Tears leaked from my eyes, and his. He came to my side of the booth and laid his arm along my shoulders. When I described the break-in itself, his muscles clenched with such fierceness that I shrank away from his chest, even as I was flooded with desire.

He wanted to avenge me! I craved his ferocity, his protection, his bloodlust against the animals who had done this to me. And at the same time, I craved his tenderness, his tears, his obvious distress at my pain. He reflected every twinned feeling back to me: fierceness and fragility, anger and gentleness, terror and hope.

When I visited the ladies' room, stumbling ever so slightly from the beer, I marveled at this illicit thing I was doing—telling intimate things to a married man. I knew I should leave. I should at least resolve to leave. But I talked back to my internal rule wielder. After what I'd been through, didn't I get a free pass? Ed was my consolation prize. He was my guide to this new world I inhabited, this world called *after.*

Later, when he brought his face close to mine, I turned away and his lips grazed my cheek. By turning my head, I was able to feel virtuous. And to stay.

In retrospect, I see the seduction of this sense of virtue—how I sliced it thinly, monitoring exactly how close we sat, how intimate a tone I used, where I allowed his arm to rest. On some level, I knew that by slicing each wrongdoing into so many increments, I was simply creating more transgressions. But the delaying was essential. I knew that if I kissed him once, the whole structure of my life would come crashing down.

Occasionally one of Ed's seminary friends would stop by the booth and ask Ed pointedly, "How's your *wife?*"

I'd sit up straighter as they studied me. Was I supposed to wither under that look? My year as the object of pity had inured me to scrutiny. I wanted to say, "Go ahead. Gossip. I know those arrows."

As the evenings passed, Ed confided in me that things were bad and getting worse between him and his wife. She was pleasant enough but was mainly concerned with laundry and cooking and her receptionist job. He couldn't talk to her the way he could talk to me. She had lived a sheltered life. Ed said this sadly. His voice grew husky and his eyelids dropped partway down, like curtains around the two of us. He put his arm around me, and I snuggled into him. He kissed me on the cheek, the neck.

"I don't know who I am anymore," I told Ed. "I don't know what I want."

"Yes you do," he said. "You just don't dare."

22

One evening in March, I invited Ed to meet me at a party that some of my old college friends were throwing. I was nervous about introducing him around, although I suspected many people already knew his story.

I arrived alone. Everyone had congregated in the dilapidated kitchen, and some people were perched on the counters. I hadn't seen Marty, Teresa, and Sam since the verdict, and I wondered if they knew my secret.

It was fun to catch up. Marty had gotten another dog. Teresa had a new job. Sam had a timeline for graduate school. When Ed came through the door, he made a jovial comment and then helped himself to something to drink as if it were perfectly natural for him to be there. Every eye in the room followed his movements. He either didn't notice the scrutiny or pretended not to, though I was knifed with self-consciousness.

Everyone knows he's older—and married. Everyone is judging me.

Someone put a Rolling Stones album on the stereo and cranked it up. We all went into the dining room, which was dark and empty except for a beat-up light fixture that hung low over a nonexistent table. We began to dance without restraint. We jumped up and down and propelled ourselves off the walls, singing along at the top of our lungs.

> *I can't get no satisfaction!*
> *'Cause I try and I try and I try and I try*
> *I can't get no!*

The light fixture swung wildly on a long chain, spinning out of control whenever someone ran into it, which was often.

Ed's method of dancing was to swivel his hips while grinning provocatively. He was wearing a pair of tight jeans, quite different from the baggy jeans the other guys wore. He pulled me against himself, grinding. I pulled away. I did want some satisfaction, whatever that was, and I suspected he could give it to me. But I was embarrassed to be feeling what I was feeling and mortified that someone might be able to tell.

> *Let's spend the night together . . .*
> *Now I need you more than ever*

Teresa and Sam were dancing on the other side of the room. As the hanging lamp swung between us in wild gyrations, I realized that Teresa was keeping an eye on Ed and me. I pushed him away with more energy.

"Dance nice," I said.

But he didn't. He kept circling his hips, kept reaching for me. His expression both attracted and repulsed me. It said he could devour me on the spot.

And if he did, what would be left of me?

I walked out of the broken-down house, and Ed followed. We

stood on the street, between our two vehicles, my Valiant and his Scout.

"Let's just sit and talk," he said. "I need a smoke." He opened his passenger door and motioned for me to get inside.

I was furious that he'd embarrassed me in front of my friends. Worse, I was frightened by what I might do if I got into his Scout.

"You're a married man," I said. Then I got into my Valiant, slammed the door, and drove away.

———

The next time I saw Ed at the White Rabbit, he told me that he and his wife had separated. I assumed he meant physically and legally separated, since they'd been emotionally and spiritually separated for a long time. Seeing the boyish eagerness that lit Ed's eyes, I decided that I wouldn't force him to explain himself.

Actually, I liked that word: *separated*. Maybe Ed wasn't the only one who needed a formal separation. Maybe I needed one too. Maybe I needed to separate from the Ruth I'd been raised to be.

Looking back, I feel compassion for that young woman, stuck in an internal no-man's-land. The past made me angry, and the future made me fearful. The right path seemed so narrow. Who would I be if I didn't marry someone from my same background? If I didn't work in the Christian school system? What if I really did go to seminary? I felt fenced in. Even combative. After all, I hadn't chosen this path. My laid-out life had been ruined through no fault of my own. And I was tired of feeling like a failure about it.

Impulsively I said to Ed, "There must be places where the Christian Reformed world doesn't even exist!"

"Marry me and we'll go," he said.

I studied the beautiful, clean lines of his cheekbones and saw his eyes shining above them. "You're already married," I said.

"Separated. Marry me as soon as I'm divorced."

"As soon as you're divorced," I echoed.

I let that word, *divorced*, roll around in my mouth, tasting it. I could love a divorced man, couldn't I? After all, I was conversant with pain.

———

My bad dreams returned. They had abated the previous summer, but testifying at the trial sharpened my recall of the night of the crime, and spending time in physical proximity to Ed stirred sensory memories. His warm breath on my neck could be arousing in the moment but terrifying in memory. It was difficult to fall asleep, knowing that a masked man might crawl through the windows of my dreams.

After a stretch of bad nights, I was simply weary. I began to wonder if sleeping with Ed would cure my night terrors. Didn't love cure all sorts of ailments? And would it help heal the sexual part of me? When we were together, I sometimes felt wildly aroused. The idea of the sexual act both tantalized and terrified me. Part of me wanted to get it over with so I could quit dreading it.

Or perhaps this was an elaborate justification for doing something I knew to be wrong.

In the end, I simply made the decision and told Ed what kind of birth control to buy. When we slept together, I was tearful, but the tears were an overflow of emotion, and not all the emotions were painful. I did feel loved and protected under the press of his body. Then I fell asleep and woke myself up with a piercing scream. I wouldn't have recognized the high-pitched cry as coming from me if I hadn't become so used to my own screams.

For the first time, I wasn't alone in my bed during a night terror. Ed wrapped himself around me, soothing me with the circle of his arms, the deep murmur of his voice, and the musky scent of his chest, which was itself scarred and imperfect.

Ed told me more about his experiences in Vietnam, stories that are not mine to repeat. The violence and bloodshed made us both weep and shake, and this time I was the one to offer comfort and reassurance.

Post-traumatic stress disorder hadn't yet entered the common lexicon. And it would be decades before the language and lens of PTSD would be applied to the victims of sexual violence. So Ed and I didn't have the benefit of diagnostic acronyms. Instead, we simply reflected our damage onto each other and felt less alone. We were a perfectly imperfect pair.

Getting a divorce seemed complicated, but Ed knew what to do. I found his aplomb reassuring. Within a day he had rented a semi-furnished apartment. Within a week he had a full-time job as a counselor at a rehab center. When I asked him what his professors said about the divorce, Ed told me he hadn't been going to class.

"All week?" I was nonplussed.

"I withdrew from three of my classes last Friday. By the grace of God, it was just in time to get a refund."

"It's your last semester!"

"There will be other semesters. I've gotta work. Divorce takes money."

"But school is important. I don't understand."

"I know you don't," he said. "It's one of the things I love about you."

I really didn't understand. I had pushed so hard to finish college. Quitting a degree program, for any reason, seemed like opening the door to chaos. I must have looked at Ed with an expression of alarm.

"Don't worry, baby. I'll finish," he assured me. "I'm not going anywhere."

A few days passed before I wondered about the timing of events. Had the course withdrawal deadline really been evidence of the grace of God? Or had Ed known about it and felt impelled to initiate the divorce?

When Ed drove me to his new apartment, I thought he was playing a joke. He pulled into the driveway right next to Jim's newlywed home.

"Are you kidding?" I said. "My old boyfriend Jim lives there."

"Skinny guy? I think I met him," Ed said. "That's his driveway, and this one is mine."

I stared out the window in disbelief. The pavement of the two driveways touched.

"See? Great neighbors!" Ed was genial. "And wait till you see inside. It's fully furnished."

We went up a narrow interior flight of stairs. The door at the top opened to reveal a small, dark-paneled room furnished with an enormous wooden desk. I was too flustered at first to realize what the problem was, but there was something not right about that desk.

Ed proudly showed me the tiny kitchen, bathroom, and bedroom. I immediately went to the bedroom window to check the view. Sure enough, Ed's bedroom window looked across those kissing driveways and into Jim's kitchen. In my imagination, I could see through the walls to those carpeted steps where I'd wept in such despair after Jim's wedding. The memory filled me with humiliation.

"Check out this desk I bought," Ed said. "It was salvaged from the old Franklin campus. I got it for fifty bucks."

He surveyed the piece with satisfaction. It occupied the entire living room like a squatter who had no intention of leaving. To my thinking, Ed may have paid fifty bucks too much for the thing. Didn't he realize that the desk's surface was too close to the floor? Then I saw the problem: the desk had no legs. When I pointed that out, Ed told the story. When he and Don tried to carry it up the stairs, the desk got stuck in that narrow stairwell, wedged between the walls. It had been the biggest joke! They had to borrow a hacksaw and saw off the legs.

"But how will you reattach them?"

"Why bother? This is temporary. We'll just have to saw them off again when I move out."

Even though he couldn't sit at the desk, Ed had organized his work on its surface. His textbooks were stacked according to subject, and each stack was topped with the appropriate legal pads. My eyes were drawn to the yellow pages, which were covered with his flowing handwriting. I wanted to sit down and read. I wanted to know everything he knew about theology and religion and God.

As it turned out, we spent very little time in the living room. Instead, we sat in the bare-bones kitchen at a tiny speckle-topped table. There was one window, which wore a pair of frilly curtains. The curtains had no view to frame, just the gray shingles of the neighboring house—the one on the opposite side from Jim's house.

Breakfast was the only meal Ed ever made in that kitchen, no matter what time of day it was. I sat at the table and watched as he made coffee and toast, fried eggs and salt pork. I could have reminded him that I spent whole days smelling breakfast, but I didn't. While he cooked, I studied the refrigerator, a 1950s model with sloped shoulders and a silver logo that was reminiscent of airplane wings.

"Let's fly away together," I said to Ed. "When the divorce goes through."

"Paperwork and money—that's what a divorce is. That's what we're waiting for. The lawyer wants his check."

I wished I could believe what Ed believed—that marriage and divorce were just pieces of paper. It would be a convenient thing to believe. I ate the breakfast he fixed for me.

I never cooked in Ed's kitchen. This was perhaps the most illogical of an elaborate set of rules I had made up for myself—rules that allowed me to negotiate the narrow corridor I found myself in: how to be with Ed but still be (kind of) a good girl. The lines I drew were rather fine. I could eat at Ed's table. After all, I could be a guest. I could cook for Ed at my own house. After all, I could be a hostess. But I couldn't cook at his house. If I did, that would make me a home wrecker.

The boundaries about sex were even less logical, but in practice they were simple. We could have sex if we made *absolutely sure* I didn't get pregnant.

Much later, I realized that the rules were not what I pretended they were. I thought I was navigating a complex dynamic between right and wrong. In reality, I was using rules to hide what I was doing—not from other people but from myself. That way I wouldn't have to face the self-loathing that was underneath my behavior.

Perhaps as a result, sleeping together was a minefield. The first time brought with it feelings of comfort after a nightmare. But as time went on, there were moments of pain, when intimate touch triggered memories of the attack. Ed's caress would remind me of the assailants, who had stroked my skin with one hand while holding a gun in the other. Sometimes I would push Ed away in anger and revulsion. Sometimes I would will myself to be still, telling myself that this was part of the healing process.

When Ed's touch was arousing, there were other problems. I would involuntarily think about his wife, whom I had never seen—not even in a picture—and be slain with guilt. Or I would imagine what would happen if my parents found out, how deeply disappointed and angry they would be.

So I discovered that love has the power to heal, but only a partial power. I could control what I thought at least some of the time, but I couldn't control my body's reactions. I could make elaborate rules, but I couldn't make myself believe them.

23

It was April again, and like every April in Michigan, it was still cold. I consciously began to build a new sort of life. I kept my apartment clean. I planned menus and bought groceries for certain meals. I cooked thrifty dishes, like lentil soup and casseroles with ground beef. Ed was effusive. "Make this all the time," he'd say. "It'll be perfect for raising a family." His smile was wide, and his hair flapped on his forehead like a boy's.

I rarely spent the night at Ed's apartment. I couldn't bear for Jim to notice my car in the driveway early in the morning. I didn't want to prove him right—that I hadn't been good enough to marry.

Occasionally we stopped by Ed's apartment in the early evening so he could make phone calls. I avoided his bedroom, especially the window that looked out at Jim's house. While Ed was occupied on the phone in the kitchen—talking to coworkers, professors, and his lawyer—I went into the other room, ostensibly to give him privacy, but really because the phone calls worried me. Everything seemed complicated. I studied the books and notes spread out on the desk, which always stayed in the same configuration.

Isn't he studying at all? Doesn't he intend to finish his degree?

"I'm setting up a meeting with the dean," Ed said from the kitchen. "Come with me."

"Why? Are you in some kind of trouble?"

He came into the living room and looked at me.

"He's blacklisting me. I'll never get a church, even if I graduate."

"But how can he—"

Ed exploded. "Because he's the f—ing dean!"

I paced back and forth in front of Ed's crippled desk, my anger rising. "First they keep women out, and now a perfectly good man! This is crazy. You can't be the first seminarian to get divorced—"

"Ruth, listen," Ed interrupted. "There's something you need to know. Becky doesn't want the divorce. She's fighting it."

I couldn't speak. A wave of guilt crashed over me.

"That's why you need to come with me, don't you see?" Ed said. "To show them that this is real. That God will use this pain. That there's some other plan."

———

I was uncertain about my role in the meeting, but I wanted to believe Ed—that there was some greater purpose to our coming together. God must have a plan. Ed believed that someday we'd have a joint healing ministry. I couldn't wrap my head around that, but I wanted to believe there was something wonderful waiting for us somewhere down the road. Isn't that how God works—bringing redemption through pain?

I dressed carefully in a skirt and blouse for the appointment. Walking into the seminary building beside Ed, I was as self-conscious as a seventh grader. As we walked through the halls, every look cast in our direction felt like a lightning bolt. Every eye happened to be male. We entered the office, and a secretary—the only woman visible—ushered us into the dean's inner office.

The dean stood to greet us but remained behind his desk. Ed

and I took seats across from him, side by side. I sat primly in the straight-backed chair.

Ed did the talking—about the grace of God and how grace alone fits a person for ministry. About his internships and the things he'd learned. About the change of heart the Spirit had worked in him.

The dean listened without speaking. I observed his tailored suit; his perfect, plastic hair; his smooth, tanned skin.

Ed kept talking. He spoke about his joy in our relationship, about what it meant to have a potential partner in ministry, about what a gift from God I was. Could the seminary see a future for the two of us together? They had invested so much in him, and he was so grateful.

The dean sat back in his chair and steepled his fingers. He enunciated each word. "Perhaps, by the grace of God, you two might have a future together." He didn't look at me or say my name. "But I assure you of this: that future will not be within the Christian Reformed Church. What's more: there's not a denomination in the Reformed tradition that will have you." His voice was cold and smooth.

After that meeting, Ed and I quit talking about seminary. When my GRE scores arrived, I ripped open the envelope with a fast-beating heart. I read the numbers once, twice, and a third time. Yes, the scores really were that high. I stuffed the paper into my underwear drawer.

——

As a young person in catechism class, I had been taught that a person can't hold a belief system that is at odds with his or her behavior. At some point either the belief system or the behavior must change. I began to wonder which I would choose. My invented boundaries were not working.

While Ed worked late one evening, I sat at my kitchen table to write a letter to my parents. For all four years of college, I had written them every two weeks or so, on whatever paper was handy. My letters were usually long and chatty, but I hadn't written them a real letter in months. Instead I'd just dashed off a few lines on a note or a postcard. What would I say if I wrote more? I would have to at least mention Ed, since he consumed all my thoughts and hours. Writing about other things to step around him would be a lie by omission. It was easier to say nothing than to do that. I couldn't lie to my parents. I couldn't be that person. Or if I'd already become that person, I wasn't ready to admit it. Maybe that was more truthful. I put down my pen. I felt uneasy in my own skin.

I would take a bath. The hot water cascaded into the tub, promising comfort. I undressed and lowered myself into the water in stages, gasping as the heat inched up my skin. Once seated, I bent my knees so I could lean back and submerge my whole torso. When I was up to my neck in hot water, I could finally cry. My salty tears trickled into the water.

Then I had a vision: a brick wall formed before me, the red bricks being stacked by invisible hands, the mortar appearing instantly. The wall stretched out of sight in every direction. My tears stopped as I studied this wall. There was no way through it or around it or over it or under it.

"Oh God," I said. "Are you there?"

For the first time in my life, it occurred to me that the answer could be no.

The thought was so surprising that I filled my lungs with air and submerged. As my head went under the water, the wall crumbled. Brick upon brick tumbled until the whole wall was a heap. I rose out of the water, and the image was gone.

I lay there replaying the vision in my mind. I hadn't had a waking dream since childhood, and this felt like a gift. What did it mean? What, exactly, had crumbled?

Perhaps God didn't exist. After all, I had questioned God's

existence, and I hadn't died. In fact, not only was I still alive, I felt invigorated.

Or perhaps God *did* exist, but it was permissible to question His existence. To question God.

Whatever it meant, I knew something was about to change. I didn't tell Ed about the dream. It held a key, and I wanted to keep it to myself until I understood it better.

My parents called one evening shortly after Easter. Ed and I had just finished supper. When I picked up the phone, the static on the line told me that my parents were each on an extension. I could picture my dad pacing the few steps allowed by the cord of the kitchen's avocado-green wall phone, while my mom perched on the edge of the bed in their lavender bedroom. My mom usually did most of the talking when they called.

But there was nothing usual about this conversation. My mother said something but was too upset to be comprehensible.

My dad spoke over her. "Is it true? Are you seeing a man named Ed?"

I was too stunned to answer.

My mother's broken voice said, "My mother—" before faltering completely.

I immediately realized what must have happened. As luck would have it—or, perhaps, as Dutch settlement patterns would have it—my grandmother lived in the same small town as Ed's wife's parents. I'd discovered this just a few weeks before, and Ed and I had joked about "Dutch bingo." The connections had seemed inevitable—funny, even. Somehow it hadn't occurred to me that the news would spread this way.

"Your mother is terribly upset," my father said. "Your grandmother called. We know what's going on."

My mother had found her voice, which quavered with emotion. "Is it true? Are you shacking up with him?"

Because Ed and I weren't living together, I said, "No."

She didn't believe me—I could tell from the growling sound that came through the phone line. I realized that my mother had no other way of asking her question, no other vocabulary to use.

I amended my answer. "We're not living at the same address."

"Don't throw semantics at me!" Her voice was piercing. "You know what I mean. Are you shacking up with him or not?"

"It's none of your business."

"My mother calls and tells me what my own daughter is doing, and you say it's none of my business?"

I couldn't speak. The sins of the children—my sins—had passed upward to the third generation and were now passing down again, in guilt and shame. I could no sooner sidestep this than sidestep my own lineage.

"I can make my own decisions," I said.

"But you aren't yourself. You don't know what you're doing. He's taking advantage—"

My mother's voice broke off, and my father jumped into the open space. "If a man sleeps with you when he's married to someone else, what makes you think he'll be faithful to you?"

I could dismiss that, so I did. "You don't know Ed. He's a good man. We're building a life together!"

"And what if it doesn't work out?" my mother said. "Your reputation is all you have. And now you've gone and ruined it."

My reputation? I think I laughed—from nervousness and humiliation, and also from the size of the gulf between myself and my mother. To my mind, my reputation had been ruined more than a year before, once people started thinking of rape whenever they saw my face. Perhaps the only good news in that circumstance had been the freedom that came in its wake, a freedom I couldn't expect my parents to understand. No one's opinion could touch me anymore. My reputation meant nothing to me. I was untouchable precisely because I had been rendered untouchable. How could I explain this? I had no words for it, not yet.

My mother said, as if she were shutting a door, "You are not my daughter. My daughter wouldn't do this." There was no mistaking the pain in her voice.

I crumpled. I loved my mother. I didn't care what the Christian subculture thought of me, but I cared what my mother thought. I was still her daughter. I still wanted to be her daughter. Maybe I had built a new self, barricaded behind Ed, but it turned out that I wasn't untouchable after all. I couldn't stand to be disowned. Not today, not like this.

I sobbed for a while and then managed to ask, "What do you want me to do?"

My mother regained her composure at that question. In a more normal voice she said, "Won't you just leave him?"

"No," I said. "You don't understand. This is the real thing. This is going to last."

"Well, then." My mother's voice measured the distance between us. "Prove it."

"How?"

"Leave him. Just for a while. Let him get his divorce settled. If you get back together after he's divorced, I'll accept it."

"How long would I have to be gone?" I had an idea, like a lightning bolt. "What if I go to Yellowstone? The summer. Three months—"

"Yes!" My dad broke in. "That sounds fine."

"All right then. I'll make the call. I'll arrange it."

We hung up. I didn't even wait to explain the situation to Ed, who was still sitting at my kitchen table, listening to my end of the conversation. I went to my cache of papers and found a pay stub from my former employer. There was a phone number on it. It was two hours earlier in Wyoming, still a few minutes before five, so I called. They looked up my employment record and immediately offered a choice of two jobs with similar pay rates: main cook at Tower Falls or assistant cook at Canyon Village. I barely thought before choosing Canyon Village, which was less remote. They told me a start date and where to report. I wrote down the facts and hung up with a sense of jubilation. The entire transaction had taken less than ten minutes.

I was so happy I practically spun. "My parents will accept you!" I told Ed. I chattered on about calendars and train schedules and pay rates.

Ed was puzzled. What was all this? Was it necessary? And why so soon? Everything was fine. We were happy, we were together, and now I was leaving?

"It's temporary, don't you see? When I get back, we can build a life together!"

I was euphoric. My parents had given me a way out of my dilemma, and I recognized it as a gift. Surely Ed could see it too. Soon I could have both lives at the same time: my new life—being with Ed—and my old life—being a good daughter. All that was necessary was this slight delay, three months in Canyon Village.

"Don't you see?" I asked Ed. "This is my big chance. If I don't go, my parents will disown me!"

As a mother myself now, I have come to see that phone call differently. I don't think that my mother was trying to disown me. She was calling me back to myself. When she said, "My daughter wouldn't do this," maybe she knew that my actions weren't in alignment with my real self. Maybe she knew that I'd lost myself along the way.

At the time, her words caused me great pain, but perhaps that's because they flew straight to their mark.

24

I left Grand Rapids in mid-May, and when I arrived in Yellowstone, snow still pillowed the pine woods. I breathed deeply, inhaling the scent of juniper. I had almost forgotten how big the sky was here and how much I loved being in the park.

People usually visit Canyon Village so they can see Inspiration Point. It's a postcard scene—a plunging waterfall at the far end of a steep-walled canyon with shoulders that are covered in evergreens. In case anyone missed how scenic the sight is, there was even a sign that designated the point as a "Kodak Spot." Most tourists obliged by snapping a picture and returning to their cars, unless they were spending the night in Canyon Lodge. We employees called them "turkey tourists" while we were "savages." We didn't just snap a picture from behind a railing; we hiked the canyon and the back country trails. We lived there and knew the whole area intimately.

Except me. For the first few weeks of that summer, I knew only my kitchen and, beyond that, one tiny part of the canyon: the lobby of Canyon Lodge. Each day after the kitchen crew and I finished the supper dishes, I would scrounge up a pocketful of change and walk to the lodge, which was at the other end of a horseshoe of buildings.

The lobby was paneled in wood and had a rustic feel, with decorative accents in a native turquoise. There were three pay phones, each with its own booth. I would step into one of the booths and shut the accordion-style door. Then I would take a seat on a small metal perch that faced an enormous contraption of a phone. I knew the complicated directions for making long-distance calls by heart. To call Michigan, I would deposit three dollars and sixty-five cents in coins, listening to each coin clang before adding the next. Once the connection was made, I had three minutes. After that, I had to feed another dime or quarter every minute or so.

I spent most of my evenings behind those accordion doors, blocking out the world. My left hand clasped the phone receiver to my ear. My right hand toyed with the metal cord that tethered me to the phone . . . and to Ed. The metal cord was tightly spiraled, and no matter how I manipulated them or pulled at them or tried to peel them apart with my fingernails, those metal loops would not yield.

Turkey tourists needing to use the phone would sometimes pound on the door, but I simply shook my head and held the door shut with my feet, choosing to stay in a world made up of Ed and me and the umbilical cord between us.

"Why did you leave?" he would always ask, as if I had never answered that question.

"To make things right with my parents," I'd say.

"But why did you leave me?" he would ask again.

"It's temporary. It's for our future."

"When are you coming back?"

"You know," I'd say. "At the end of the summer."

"But why did you leave me?"

Eventually my stash of coins would run out. A distant-sounding voice would come on the line and inform us of our impending disconnection. Reluctantly, I would hang up.

With the next day came a new pile of coins and a new hope. As soon as the supper cleanup was done, I'd hang up my apron, make my way to the lobby, push open the glass door, step into my time capsule, and try, once again, to connect with the man I loved.

After a few weeks, Ed asked, "Are you seeing anybody?"

"Nobody," I said. I felt a twinge of guilt that I didn't mention one fellow who was pursuing me, a sheepherder from Montana. He was one of the gentlest men I'd ever met, with a beard to his midchest, a Harley-Davidson, and a daughter he was raising alone.

"Not to lay a heavy trip on you," the rancher had told me, "but my old lady started doing angel dust and split. It's been four years. The daughter's seven now. She needs a woman around, but it's just me and her and the sheep. And the ever-lovin' wind."

I didn't tell Ed about the sheepherder because I'd resisted him, even though his windswept ranch had wooed me.

At least I thought to turn the question around. "What about you?" I asked. "Are you seeing anybody?"

"We said we could. Other people aren't the problem. Your parents are the problem."

I raised my voice at that, and we argued. I didn't put in more quarters.

Was Ed right? I pondered that during the solitude of my afternoon shifts as I peeled the inevitable potatoes. Were my parents the problem? I imagined their faces, which I hadn't seen since Christmas. Complicated feelings swirled through me—a mixture of longing and dejection. I still wanted to please my parents, even though I would never be who they raised me to be. Was that because I was raped, or was it because of something more essential? When had I set out on a different road from the one they'd laid for me?

I picked up another potato, large and oblong. I had become an excellent potato peeler. I peeled a twenty-five-pound bagful every day. I would hold the potato in my left hand and shift it counter-clockwise with my thumb as I sliced rapidly with the peeler, held in my right hand. Then I would drop the skinned potato into a pot of cold water, where it bobbed beside its naked mates. There was always another potato in the bag, its gritty skin waiting to be sliced away with a few deft strokes.

If I were honest with myself, I had to admit that I'd chafed against my denomination all through college. I thought the church subculture was monochromatic. Its strictures for women felt overly tight. Its doctrine was too tidy a package. I wanted to be part of a wider world, a messier one. I wanted a more active role in that world. I bristled against the knowledge that my life would be defined, in large part, by whatever man I married.

I hardly saw the potato in my hand. Instead I pictured Ed's wide cheekbones and quick grin. He wasn't the type of man my parents envisioned for me, with his divorces and his checkered past. I pictured the sheepherder's kind, baffled eyes and long beard. He would be just as disappointing to my parents. As the strips of potato skin curled from my peeler and dropped into a bucket, I understood one important thing that my parents didn't seem to understand. I needed a man who wasn't afraid of some dirt.

When I finished the last potato, I slipped my peeler into the pocket of my uniform. Tomorrow there would be another bag of potatoes to peel.

———

I let a few days pass, and then I entered the phone booth with fresh resolve and another pocketful of coins.

"I knew you'd call," Ed said. "Come home to me, and we'll work it out."

"Soon enough," I said.

"If you really loved me, you'd come home. You wouldn't care what your parents say."

"We're halfway there," I said. "Six more weeks."

"Are you seeing someone?" he asked. "Are you sleeping with him?"

This time I pushed back. "What about you? This person you're seeing—are you sleeping with her?"

"It doesn't mean a thing," he said.

My heart dropped as he filled the distance between us with words, a long peel of words. "You said yourself we needed to figure it out, whether this thing between us is real and whether it will last. What better way—"

"Stop talking!" I said.

I clamped the phone under my ear so I could put both hands on the spiraled phone cord. I pulled as hard as I could, trying to straighten the metal coils. They didn't budge. They couldn't. They never would.

There was silence. Then Ed's voice came through the twisted wire in a sentence I would never forget: "My dick may have strayed, Ruth, but not my heart."

Right.

I sat up straight on the little perch. I didn't wait for a distant voice to terminate the conversation. I didn't eke out the last moment from the last coin. I opened the accordion door and walked away, leaving the receiver to sway at the end of its unyielding cord.

I could think about nothing else for days. I went from anger to sorrow to despair and back to anger. How could he have cheated on me? I had given up so much for him! And he had thrown it away. After six weeks?

I began to get glimpses of a new realization. I saw that I'd been hiding behind my parents' lack of approval. But the truth was, I didn't approve of our relationship either—not entirely. I didn't like that it began while he was married. It was an affair—that's what it was! Maybe the real reason I left town wasn't to please my parents but to purge the taint of our beginning.

For the next six weeks, I fantasized that things would still work out between us. Ed would climb into his Scout and drive the six-teen hundred miles to Wyoming and walk into the kitchen, and we would begin again. I pictured his arrival so frequently and in such detail that it's one of the clearest images I have from that summer, even though it's a memory of something that never happened.

Ed never did push open the swinging door of the kitchen like a sheriff. He never did run his hand through his blond mop of hair or tuck his sunglasses into the pocket of his yellow shirt and say my name as I ran across the kitchen to him, burying my face in his shirtfront.

—

I had made friends with one of my coworkers and began to confide in her. Her name was Faith. Maybe that made the confiding easier. Faith was a nursing student and was going to spend the coming fall semester at a hospital in downtown Minneapolis. She was an energetic person with a huge heart, prone to telling stories that made everyone laugh. Faith could turn the most ordinary experi-ence into an adventure. She was from Iowa and was eager to explore the world. When she heard that my life was falling apart, she urged me to move to Minneapolis.

"You'll love it!" she said. "There's all kinds of culture. Lakes. Outdoorsy stuff. You can stay with me until you find a place. We'll have a blast."

"Outdoorsy stuff?" I asked. "Are there mountains?"

"Depends what you mean by mountains," she replied.

I had to start my new life somewhere, didn't I?

25

When my contract at Yellowstone was up on Labor Day, I took a train to Chicago, then a bus to Grand Rapids. My Valiant was parked on the street where I'd left it, looking much worse than I remembered, mottled with rust. I opened the door with trepidation. The round piece of Formica on top of the driveshaft seemed to have shrunk, or maybe the hole had expanded. I could see a ring of pavement through the floor. I climbed into the driver's seat, turned the key, and pressed my foot on the accelerator. Nothing.

A friend of a friend knew something about cars, and he pronounced the Valiant beyond repair. We studied the classified ads to find a replacement. We zeroed in on a Datsun hatchback that was listed for $1,800. He told me to get $1,300 in cash. "Make it twelve $100 bills and two fifties. Put it in one of those bank envelopes."

That was almost everything I'd earned at Yellowstone, but I went to the bank and did exactly as he said.

"Give me the envelope," my new friend said, "and let me do the talking."

The Datsun was white and oval shaped. To my eyes, it was sleek and beautiful, like an egg. It looked like it could drive into the future.

We took it out for a test drive. The owner rode in the backseat and kept saying, "It's a great car—you'll love it."

As instructed, I stayed silent. We got out and slammed the doors. We circled the car, inspecting the paint job—as if a ding would matter. I tried hard to look uninterested.

Eventually my friend leaned against the driver's door and plucked a cigarette from the pack in his pocket. He leaned through the open window and punched the car's cigarette lighter to heat it up. Then he took the cash envelope from his breast pocket and counted the bills as he peeled them apart.

"Thirteen," he said, the cigarette dangling from his lips. "Thirteen hundred in cash, here and now, and she drives away."

To punctuate the sentence, he pulled out the lighter and brought it to his cigarette.

"It's busted," he said in disgust. "Make that twelve-fifty." He peeled a fifty from the wad and stuffed it in his pocket.

A few minutes later, we drove away in the Datsun. I let my friend keep the fifty he'd saved me, and we went to the White Rabbit to celebrate.

———

By coincidence, my former roommate Cindy had just returned to Grand Rapids after an all-summer visit to a convent in Kansas. We were both staying in our old apartment for a couple of nights. Cindy was driving a dark blue Volkswagen bug that she'd just bought with most of *her* savings. We admired each other's new-to-us cars, then walked a block to the corner store to buy a warm packet of unshelled peanuts and a six-pack of Vernors ginger ale. Back on our front porch steps, we crushed the fragrant peanuts from their shells and swigged the cold pop.

"This is the only part of Michigan I'm going to miss," Cindy said. "Vernors and peanuts on a porch."

"Where are you going?"

"Back to Kansas," she said. "For good."

"I'm thinking of Minneapolis," I said. "I have a friend there. At least I'd have a place to stay for a few days."

"Minneapolis is nice, as cities go," Cindy said. "You'll be like Mary Tyler Moore!"

"Throwing my beret in the air?"

She sang out, "You're gonna make it after all!"

We laughed and lifted our bottles in a salute.

"So you're joining the convent?" I asked.

"I am." Cindy had a way of lifting her face and shaking it slightly, as if she were shaking rainwater from her cheeks. When she made that motion now, the streetlight shimmered over her cheekbones. "It'll be a whole new life!"

After a long silence, I asked, "Are you taking your stuff?" I wasn't sure how a person goes about making a new life.

"I am. Loading up and driving away."

So that's how you do it.

That night we hatched the idea of traveling in tandem part of the way. It took a couple of days for us both to get ready. I loaded my car with everything I owned: my clothes and shoes, a dozen or so books, four or five records (but no stereo to play them on), my flute from high school, the towels and blankets my mom had ordered from Sears before I went to college, some thrift store dishes and pans I'd acquired along the way, a desk lamp, and my backpacking gear. The boxes and loose possessions mostly filled the hatchback and backseat of my little car.

The next morning it was time to leave. I called Ed and told him I wanted to say good-bye.

His voice was warm and friendly, as if we had never hurt each other. "Now is a good time," he said. "Come on over."

I drove to his place right away, before I could think about it too much or change my mind. Ed was waiting for me on the street, dressed for work. I got out of my car and slammed the door. Ed made some lighthearted comment about my loaded Datsun. It was a relief to hear his tone. I was bringing enough baggage to Minneapolis as it was.

"I'm sorry your marriage ended," I told him.

"Why? It had to end." That boyish lock of hair still caressed his forehead.

"What about seminary? Did that have to end too?" I still couldn't believe he'd thrown his degree away, so close to the end.

He laughed. "I still believe in God. But not this church crap."

It struck me as a dangerous thing to say. I had the urge to check the sky for a lightning strike. Part of me still believed that God was powerful and capricious and punitive. But the sky was silent and beautiful and blue. It was a perfect September morning, the kind when anything seems possible. Ed and I stood looking at each other. There were so many things I could have said, but none of them seemed important.

He didn't ask me to stay.

I got back in the Datsun.

"Enjoy your adventure!" he said. "Someday you'll tell your grandchildren about this day, mark my words. The day you drove away and started a new life."

So I did. I drove away from all the things that would never be mine again. I drove away from Ed, who waved from the middle of the street, his blond hair glinting in the sunlight. I drove away from the White Rabbit and its pool tables, and from Breakfast Just Breakfast and its eggs. I drove away from the house on Alexander and from the Grand Rapids Hall of Justice and from the Calvin College campus. I drove away from everything that was Christian Reformed, from everything that had once told me who I was. I drove away with everything I owned rattling around in a hatchback that cost me nearly everything I had.

Cindy and I traveled north in two cars, following the shore of Lake Michigan. Every night we camped in her tent in a state park. Since it was past Labor Day, the crowds were thin and the weather was cool. We ate peanut butter sandwiches and apples. We built a small fire each night to warm ourselves and toast marshmallows. We did touristy things too, as long as they were cheap. We hunted for Petoskey stones along the lakeshore; we rode the ferry to Mackinac Island; we split a pasty from a roadside shack. We crossed the border into Canada and looked at the locks at Sault Ste. Marie, then crossed back into Michigan.

We headed west through the northernmost part of upper Michigan, hugging the shore of Lake Superior. With every mile, the wind picked up and the number of people dwindled, as if they were being blown away. We felt like we were driving to the end of something. In a little town called Paradise, we stopped and bought postcards with pictures of enormous fish under a banner that read "Hello from Paradise." We each bought ten for a dollar, then wrote notes to everyone in our little address books. Cindy, who was on her way to join a nunnery, couldn't stop laughing as she wrote: "I greet you from Paradise."

Not far outside Escanaba, Cindy and I went our separate ways, and I stopped to tank up. I got out my Rand McNally atlas and estimated it to be eight hours to Minneapolis. Faith had marked the location of her dorm on the inset map of downtown Minneapolis. It was on the campus of Abbott Northwestern Hospital, so she told me I could follow the signs with a blue "H" on Highway 94, where it intersected with Highway 35W. Easy.

I got back in the car, intending to stop for the night if I got tired. But I didn't really want to spend money on a motel, and I didn't have a tent. So I made another peanut butter sandwich and kept going. I could always sleep in the car later. One more hour. Maybe

I could make it after all. I sang the Mary Tyler Moore theme song aloud, accompanied by the clatter of dishware from the backseat.

It was late when darkness fell. Finally I saw what I was looking for: a sign for Highway 35. I turned onto it, thinking I was headed into the heart of Minneapolis. But this appeared to be a minor highway, passing through empty, dark country. Now and then the road wound through small towns, which I hardly noticed as I whizzed along. Where was the city?

I didn't notice the blinking red lights in my rearview mirror until I heard the siren. The state trooper who stopped me was not smiling. In fact, the planes of his face were as creased as the brim of his hat. I handed over my license and registration. Then he was gone for a long time. It occurred to me that the sale of my Datsun was awfully recent.

Finally the officer reappeared. "I need to make a call," he said curtly. "You'll need to follow me to town."

"Town" turned out to be Prescott, Wisconsin. I noticed the sign as we drove slowly down quiet streets to the police department. We both parked, and he headed up the steps into the brick building. I followed, thinking he would turn around any minute. "Be on your way," he would say. Or maybe, "Would you like a cup of coffee?"

I could use a cup of coffee.

We just kept climbing the steps. I must have slipped into someone else's life by mistake. Was I really being hauled in by the law? This wouldn't happen to Mary Tyler Moore. If it did, it would be funny. Rhoda would make it funny.

There was only one other person in the building—an officer who didn't even look up when we entered. I tried to catch his eye to reassure myself that this was all a humorous mistake, but the officer was entirely disinterested in me and my plight. There was a map on the wall. I studied it and found Prescott. That's when I realized I had turned down Wisconsin State 35 instead of Interstate 35W. As unlikely as it seems, the two highways bear the same number and run parallel. This fact struck me as pretty ridiculous, and I wanted to point it out. Then it occurred to me that they already knew.

"You can call someone before I put you in a cell," the officer said, which made me realize I had no one to call. What could Faith do if I called her? I didn't want to be the friend who needed rescuing. I shook my head, and the officer led me to a cell. I didn't trust myself to speak, because if I unclenched my face, I would cry. And I refused to cry. This was my new life, and I was done with tears.

When the metal door clanged shut behind me, I found myself in a windowless room made of cinder blocks. I sat on the stainless steel bench built into the wall and pulled out my wallet. I had $125 in cash. I also had a cashier's check for almost $200—all that was left from my checking account. I had hoped that amount would cover my first month's rent plus a deposit.

I studied the small cell. At least it felt safe. I told myself that things could be much worse. I curled up on the cold steel bench. The next thing I knew, the officer was clanging the door open. "All clear. Pay up, and you're free to go." The speeding ticket cost $75. I peeled the bills from my wallet and got back in the car. The ticket had almost cleaned me out. Maybe that was a good thing. Didn't I want to start my new life clean?

26

By the time I arrived in Minneapolis, it was well past midnight. Faith made a nest on the floor of her dorm room with some sleeping bags, and I slept soundly. I woke to the smell of eggs frying. Faith was using the hot plate of her popcorn popper like a frying pan. She cheerily set breakfast in front of me and then went to class.

I needed to find an apartment and a job, but both of the Minneapolis newspapers had just gone on strike. Without any classifieds, I decided to look for an apartment by inquiring at whatever "For Rent" signs I came across. I found a cheap single-room apartment in Loring Park, at the south edge of downtown. It was mine for just under $100 per month, with a six-month lease. I wasn't sure what kind of neighborhood it was, but the three-story brick building was full of elderly women, each in her own efficiency apartment, so it seemed safe enough. I parked my Datsun on the street and unloaded.

My apartment was on the first floor. It had an old-fashioned bathroom with a claw-foot tub and no shower. There was a tiny kitchen with a two-burner stove and a minifridge. I was grateful for the new, plush carpeting in my single room, since I'd be sleeping on the floor in my sleeping bag.

When I checked the basement laundry, I noticed a straight-backed chair in a corner. I put a note on it: "May I borrow this?" and included my room number. The next day an older woman in a housedress knocked on my door and told me to just take the chair, if I could use it. She also offered me some dish detergent, saying she didn't like the scent, along with a bag of gently used bras and half a package of English muffins. I accepted everything and thanked her. I set my lamp on the straight-backed chair and put my pillow on the floor beside the chair. The light was perfect for reading, and I had books. That night I looked up from my page and felt content. So this was how my new life began: with a room and a lamp and a book.

I cultivated a taste for the ordinary—quite a change from the high-intensity diet I'd been subsisting on. I began to see that part of Ed's appeal had been the sheer intensity of our relationship, with its secrecy and high stakes. Maybe I'd become accustomed to living life at a high pitch during my year of trauma. Maybe Ed's stories—always colored by extremes—matched my own inner story. Maybe it was time to rethink that. Maybe instead of living at the edges, I needed to find the center of my life.

A thrift store down the block sold used books. I bought a thick paperback copy of *The Source* by James Michener, swayed by the number of pages that thirty-five cents could buy. In a few weeks, when I had the paperwork to prove Minnesota residency, I got a library card. Mainly I checked out fiction: Anne Tyler, John Steinbeck, Flannery O'Connor. That fall I lost myself in the stories of other people's lives.

⁓

The newspaper strike dragged on for weeks, making it hard to find job openings, so I went downtown and applied at all the employment agencies. One agency arranged an interview with Target for a management trainee position. But when I arrived, the agent refused to send me to the interview until I looked more professional.

"Get a suit and come back," she said.

I couldn't buy a suit until I got a paycheck. I had thought my skirt and blouse were fine. My hair looked great. Dispirited, I wandered through the skyway, which connects the downtown buildings at the second-floor level. I paused at a balustrade to watch the people below, in the atrium of the IDS building. Would I ever be one of them, hurrying to a downtown job?

I noticed a handsome black man in a well-tailored suit riding the up escalator. When he got off at the top, he walked in my direction with long, purposeful strides. Other than having dark skin, he bore no resemblance to my assailants. Perhaps he noticed me noticing him. He stopped and struck up a conversation. He said he was in town to meet with his patent attorney. As we chatted, another man came by and told him some news. The two backslapped and high-fived, jubilant. I allowed myself to get caught up in their good mood. When the handsome man invited me to have dinner with him that evening, I said yes, and we arranged the time and place.

Watching him walk away, I immediately had second thoughts. As the afternoon passed, I grew increasingly restless. Perhaps he meant me harm. Perhaps the interaction with his friend had been a setup. Oh, that was ridiculous. Why would he do that? Why should I be suspicious of him, other than the color of his skin? He was better dressed than any man I'd ever dated. Certainly better dressed than I was! I ping-ponged all afternoon, unable to decide whether meeting him would be foolish or brave. At last I realized that foolishness and bravery may well be identical, at least until after the fact.

In the end I met him, as agreed, at an upscale burger place in Uptown. My stomach was in such knots that I didn't think I could eat. After we ordered, he asked if I liked theater and talked about the plays showing at the Guthrie. I didn't say I'd never been there, that I had no money for tickets. I didn't want to let him know how destitute I was. I realized I wasn't in his league, in either income or sophistication.

I also couldn't concentrate on the words he was speaking. I was uncomfortably aware of his full lips—their precise coloring and the way they were lined with a slightly darker color. My head was so cluttered with things I couldn't say that I became tongue tied. When the conversation petered out, I knew it was my fault, and felt guilty for dampening his celebratory evening.

After dinner, he suggested we walk around Lake of the Isles, which I thought was game of him. It was a crisp fall evening, and the sun had just set. The sidewalk around the lake was full of people running and pushing strollers. We threaded our way through a crowd of adults and children gathered around a small flock of Canada geese. He told me that a few pairs of geese had been introduced to the lake recently and were so novel that families drove in from the suburbs to feed them. A toddler bravely held out a piece of bread to a goose as tall as he was. Behind the child's outstretched arm, the lake glimmered as the street lamps came on. As we followed the winding path around the odd-shaped lake, we occasionally caught glimpses of the Minneapolis skyline in the distance, its lights a promise of culture and safety. My companion pointed out the road that ran past the fictional Mary Tyler Moore house. I thanked him. I tried to be present to the loveliness of the evening, but I kept noticing where the path was darker and where there were pools of light. My mind raced to scenarios of abduction.

I felt both helpless and ashamed. Here I was in a beautiful place with a handsome, accomplished man who was doing everything possible to make me feel comfortable. But because he was black, I was uneasy. Did that make me a racist? If I was uncomfortable with a man simply because of his skin color, what do you call that? Was race aversion the same thing as racism?

I didn't know. But I knew that two years had gone by and this had to end. I couldn't continue to be a prisoner to my past.

———

Meanwhile, I had pressing financial problems. The newspaper strike was dragging on, and I needed to pay rent again. I took my flute to a pawn shop, where I got thirty-five dollars for it. I brought my high school class ring to a "Cash for Gold" place. The man put it on a scale and offered me sixty dollars, which was more than I'd paid for it. Between the two sales, I could cover rent.

But I had nothing else to sell. I was down to three dollars in cash—three single bills in my thin wallet—bills that lasted a long time, because really, what's compelling enough to make you pull them out? Every purchase could wait. I had a few cans of soup in the cupboard. Some oatmeal and brown sugar. Packages of ramen. And Faith brought me fruit she pocketed from the cafeteria—apples and oranges and bananas. Also small packages of oyster crackers and tea bags. She gave me the food breezily, offhand. We both pretended that I didn't really need it.

Faith was exactly the friend I needed at the time. She was light-hearted and upbeat, and she acted as if it were perfectly normal for me to be young and destitute, to have moved across multiple states to escape a denomination as well as a boyfriend, and what's more, to have bought her story about Minnesota's mountainous terrain. I never confronted her about it directly, but after several months it occurred to me that I'd been coaxed to Minneapolis under false pretenses. There are no mountains in Minnesota.

My parents phoned weekly, sometimes more frequently. We chatted casually. They never mentioned how much the phone call cost. We talked about my job prospects. They were always supportive.

I told myself I would ask for money the next time they called if I hadn't gotten a job by then. Just a few more days.

The newspaper strike finally ended after a record-breaking four weeks. When the newspaper publication resumed, I was elated. My heart beat hard as I circled every position I was qualified for—a dozen or so. I lined up a series of job interviews, and within a week I was offered a secretarial position at a hospital consulting firm in suburban Roseville. My college degree meant nothing, but I aced the typing test.

A few months later, on a spring day, I was riding the city bus when some young black men boarded. The weather was perfect, and they were in high spirits, joking and slapping hands. My reaction was immediate and visceral—rapid heartbeat, shallow breathing, perspiration. The distress involved my brain and adrenal glands and involuntary muscles, and I couldn't stop it.

So this is how it is and ever will be, I thought. *Young men with dark skin appear and I have no choice but to manage an onslaught of symptoms?* I hated them. Not the young men; the symptoms.

This is not who Jesus wants me to be. The clear thought descended from nowhere and steadied my heartbeat. I suddenly saw a way out. I needed to find some black men who loved Jesus too. I needed to find a church.

I asked around at work to see if anyone knew of a church where black and white people worshipped together. Someone suggested Prince of Glory, a small Lutheran church that was intentionally multiracial. It was located in a rough part of downtown Minneapolis— a mission church. My coworker gave me directions.

The next Sunday morning I steeled myself and headed to Prince of Glory. I had to navigate through one-way streets to find my way beneath a tangle of overpasses. Then I had to pass the city's impound lot, with its stern warnings and imposing fence, and head into the housing projects. The streets were not quite as narrow as the ones my father drove me through in Paterson, but they were littered with broken glass. There were high-rises with boarded windows on either side. Even though it was springtime, there was nothing green growing anywhere. *What am I even doing here?*

Is this brave or foolish?

I will soon find out.

The church was a small brick building, and the parking lot was in terrible repair, as if tectonic plates were shifting right beneath its surface. But there were other cars already in the lot, so I parked beside them. Then I talked myself out of the car and into the building.

Once inside, I felt more at ease. The sanctuary was noisy and full of energy, with a group of people singing a spiritual around the piano—probably a last-minute choir rehearsal—and other people standing around, talking and laughing. The majority of the people were black, mainly women, mainly older. Within a few minutes the choir rehearsal ended, and one of the singers, an elderly black woman, came over to welcome me. Then she took me to meet the one other young white woman in the room, who'd also been singing by the piano. Her name was Barb, and she had silky brown hair that hung straight to her shoulders, with heavy bangs. Behind her glasses were large gray eyes. She had a beautiful, shy smile.

Barb told me she had just graduated from the University of Wisconsin at Madison and had moved back in with her parents, who were also at church. She introduced me to her mother, who was short and effusive, with a heavy German accent. Barb's dad was white haired and welcoming, a retired Lutheran minister. They joked around about Barb finding a job and a place to live. I caught a whiff of the love between the three of them, along with Barb's readiness to move out of her parents' house. I knew that mix of feelings.

"Want to move in with me?" I asked. "Too bad there's not enough room."

"Are you sure about that?" She laughed. "I don't take up much space."

"I'm on a month-to-month lease," I told her. "I'm what you might call extremely flexible at the moment."

Church began, and Barb and I worshipped side by side. That afternoon we went looking for places we could live together. We found an upstairs apartment in a Victorian home in the Whittier neighborhood and signed a joint lease that began the next week. The following Sunday I was back at Prince of Glory, only this time I was with my roommate Barb and singing in the choir.

The choir had a dozen or so members. They disagreed about everything except loving to sing, so the rehearsals were full of energy and arguments. Our choir robes were a hodgepodge of discards from other churches, and there was a great deal of wrangling over which ones to wear on a given Sunday. I loved it when we all wore different ones.

I learned to sing a looser way—to sway and clap—and to sing like no one but God was listening.

Soon and very soon
We are goin' to see the King

I had grown up singing alto, but now I dropped down to tenor, which allowed me to trace the melody and was more fun to sing. I enjoyed harmonizing with the male voices. From the back row, a tall man boomed out a steady bass line. If I caught his eye, he would nod his head, almost imperceptibly.

No more cryin' now
We are goin' to see the King

Occasionally some teenage boys showed up—usually at the request (or command) of their mothers or grandmothers. There was a good bit of joshing around. I was happy to stand beside them, singing tenor. They were young and black and male. But they were just people, singing. They weren't potential rapists. And I wasn't a potential rape victim. We were just children of God, singing. Clapping. Shifting side to side.

Elbow to elbow, week after week, our songs sanded away the jagged edge between us.

Hallelujah, hallelujah
We are goin' to see the King

PART 5

THE FUTURE

June 1981–December 1989

Jesus said to her, "Daughter,
your faith has made you well."

MARK 5:34

Writing . . . is like driving a car at night.
You can see only as far as your headlights,
but you can make the whole trip that way.

E. L. DOCTOROW

27

I didn't expect that Barb and I would spend so much time in the kitchen, but cooking is one way to warm up a Minnesota winter. On weeknights we fixed supper and ate together, then did the dishes side by side. On the weekends we cooked for friends, attempting complicated recipes and experimenting liberally. Fortunately our friends were hungry and forgiving, which meant that no dish was an utter failure.

As Barb and I clattered about the kitchen, we talked about everything: our jobs and how boring they became by midafternoon, guys and what was wrong with the ones we were seeing, our parents and siblings and the complicated feelings we had about them. We told each other our secrets, even the things we were still revealing to ourselves—what we wanted out of life, or might want, or didn't dare want. At any moment our conversation could be suspended while we debated which of our battered pans was best for popping popcorn or we exclaimed that someone had eaten the Butterfinger bars we'd been saving to make milk shakes.

On Sundays we usually attended Prince of Glory and then ate

dinner with Barb's parents. Her mother was generous with her good cooking and her jokes, both of which were flavored by her native Germany. "Try the lingonberries with the pork. Did I tell you the one about the Swede and the Norwegian? More coffee?"

Barb's retired-pastor father was studying liberation theology— James Cone, Gustavo Gutiérrez—and was eager to discuss it. "What's the meaning of the Exodus narrative today? In what sense is Jesus a liberator?"

I loved the way our conversations pinged between the deeply serious and the silly, and the way they traveled around the globe. After we praised the lingonberries, we might wonder aloud if the easy availability of German luxury food was a good thing or if multi-national corporations were a form of modern-day colonialism. After we laughed about the Norwegian and the Swede who walked into a bar—the punch line invariably turned out to be a laconic Finn— we'd ask, "Why *do* people tell jokes about their nearest neighbors?"

And there was always another cup of coffee.

Like all roommates, Barb and I sometimes argued over minutiae: her tendency to leave a trail of used tea bags or my habit of parking a bicycle in the living room, to become imprisoned for months by the snow. But there was no doubt that the cup of our companionship was full. I felt deeply known. I didn't have to pretend to be better than I was or to have a purer past than I had. Barb and I were able to tell each other our stories as if the endings were yet to be written.

Occasionally, and often unexpectedly, my thoughts would turn to the rapists. What were they doing at that moment? I couldn't imagine what it was like to be incarcerated. To have served four years of a sentence that stretched for decades. I wondered what it would be like to look at them now across a table in some safe place. Their faces were a blur, a smear in my memory. Thinking of them didn't fill me with hatred and revulsion anymore. Maybe that's what healing looks like. Or maybe hatred is just too exhausting to sustain. Maybe revulsion is too miserable to keep as close company. Maybe the brain skips to the other side of both emotions, just to be done with them.

I wondered: Did the rapists have remorse for what they'd done? Did they at least regret destroying their own lives? Or were they hardened and bitter and full of hatred? Would they do it again in a heartbeat?

Thinking about the rapists now, their blurry faces safely behind bars, filled me with a new emotion—something closer to sorrow. Maybe you could call it melancholy. Maybe it was a lament for the deep pit of evil and depravity that exists in the cosmos. Maybe I felt regret, even if the rapists didn't. Regret that they'd stood on the brink of evil, as if it gave them a foothold, a lodging place from which they could lunge into our lives as they fell. Regret that people could pull each other to such dark places, and for what?

Sometimes the aching feeling that welled up in me was even a form of pity. I couldn't tell anyone that, not even Barb. Whatever words I used would sound ridiculous. They would sound like an indulgence. A liberal white woman's indulgence, pitying a black man in prison.

I was also aware that *indulgence* was perhaps the appropriate word. I could indulge in this emotion because of what the justice system had done for me. Justice had purchased this emotion, whatever it was—this emotion that lay on the other side of hatred and revulsion.

Eventually Barb and I moved to another apartment, one that allowed pets, and we decided to adopt a cat. We chose a solid black female from an animal shelter. She had green eyes and a kinked stub of a tail. Barb named her Bo.

We invented backstories to explain the missing tail—tales that rivaled Rudyard Kipling's *Just So Stories*. "How Bo the Black Cat Lost Her Tail": Bo was scavenging for food for her starving litter mates when a garbage truck scooped her up and the crushing jaw descended! Bo rescued a baby rabbit from an evil farmer with an ax! Bo was strolling through the countryside when a sinkhole opened . . .

One thing we were sure of: Bo didn't miss her tail, not when she had such tales to tell—tales of bravery and fortitude. I knew we were inventing stories about ourselves, too. About the troubles we had escaped. About what we had lost and what we had gained.

———

Meanwhile, I was surrounded by words all day. My work involved document production at a time when the word processing field was exploding. I changed jobs as my skills progressed, from the hospital consulting firm to the agribusiness Cargill to a downtown law firm. My word processing equipment was as large and heavy as a washing machine, but it could do amazing things, at least by the standards of the early eighties. Maybe I was typing other people's words, but I took pride in making sure those documents were perfect.

Eventually I itched to write again. I began staying after hours at the law firm so I could use my beloved machine to compose stories. Then I bought a secondhand typewriter so I could write at home; I would retype the pages into my word processing machine during breaks. I even scaled back my hours to four days a week, giving up my law firm benefits to have one solid day to write.

A cooperative in south Minneapolis called The Loft offered writing classes, so I signed up. In small groups we shared our work and learned about character, plot, and setting. The critique process was difficult but eye-opening. I realized that most of my characters were suspiciously like me, yet my best writing was about the characters least like me. It was a painful pleasure to be pushed out of my own skin. I began to understand the importance of distance and what it meant to have a point of view.

People sometimes say that authors are like gods, manipulating the fates of their characters. But I prized my characters' autonomy and agency. I wanted to see what they would say or do next. The words they said mattered. The choices they made mattered. As the author, I set characters in circumstances, but their choices soon altered those circumstances. Plot was a dynamic enterprise, not a foregone conclusion. Events had a certain randomness to them, yes, but they also had causality and connection and consequences.

I resisted reaching into my stories *deus ex machina*. That might have been how fate operated, but not my world. Once a scene was set in time and place, I allowed for no rewinding of time to undo the action, no escaping to another locale, no otherworldly power or white knight appearing to rescue the protagonist. Once the plot was in motion, I wanted to see how a character managed. Let's say you didn't get that job after all. Move on! And let's say that in order to move on, you have to drive across Iowa. Yes, the whole state. I'd like to see that scene. Show me the corn. Churn out some dialogue! What happens next?

I'm not talking about revision. Of course, I had a Delete key. And I knew how to use it. Writing is nothing if not rewriting. But I sometimes wanted to let my character's choices stand to see how they would handle a setback. No matter how beaten down a character seemed, there was always a way to rise up again.

Unless I killed them, of course. But I didn't kill my characters.

Thinking back, I see how writing fiction set the scene for me to become a theologian. My power of revision helped me wrestle with what it means to be made in the image of God, with creative powers and the ability to make choices that matter.

Writing also helped me redeem my past. Redemption not in the transactional sense, like when I bought my flute back from the pawnshop, but in the compensatory sense, like uncovering a hidden gift. No one—not even a character—wants to pass through the valley of the shadow. But once you've done it, at least you know one way to get through.

⌒

My sister-in-law, Annette, served on the board of a progressive Christian magazine in Chicago called *Daughters of Sarah*. She asked if I would be interested in writing a book review of a rape memoir. The author was a Christian who'd been raped as a young woman while doing inner-city mission work. In her memoir she chronicled her years-long recovery, pinpointing the experience of giving birth as the key to her restoration to wholeness.

Reading this woman's story threatened my sense of self. Even if I felt fully recovered, was I fooling myself? Would others see me as recovered if I didn't have a husband and a baby? The idea grated on me. It echoed so much of what I'd heard growing up: that a woman's life is defined not by her actions but by her relationships. Is she a wife and mother? Then she is blessed.

I wanted to raise my fist against such a thought, to claim the healing I'd found. I was no longer a victim but a survivor. I bore scars rather than wounds.

⌒

One day in 1982 I got a call from Marty. We spent some time catching up on each other's news, and after a bit she asked, "Have you heard about Hayes?"

"No," I said. "What's to hear? Is he dead?"

"We're not that lucky," she said. "The SOB. He's been convicted again. This time it's murder."

I sat down quickly as the blood thumped in my heart. "How is that even possible? Did he get out of prison?"

"It's an old case. From before us," she said. "Remember that Jerry Freid case? The community college professor?"

I did remember, vaguely. Jerry Freid lived in the Heritage Hill neighborhood and was murdered around the time of our crime. There'd been speculation about a connection, which was why I knew anything about it at all. But I hadn't paid much attention. It didn't seem connected. Maybe I just didn't want to acknowledge that it could be.

"You're saying Hayes was convicted of killing Freid?"

"That's what I'm saying. Hayes murdered someone *before* he broke into our house."

I could hardly absorb the fact.

We talked for a long time. Marty filled me in on what she knew, and later I read articles from the *Grand Rapids Press*. The more I learned, the more awful the story became. Hayes had murdered a good man. Not only was Jerry Freid a well-liked professor, but he loved the Heritage Hill neighborhood. He believed in the power of racial integration. He held block meetings in his home, including one shortly before his death.

In reconstructing the timeline, I realized Freid's murder may have been the first crime Hayes committed. He and another criminal (not the same person as my rapist) broke into Freid's home, apparently planning to rob it. They knew Freid had a large dog, a Russian wolfhound, so they came armed with a baseball bat.

What they didn't know was that Freid was at home, watching TV in the darkened living room. When the dog barked, they cracked the dog over the head with the bat. Then the criminals must have seen Freid. One of them leaped over the couch and attacked Freid with the bat, bashing him over the head too. They broke his skull. Amazingly enough, Freid didn't die immediately. Maybe they thought he had. They seemed to take their time ransacking the house. Sometime later—perhaps when Freid made some sound or movement—the criminals must have dragged his body up the stairs and stuffed him into a bedroom closet.

Later that evening, when Freid didn't answer the phone, his

girlfriend came to the house. She glimpsed the disorder and called the police. They found a gruesome scene, including the beaten dog and blood everywhere. At that point Freid was still alive, shut in the closet. He lived for nearly a day but never regained consciousness.

The account of the crime was heartbreaking. I was flooded with sorrow for Jerry Freid and all the people who loved him. I was glad that justice had finally been meted out, some five years later. But I was also stunned. To think that Hayes had done these things before he broke into our house! I had resisted thinking that the criminals were truly evil. I didn't want them to be capable of such atrocities. I wanted to downplay the danger we had been in.

They were young! They said they wouldn't hurt us! They stole trinkets! They asked for bologna!

I saw that it was taking an easy way out to feel regret without first coming to terms with the horror. It was easier to hold on to a fantasy of forgiveness someday in the future—to indulge in such a thing—than to feel the revulsion of an encounter with true evil. Death by baseball bat.

Most of all I felt a harrowing sense of escape. Narrow escape. We'd been raped, but not killed.

November 5, 1978, had been the night that changed my life. Suddenly I realized that it might have been otherwise.

28

IN THE SPRING OF 1983, I joined a bicycling group that went on long-distance rides on the weekends, often overnight. A few days before the Fourth of July holiday, a friend from the law firm, a paralegal named Anitra, invited me on a three-night canoe trip to the Apostle Islands.

"Sorry," I said. "It sounds like fun, but I'm signed up for a two-night bike trip."

"So cancel!" Anitra said. "You're my last hope. Some bozo dropped out, and we're short a paddler. We need a full dozen."

"I'm not a paddler," I told her. "I don't really love canoeing."

"You've just done little lakes, right? This is different. This is Lake Superior! We use a huge canoe, like the voyageur canoes. This is living history. Come on, Ruth. You'll love it! Without you, the trip is a bust!"

I let myself be persuaded.

Anitra had just started dating Tom, one of the summer interns. They were both heading to law school in the fall. Besides being brilliant, they were outdoorsy. After work, Tom and Anitra picked me up in a tiny, red Toyota. We were headed north about four hours, to a church camp on the shore of Lake Superior. The plan was to arrive by dark.

"Oh, and on the way we're picking up the trip leader," Anitra mentioned.

Doug was waiting for us on the steps of his apartment building. He had dark blond hair that curled around the edges of his ball cap, and he was wearing a light-blue T-shirt that said something about rowing. He wore glasses and had a mustache resting like a caterpillar on his upper lip.

We loaded Doug's gear into the trunk and then discussed seating. Doug ended up in the front seat beside Tom, who was driving. As Anitra and I climbed into the tiny backseat, Anitra teased that we were sitting "married style." We headed north out of Minneapolis on Interstate 35.

"So, Ruth, what did you do all day?" Tom asked.

"I typed a prenuptial agreement," I said, "and the supporting documents."

"Don't tell me," Tom said. "The wife is young, and the guy is old."

"Old and rich. And honestly? A real piece of work. You should see his asset sheet—what she's signing away. Does she have any idea?"

"Probably," Tom said. "I'm sure she's marrying him for his money."

Anitra jumped in to defend the faceless woman.

The two lawyer types were equally passionate and articulate. It was fun to listen to them argue the subject of prenuptial agreements, especially since they had just started dating. I threw in a few comments, but Doug was quiet. Eventually Anitra asked Doug his opinion.

"Marriage must be hard," Doug said, "but I don't believe in divorce. I think you have to be really mature. You have to say, 'This is it. No back door.'"

From the backseat, I perked up my ears. Did that cute, outdoorsy guy just say what I thought he did? Was he single? A hundred and fifty miles later, I knew that he was. I also knew where he worked, that he was a Christian, and that like me, he was a middle sibling, third out of five. Not only that, but Anitra was also the third out of five siblings, and Tom was third out of four. Our shared birth order seemed miraculous and significant. What were the chances? The four of us joked about how well-rounded middle children were—how adaptable, how balanced. Our canoe would do just great!

By the time we got near our destination, darkness had fallen. Just before the final turn, we stopped at a place called the Silver Star. A live band was playing, and the building thumped with sound. While we made our way onto the crowded dance floor, Doug managed to pour the entire contents of his glass down my back. How clumsy! I laughed, grateful to have found a flaw—one I could live with.

We all danced with abandon. "Wipe out!"

⌣

That night the four of us spread our sleeping bags on the thinly carpeted floor of the camp's deserted lodge. The next morning we headed to Bayfield, Wisconsin, where the canoe was stored. We would meet the other paddlers there. Along the way, Doug suggested that Cornucopia would make a good pit stop. It wasn't really a town—just a few buildings connected by a boardwalk along the shore of Lake Superior. Tom parked by a store that advertised marine motors, T-shirts, and cigarettes. He and Anitra headed inside.

"Do you want a drink of water?" Doug asked me.

"Sure."

He headed away from the store. I followed him up an embankment to where a pipe projected from a mound of lush grass. Doug warned me to stand back; then he turned a valve on the pipe, like a wheel. There was a thumping sound, and water gushed out in a torrent. I reached out my hand and let out a cry of surprise. The water was as frigid as glacial melt.

"Well, we don't need ice," Doug quipped.

He plunged his hands under the flow of water and then drank deeply. I followed suit. Doug cranked off the valve, and we stood gasping from the cold, shaking the drops from our hands.

"I think you call that refreshing," I said.

"It's an aquifer. It's why I like to stop here. Just think: a few minutes ago, that water was deep underground. For thousands of years. Hundreds of thousands. Millions! Just waiting under a rock shelf—a giant ocean. The freshest water in the world, and the most ancient."

I studied Doug's face, the way a deep dimple creased his right cheek when he grinned. He seemed totally alive in the moment. Fresh and ancient at the same time, indeed. Isn't that what love is?

Tom and Anitra emerged from the store carrying cups of coffee.

"Coffee!" Doug said. "My other favorite drink! You want a cup?"

Of course I did. The coffee smelled wonderful. My fingers were still tingling from the frigid aquifer when I wrapped them around the steaming paper cup.

———

The other eight paddlers met us in Bayfield. There were two married couples who were Doug's friends, plus four single women who were all PhD students in anthropology.

Anitra was right. The canoe was unlike any I'd ever seen, so long and broad. Doug called it a Montreal canoe and said it was a replica of what the French voyageurs had used for fur trading on the Great Lakes. Before we could load it, all our gear had to go in Duluth packs, in case the canoe overturned. The Duluth packs were large, square bags—basically canvas pockets secured with leather straps.

"Everything goes in a Duluth pack," Doug announced. "Sleeping bags. Clothes. Everything. And we need to share. Two people to a pack. Pack it tight."

Then he turned to me and asked if I wanted to share his pack.

I felt fluttery at the thought of our personal items being smooshed together. We stuffed everything into the canvas bag and worked together to do up the straps. There was air trapped inside, but Doug said that was good. It gave the bags a tiny bit of buoyancy.

"So if we capsize and drown, they'll find our Duluth packs floating?" Tom joked. "Good to know."

Once the canoe was loaded, each of us could choose a position. The widest seats in the middle were two abreast, but the rest were solo. I saw Doug head for the stern, which made sense, because he'd be the one to steer. I drifted inconspicuously to the rearmost seat. The canoe was so long that the paddlers along each side could stretch out both arms and barely touch the fingertips of the person ahead and behind. We'd have plenty of room to paddle.

The sun was bright, and we were all in high spirits. Doug distributed paddles and showed us the long oar he would use as a rudder. He explained how he would navigate and the commands he might call out. Then he demonstrated paddling technique. "Stroke in rhythm to maximize thrust," he told us. "Use all your muscles from the hips up, not just your arms. Keep your shoulders square to the front."

Doug was in command of the situation—thorough, but also lighthearted. "I want you to imagine that the bottom of the canoe has cargo, not just our gear. Imagine it's heaped with furs. Wampum. Something valuable."

I wondered what Doug would find valuable. What was his wampum? I would have to watch and listen and find out.

The water was sparkling as we slid the canoe in and splashed in after it. We settled into our seats and practiced paddling back and forth across the sheltered bay. There were a few sailboats out, their sails fluttering like handkerchiefs. Once the dozen of us had mastered the ability to stroke in unison, we headed into the open water. We were immediately surrounded by blue.

Blue below, above, behind, ahead. Blue horizon.

I dipped my fingertips into the icy water and thought about how deep it went. Superior had depths I couldn't imagine. In our rudimentary craft, we were perched on its massive lap, rocking gently as small waves licked our sides. As we paddled, I began to hum "The Wreck of the Edmund Fitzgerald." The Gordon Lightfoot song is an anthem to this big lake—a mournful ballad with a million verses that tells the story of a freighter that went down in the 1970s, taking the lives of everyone onboard. The song is strangely singable, a rhythmic dirge with upswings on the refrain. Doug joined my humming, his voice a deep growl behind me. I felt emboldened to sing but couldn't remember the words. I strung together whatever bits of lyric came to mind.

The lake, it is said, never gives up her dead

Here Doug joined in:

Of the big lake they called Gitche Gumee

We botched the lines, but it didn't matter. We only had to end each one with the up-swelling "Gitche Gu-MEE." Our terrible singing only made the scene more incongruous. We were singing about dying in a lake while we paddled on top of it in calm water on a cloudless day.

Sometimes we all paused our paddling just to look around. Our canoe bobbed gently, as inconsequential as a life raft in the Atlantic. Doug pointed out dark blue shapes on the horizon and named the islands: Basswood, Hermit, Oak, Raspberry. We were headed to tiny York Island, where there was a campground.

That night we camped in army surplus tents. We built a big fire and roasted hot dogs and marshmallows and told jokes. The next morning we intended to cross over to Sand Island, about three miles west, which would be the longest stretch of open water during our three-day trip.

In the morning, the sky was cloudy. Doug consulted his weather radio, which was little more than static. "I can't get much, but it sounds like a storm is on the way." By the time we cleaned up from breakfast, it was already starting to sprinkle.

"Now's the time!" Doug yelled. "Paddles in the water!"

We were entering the three-mile open stretch when it began to pour. The rain immediately soaked us. The stinging raindrops struck our heads and faces, blinding us. I squinted and locked my eyes on the paddle of the person in front of me, doing my best to stay in rhythm. I tucked my chin, pulled myself up out of my hips, and tried to keep my shoulders square. As the canoe rocked, my paddle plunged well past the blade on one stroke and sliced uselessly through air on the next. I wondered how Doug could possibly see to navigate. I just trusted that he could. I myself could see only three things: my paddle, my neighbor's paddle, and the side of the canoe. We continued this way for more than an hour. It was exhilarating and unnerving and exhausting.

—⁓—

By the time we pulled onto the beach at Sand Island, the canoe was half filled with water. We tipped it over to drain it and stashed the gear underneath. What next? Our gear was more protected than we were. The rain and wind were bone chilling and showed no sign of abating. We huddled. The anthropologists decided to build a shelter of some kind, but the rest of us opted to run to keep warm. As Anitra said, "I'm already so miserable—what can it hurt?"

We found a wooded path not far from the shore, so we followed it. It was darker in the woods than we expected, and we were reduced to stumbling through the trees. After two miles or so, we arrived at a clearing at the northernmost tip of the island. There was a bit more light without the trees, but in the open, the rain pelted us. We squinted and through the rain could see, as if an apparition, a brick building. When we got closer, we could see that it was a house with a lighthouse attached. The light wasn't lit, and the windows were shuttered.

"Look at the chimney," Anitra yelled. Sure enough, a tendril of smoke was rising, barely visible through the rain. Then the door of the house opened, as if by magic, and a woman wearing an apron beckoned us across the yard.

"Come in, come in, all you drowned rats."

We clomped into an old-timey kitchen and were greeted by warmth and the enveloping aroma of ginger. A younger woman was just inside the door. "I knew there was a reason we had the urge to bake those cupcakes," she commented to the aproned woman.

At the women's urging, we pulled off our dripping jackets and rain ponchos and made a mess of the floor. Then we squeezed around a rough table beside a potbellied stove. The room filled with the brown-sugar smell of steaming wool. Two men materialized, an older and a younger, to match the women. They explained that the young couple was serving as volunteer lighthouse keepers and the woman's parents were visiting for the long weekend.

"But don't you have to go up there and turn on the light?" someone asked.

"It's on," they assured us. "It's been moved to a steel structure at the water's edge. See for yourself."

We looked out the lakeside window and saw a light, blinking in sequence.

"It's fully automated. We're here to tend people like you, not the light."

"So you mean this lighthouse is useless?" one of us said.

"Not useless. It's the best place in the world during a storm. Go on up there and see. You'll never forget it. The glass is triple-paned, and still the wind and rain come right through."

We listened as the wind howled and the rain pelted the house. Lightning flashed.

"Imagine if you hadn't opened that door," one of us said. "We'd be out in that."

"You'd be even drowned-er than you are, but you'd survive!" the aproned woman said. "You're all young and strong."

She poured tea into chipped cups. We gulped it down, and she poured more. We devoured the spice cupcakes, which were still warm.

"They're not even frosted," she protested, but we just laughed, our mouths full.

Then the eight of us took turns ascending the lighthouse tower in pairs. Doug and I were the last to go. The staircase was circular and metal—the kind that clangs with every footfall. But we couldn't hear our steps over the howling wind. The whole tower reverberated. When Doug and I emerged into the tiny circular room made entirely of window glass, the storm engulfed us.

The lake writhed like something alive. It was black, then white, constantly alternating as the beacon blinked its warning. The powerful light illuminated the waves crashing onto the rocks at the point. The light seemed to cling to the white edges of churning water. Great spumes blasted the windows of the lighthouse tower on every side. I couldn't tell if the water coming in was horizontal rain or spray coming up from the lake below. Everything was a froth. On all sides of the tower, the panes of glass rattled in their frames, a cacophony. A foghorn sounded its baleful warning over and over. Thunder crashed at the same instant lightning streaked the sky.

I shivered uncontrollably. Doug was wearing a thick wool sweater, which he took off. He bent down and put his lips against my ear. "Put this on. It's oiled wool. It's warm even when it's wet."

I gladly would have let him pull a garbage bag over my head, just to be close to him. I nodded, and he pulled the too-big sweater over my head. I could smell his scent along with the wet wool. He settled the sodden sweater around my shoulders and hips and then kept his arms around me. In that embrace we kissed for the first time. I was still shivering, and he clenched me against his chest.

I couldn't hear anything over the thumping thunder. Or maybe that thumping was the beating of my heart. I wished the moment would never end. I would be content if the tempest whirled and whipped and walloped around me forever.

29

I RESOLVED TO TELL DOUG about my past on our second date. I hadn't told other guys this soon, but Doug was different. Emotionally, I was already in deep. If he was going to walk away, the sooner the better. My head said that my history shouldn't matter. But in my heart I feared that he would see me as damaged goods. Not just because I'd been raped but because of what I'd done in the aftermath.

We were in his apartment, sitting rather formally on a too-narrow couch—a hand-me-down from his parents. I was terribly nervous, afraid that this magical thing between us would vanish as soon as I said what I needed to say. I faced him as I spoke, the words sticking in my throat. Everything hinged on his reaction. Finally I let the words out in a rush.

"I have something important to say, so please listen. When I was in my last year of college, living with my friends, some men broke into our house with guns and raped us all and they caught the guys and there was a trial and they were convicted."

Doug's face went pale.

"Men always ask about the guns and all that, and I can't bear it if you do that."

After a moment, I barreled on. "And after that I felt rotten about myself, and I had an affair with a married man. He was older, a seminarian, and I fell in love with him. I shouldn't have done it, but I did."

"How much older?" Doug asked.

"Ten years."

"Then it's his fault," Doug said.

"I'm really sorry I did it."

"It's not your fault," he said.

I didn't agree, but I wished I could.

As I'd requested, we didn't speak of it again—not for a long time. Much too long.

—

We'd been dating about two months when Doug came to church with me at Prince of Glory. We drove in his rattletrap Plymouth Volare, another hand-me-down from his parents. The car was two toned, the roof darker than the body. Doug said it was two tones of brown, but I teased that it was two tones of mustard, as if the colors were competing over a fifty-cent hot dog. The ramshackle car looked right at home in Prince of Glory's decrepit parking lot.

It felt natural to sit side by side with Doug in a pew, to share a hymnal, to go forward to receive Communion together. Driving home, we discussed why I attended this particular church. I was able to tell Doug that worshiping beside black people was important to me, that it was healing after having been raped by a black man. I said I believed in God but was still figuring out what that meant and I needed church to help me do that. I said I trusted the Spirit to do something important in this hour every week, even if I didn't know exactly what that was.

Doug had grown up attending church with his family. It was

something they did together, like weeknight suppers or Saturday housecleaning. It was never discussed, simply done, and from there they moved on to other things. I explained that it was different in my family—that attending a church in our denomination wasn't just *one* thing we did; it was the *main* thing we did. Church was the center, the hub from which every other thing emanated: our social life, our schooling, my parents' employment.

That fall, Prince of Glory experienced internal conflict. As a mission church, it was always on the edge of existence, and when the minister announced he was leaving, there was much talk about the future and money and leadership. There was even talk of closing. I wasn't ready to deal with church drama. Surely there was a multiracial congregation that was a better, more stable fit.

Doug and I began to visit other urban churches on Sunday mornings. Someone suggested a church in St. Paul called Dayton Avenue Presbyterian. I couldn't imagine driving all that way just to go to church, but I took note of the name. Meanwhile, my parents kept asking if I was going to "come home" to the Christian Reformed Church. Their words echoed in my thoughts, and I felt a twinge of guilt each time we drove into the parking lot of yet another unfamiliar church.

———

In December, my law firm had an elegant holiday party at an exclusive club in downtown Minneapolis. In the six months Doug and I had been together since our first stormy kiss, we'd never been anywhere this sophisticated. We nibbled from seafood hors d'oeuvres arranged around an enormous ice sculpture of a sea monster. The ice was lit from below, as iridescent as a fantasy.

There were luminaries in attendance, including former Vice President Walter Mondale, who was preparing for his 1984 run for the presidency. We shook hands with him and made awkward small talk. Someone took our picture, but only after Mr. Mondale set down his glass. It was only ice water, but as he told us, that wouldn't show in the picture.

We sat down to a sumptuous dinner of steak and lobster tail and unending glasses of wine. After dinner a band played, and everyone danced. After a few songs, Doug suggested we rest for a moment in the elegant pink and gold drawing room. No one else was in the gorgeous room, which was softly lit with lamps all around. We sat together on a Victorian settee surrounded by portraits and brocade, like people in a fairy tale. Doug seemed nervous.

He finally got the words out: "Would you marry me?"

I tried to let two heartbeats pass before I said yes. But really, I wondered what had taken him so long. We went back on the dance floor, glowing. A friend of mine, a legal secretary, was dancing with her husband, who was a judge. I blurted our news, and the judge offered to tie the knot, then and there. Wouldn't that have made a story?

My parents thought I would want to be married in New Jersey, but I said no. Minnesota was my home now. We set the wedding date for early August, eight months away. Finding the right church acquired a new urgency. Still, Doug and I agreed that we wouldn't be swayed by color schemes or center aisles or possible reception venues. We were looking for more than a pretty backdrop for the ceremony; we wanted a church home, a community that would be an important part of our marriage. I liked that we talked about our marriage this way, as if it were an entity separate from us, something we could cultivate.

We began to search more efficiently. We attended two worship services each Sunday, one in the morning and another in the evening. Afterward we discussed every detail: the type of music, the friendliness of the people, the theology of the sermon, the version of the Bible in the pews, even the quality of the after-church coffee.

We quickly learned each other's hot buttons. Doug was especially irritated by churches where people seemed fake or perfectly dressed. I hated it when the minister began every prayer with "Father God." Doug studied the crowd while I studied the bulletin, analyzing the names in the list of elders so I could calculate the percentage of lay leaders who were female. After the service we stood to the side and sampled the coffee, which was invariably mediocre, invariably served in Styrofoam cups.

I still believed that someday I would walk into a sanctuary and everything would click. I would have that childhood experience I still craved. Call it comfort. Call it grace. Call it home.

The Dayton Avenue Presbyterian Church was a magnificent old structure, built of enormous chunks of rose-colored brownstone. A sign pointed toward a side entrance where an elderly man, spare and slightly bent, greeted us. He escorted us inside, explaining that worship was held in the fellowship hall during the winter months to save on fuel bills.

"The board decided we have more important things to do with our money than heat that gargantuan sanctuary," he said. "It takes twenty-four hours to heat it for an hour's use. That's just not good stewardship."

The fellowship hall was set with rows of metal folding chairs. We took a seat and someone handed us a hymnal. I watched as the hall filled up, noting a number of interracial couples and families. The choir filed in wearing matching orange robes. That was the only thing about the church that matched. The members were every age, size, and skin tone.

A woman walked in wearing a black pulpit robe. It was the first time I'd ever seen those vestments on a woman. She didn't look much older than I was. She was introduced to the congregation as the Reverend Julie Neraas, their candidate for the position of interim pastor. After the service, there would be a vote about whether to hire her. I was incredulous. This church was going to hire a woman pastor? Today?

A silent prayer of thanks rose inside me. I was grateful God had led us to this particular place on this particular day.

Ever since the night of the crime, I had resisted seeing God's hand in the details of circumstance. After all, if God orchestrated one event, that would mean He orchestrated all events, good and bad. I didn't want to believe that. So could I believe that God had put me in this folding chair? I resisted the thought.

Yet I felt a welling sense of gratitude. It was right and good that I was here at this moment.

I glimpsed a new possibility. Could there be some way that the working out of God's will encompasses human free will? After all, hadn't Doug and I been diligently searching for a church home?

Maybe this matter of will was not all one way or all the other. Maybe events occurred from a sort of partnership between God and people.

———

The text was Mark 5, about one of Jesus' healing miracles. A woman had been bleeding for twelve years. She'd spent every last dime on doctors, to no avail. When she heard about the miracle worker Jesus, she decided to get as close to Him as she could, thinking, *If I can just touch the hem of His garment, I will be healed.*

She crept forward in the crowd and touched His robe. It worked! She could feel healing flood through her body.

But Jesus was aware that power had gone out from Him. "Who touched Me?" He asked the crowd.

"What a question, Jesus!" the disciples said. "The crowd is pressing in on You!"

Then the woman came forward and admitted what she had done.

Jesus told her, "Daughter, your faith has made you well. Go in peace, and be healed of your disease."

I was familiar with the story. I grew up calling her "the woman with an issue of blood." As a child, I liked to imagine her, arm bravely outstretched to touch the hem of Jesus' garment. I figured the poor woman had a bloody wound that would not heal—maybe a gash on the knee or elbow.

The sermon I heard at Dayton Avenue that morning changed everything I understood about that story. The minister said that the likely cause of the woman's "issue of blood" was a menstrual irregularity. She spoke about this frankly, in the context of the purity laws of the day, which had enormous implications. A woman who was menstruating was not allowed to do normal activities. She couldn't cook or serve food or even touch a man. Can you imagine being in this state for years? If she ever had been married, her husband was long gone. A woman who can't bear children or provide meals or even go to the market—what good is she?

I was overwhelmed with compassion for this nameless woman. How did she even support herself? No wonder she was desperate.

But she was also brave. She dared to have hope. She heard of Jesus and followed the crowd. Even though she was unclean, she pushed her way to Jesus and touched His garment—a punishable offense. Imagine her fear at being found out.

Jesus knew all this, of course. When He called her out, He was asking her to risk her life in admitting what she had done. And when she admitted that she had transgressed in this way, Jesus called her "daughter."

Tears flowed from my eyes as I recognized my own experience. This unnamed woman had been an outcast, through no fault of her own. She was "less than," ostracized because of her female parts. Yet she had faith. She persisted. She took risks.

I saw my own wounded, scarred self and heard Jesus say, "Daughter, your faith has made you well. Go in peace, and be healed of your disease."

I can still recapture the floating feeling that came over me, the sense of being wafted to the rafters even as I sat anchored to a gray, metal folding chair in an unfamiliar fellowship hall.

Daughter. What a word! For the first time in a very long time, I felt at home.

30

WE JOINED THAT CHURCH. But you already knew that. The church hired Pastor Julie as their interim minister. The elderly gentleman who had showed us to our seats was named Arthur, and the next Sunday we asked him to show us the sanctuary. He didn't have the right key to open the door, so Doug and I took turns peering in through the window.

Arthur cleared his throat. "The ceiling is painted blue," he said. "A pretty blue, all the ladies say. A cornflower blue."

Seven months later, on a Sunday in August, Arthur and his wife, Martha, were among the guests who attended our wedding in that sanctuary. It was a beastly hot day, and we had the opposite temperature problem: a lack of air-conditioning. Not that it mattered, really. The ceiling was a lovely cornflower blue, as Arthur noted, and its vaulted lines helped counteract the heat and humidity of an impending storm. Barb was my maid of honor, and her father was our officiant. Every member of my family was there. The reception afterward was held in Doug's parents' backyard, and we all felt fortunate that the rain held off until the party was over.

Doug and I still have the wedding gift Arthur and Martha gave us that day: a wooden bread plate inscribed with "Our Daily Bread." It was altogether satisfying to bring our gifts home and put them away in our new apartment. The brick apartment building we lived in was close to downtown Minneapolis and had once been handsome, even stately. Now the police station at the rear of the building was a positive feature, because it made the somewhat sketchy neighborhood feel safe. Our apartment was in the back of the building, and the windows of our tiny eating area looked out at a chain-link fence and a posse of parked police cars. I loved that. I loved eating meals at that table with my husband—the thrill of that word!—and feeling absolutely safe.

I felt myself growing every day, soaking in the love and security of this relationship. It was revelatory to me that love could be as great a teacher as suffering. And ever so much more pleasant.

We attended Dayton Avenue every Sunday, and I quickly felt at home. Like the denomination I'd grown up in, Presbyterianism had its doctrinal foundation in Calvinism, and its governing structure was a representative democracy. I loved talking about these things with Pastor Julie. One day she said to me, "You seem to have a real affinity for theology. Have you ever thought about going to seminary?"

Rather sheepishly I admitted that I had. "But I don't think I'm called. Not when I've run into so many roadblocks."

Pastor Julie looked at me rather quizzically and asked two questions that changed my life: "Did you know that United Seminary isn't far away, in New Brighton, and they offer night classes?" and "Would you like to preach a sermon here in January?"

I drove out to United Theological Seminary in December, right before the fall semester ended. The campus was modest—less than modest. It was just one building, and a bit haphazard. There was a central two-story section for the offices, the library, and a small chapel. The classrooms seemed like a single-story afterthought, a long low arm jutting out into the snowy Minnesota prairie. I stood at a counter and studied the list of evening electives. I chose "Feminism and Practical Theology," because, well, look at all those words in the same title.

Which is how I found myself, a few weeks later, in a classroom that wasn't quite warm enough, crammed into a student desk that wasn't quite big enough, surrounded by third-year seminarians whose mere presence made me feel not quite smart enough. Despite the cold, I perspired as I discovered just how little I knew about feminism, practicality, or theology. I was completely and gloriously in over my head. I was hooked.

Meanwhile, I was working on my first sermon, the one I'd be preaching in the same fellowship hall where I first heard a woman preach a year before. I spent weeks researching the text, which was the story of Jesus healing a paralyzed man after four of his friends lowered him through a hole in the roof. I approached the text as a lesson about human interdependency, as well as healing.

On the Sunday I preached, Pastor Julie drove me to church because Doug needed the car to get to work. I dressed carefully in one of my legal-secretary outfits: a plaid pleated skirt and a Scandinavian-style short wool jacket. During the long drive from Minneapolis to St. Paul, Pastor Julie left me alone with my thoughts. I silently clutched the sermon in my gloved hands.

When the time came, I read the Gospel lesson, and then I preached. The earth didn't move. The universe didn't shift. Afterward, a few people told me that they appreciated my words, that they saw something more in the story than they had before. They could insert themselves into the action. Pastor Julie said I had done a fine job. Then she asked, "Now do you believe you could be called to ministry?"

I registered for full-time classes for the fall, which meant I needed a job with a more flexible schedule. Finding a position at a new law firm wasn't difficult. I was hired at a larger firm that needed someone to fill in at odd hours.

It was more difficult to choose a seminary degree program. For the first semester I could take overview classes, but then I had to make a decision. There were two types of master's degrees: a master of divinity and a master of arts. The MDiv would take three or four years and would lead to a career in ministry. The MA would take less time—two or three years, depending on what I studied—and was the kind of degree people earned on their way to a career in the arts, social sciences, or academia.

I sat in class and tried to absorb the material while part of my brain kept wondering just what I thought I was doing. Did I really think I could lead a congregation? *Me?* Maybe the MA degree made more sense. Maybe I would go into something more academic. An MA would always be handy. It might open doors—who knew? And I wanted, more than anything, to keep all possible doors open. I was terrified of shutting the wrong one. I was determined not to live with regret.

Other seminarians were making similar decisions, so we discussed our options over coffee in the refectory, which was what we called the windowless basement room where we ate our bagged lunches. More than half of the seminarians were women, many of us married. We called our quandaries "dual-career issues."

At home, Doug and I agreed we should pursue our vocations in tandem. Not only would we be egalitarian before God and each other, but we would be equal before society and our bank accounts too. The problem was that we had rarely seen couples do this, and we didn't know what it would look like. Should Doug become a teacher? He could get licensed in about a year. It made more sense than getting an advanced degree. Should I become a pastor? Or get some kind of counseling degree? And how would children fit in?

But even as we dithered, we realized we were delaying an inevitable decision. Delays waste money and time, and we had precious little of either. It was a straightforward decision, really. Either I was called to ministry or I wasn't. That was the key piece.

Decades later, I understand why I wrestled with the decision. It may have been a straightforward matter, but it was hardly a simple one. Ordination rarely is. And for a woman with my history— growing up in a conservative culture that barred women from ministry, being raped at gunpoint, taking up with a married man—the issue of fitness for ministry was especially fraught. Not just "Could a woman be a minister?" but "Could I, a woman with a history, be a minister?"

How does a person think a thought that has always been unthinkable? It takes a strategic shift. I remembered my vision from years before—the brick wall that rose before me, seemingly insurmountable, before it fell in a cascade of destruction and release.

Really, I knew what needed to be destroyed. I needed to put aside, once and for all, my sense of being not good enough. I was a woman. A rape survivor. A sinner. What's more, I would always be these things. The Spirit could use me—not in spite of them, but because of them.

⁓

During the second semester, in a class called Modes of Ministry, one of my classmates raised her hand and asked our female professor an unusual question: "Some of us have been talking about when we're going to get pregnant. What do you recommend? Should we have babies now, while we're in school? Or wait until we're in our first church? What if there's no maternity leave?"

The professor, who was the mother of teenage twins, laughed. "There's no good time to have a baby," she said. "You just do it anyway."

Perhaps it's no coincidence that my class had a rash of pregnancies soon after. I was as eager for a baby as my classmates seemed to be, but I didn't want to slow my progress toward a degree. After being derailed for years, my life was on track at last! I could hardly wait for everything to happen: graduation, a call to a church, ordination. I wanted to have children, too. I wanted to have it all.

I decided it was a matter of timing. I chewed on my pencil as I considered the calendar. I was signed up for a full load of classes for the coming fall, plus a half-time internship. If a baby were to be born in late May, I could spend three months at home before my third-year fall semester began. . . .

As I plotted, details filled my head. Whom could I borrow maternity clothes from? Would a crib fit in the hallway? And at what point, exactly, would I have to give up caffeine?

To my amazement, life seemed almost too willing to cooperate with my penciled plan. I got pregnant immediately, which made my due date sooner than I'd expected: early April rather than late May. When I wrote that due date in my calendar using the green ink I saved for important due dates—meaning when papers were due—the reality began to sink in. This was a different kind of due date. I was going to be a mother. And I was going to have to write this year's papers without my favorite study aid: coffee.

Every week I worked two or three shifts at my new law firm while Doug worked part time at a residence for autistic adults and took classes to get his teaching certification. We shared one car, a complicated schedule, and a shoestring income. But we had very specific goals. This craziness wouldn't last forever. We were building a future, and every day was exciting.

Other than being tired all the time, I didn't mind going to work. My new law firm had offices in the top floors of the IDS building, the skyscraper that had once beckoned me with its shiny possibilities. The IDS was still the tallest building in Minneapolis, and I enjoyed pushing the express elevator button labeled "44" and taking in the panoramic view of the city below. I even enjoyed the great swoosh of the toilets whose plumbing somehow traversed those many floors.

My job was to assist a busy commercial real estate attorney. Typically we began our work after everyone else cleared out on Friday at five. We created stacks of paper that covered an enormous table in a conference room. We spent all Saturday perfecting the documents: he made changes while I deciphered his red-inked scratches. The printer hummed. I have always loved a clean document.

Those silent Saturdays passed with more ease than Sundays. I was interning at a suburban church, and Sundays were noisy and full of spoken words—a whirlwind of handshakes and announcements and worship and fellowship-hall chats and visits to nursing homes and pizza and icebreaker games and Bible study for high school students, all of which overwhelmed my introverted self. On Saturdays I felt quietly competent, but on Sundays I was never quite sure if I was doing anything right.

31

Many things were gestating that second year of seminary. Suitably enough, one of my classes was called Constructive Theology. That title sounds like Tinkertoys and dump trucks, but this construction project required only ink and paper. At the end of the term a major paper was due: our very own systematic theology. Our paper should hold together all the key doctrines in a cohesive way. Our theological foundation—to continue the construction metaphor—should be a question—the question we thought was the most essential to faith.

From that foundational question, we were to address all the classic doctrinal concerns: Who is God? What is the purpose of human life? How does one approach Scripture? What is sin? What does it mean to be saved? Why does the church exist? What is the role of sacraments? What is discipleship? What does resurrection mean? What is eternity? What are the last things?

Okeydokey.

I didn't even know how to choose my question. No, that's not quite honest. I knew what my question was; I just didn't dare pose it, since then I'd have to come up with an answer. *Why does a sovereign*

God allow suffering? It didn't necessarily help that the conundrum is so common that it has its own name: theodicy. The problem of evil. Why does a good God allow suffering?

Maybe I could choose a different question. Why not behave like a normal newlywed—enjoy life and ignore the problem of evil? Because as significant as the question was, it was hard for me to approach the subject of evil academically.

Instead, a word like *rape* could flood me with sensory memories even yet. Masked intruders pressing guns into my body. My friends and I tied together and marching up the stairs. The windshield wipers slashing away my old reality as we drove to the emergency room.

On a normal day, the terror of those specific events had greatly receded. Suffering in general was no longer an abyss. But if I had to dig into my belief system, I knew I would soon discover that suffering had, in fact, carved a deep groove in my life. Sometimes it seemed that I peered at life over the lip of that groove.

I took Constructive Theology in the fall of 1986. The previous January the space shuttle *Challenger* had exploded at takeoff as the nation's schoolchildren looked on. In April a catastrophic nuclear accident at Chernobyl rained radioactivity over large swaths of Europe and the Soviet Union. In October the stock market collapsed, destabilizing the global economy. And the Iran-Contra affair was constantly in the news.

Sometimes my heart was tender for the whole hurting world; other times I felt tough and cynical. What could I do about any of those problems? Meanwhile, I spent my days crammed into a student desk, parsing words about God. Was that a ridiculous waste of time? The thing was, some of the words we parsed were helpful to me, especially the most common words, the ones I thought I already knew. Each word was like a puzzle piece. *Finitude. Sin. Evil. Temptation. Free will. The image of God. Salvation. Grace.*

In their lectures, my professors explained how different traditions fit the pieces together, though no tradition could solve every puzzle. In fact, whether you thought a tradition was successful in answering life's questions largely depended on which question you considered fundamental. It was fascinating to realize there were so many ways to approach Scripture. It wasn't interpretation so much as prioritization. There were so many texts and writers, anchored in such different times and voices. Which passages controlled the others, and why? There was so much head knowledge to assimilate. I suspected it would take a long time to let the things I was learning percolate into my heart and soul.

Sometimes I yearned to feel the simple comfort and conviction of my childhood beliefs. In bed I sometimes wished I could slip into the recurring dream of my childhood and float into the sky to a cathedral of great majesty and peace. Even though I spent all day thinking about God, I missed the easy intimacy we had when I was a child. Sometimes I wondered how I would approach doctrine if I hadn't been raped. Maybe I wouldn't ask so many questions. Maybe the questions wouldn't burn so. Maybe that would even be a loss.

Meanwhile, the baby was growing. People often call conception and birth "miracles." Certainly the process is amazing, especially when it proceeds smoothly: the sperm and egg joining to form a zygote, then an embryo, a fetus, a baby. But none of these transformations take place outside the created order, which is the definition of a miracle. Conception and gestation might feel miraculous, but they are not, technically, miracles.

Still, this process going on inside my body changed me in ways that *felt* miraculous. At age twenty-nine, I was reasonably prepared for the physical changes of pregnancy. I had read about those changes in books and had watched others go through them. But I was unprepared for the spiritual changes that pregnancy brought, especially the change in how I prayed.

Each day brought many opportunities for prayer—in class, in

chapel, at mealtimes. As I'd been taught to do, and as I'd done my whole life, I would begin to pray by bowing my head. But being pregnant changed this simple action. Dropping my chin brought my attention to my belly, which each day was a tablespoon bigger. A prayer would rise from me, a prayer that didn't need words—certainly not a specific formula. This prayer was formed by an awareness of heartbeats, of blood pulsing through veins, of nourishment moving through a placenta. This prayer was carried to God upon the exhalation of my breath, and began again with inhalation.

At first I tried to insert words into this process, proper words laid in sentences. But why? I could simply let the prayer rise and fall. It's what my awareness wanted to do: to pause and lift this growing life to God for blessing and then gather that life back to my center. This prayer loop was wordless, spontaneous, unending. This was a loop of breath that was grateful for breath.

Perhaps because of this shift in my prayer life, I experienced a shift in my theology. The fact that I was still alive now appeared to be a gift of grace—a larger gift than I had realized. The criminals had taken something precious from me that night, but they had not taken my life, my breath. Now I had the chance to pass that life and breath on to a baby.

This marvel of breath was a simple thing, a profound thing—breath's continuance, breath's persistence and vitality. This marvel of breath began to lead me back to the innocent faith of my childhood. Not to a world where everything made sense, as it once had, but to a world where life was a daily gift, if only we could get enough height to see that. Sure, life was a mess. But it was in the mess that we made choices that mattered, not only for ourselves but also for others.

The New Testament says we must "work out [our] own salvation with fear and trembling" (Philippians 2:12). In seminary I worked indeed: listening to hours-long lectures, taking copious notes, reading thick books in small print, writing lengthy, footnoted papers. But in the end it was the work of prayer, wordless and breath centered and no work at all, that helped me work out my salvation.

———

At the same time that I was undergoing this seismic shift in my prayer life, I was learning to pray in public. At the church where I interned, I spoke aloud the carefully worded prayers that people expected. But in private I kept breathing my wordless prayers. This was the first time I stepped over the cleft between a public spiritual face and a personal spiritual faith. I didn't realize it at the time, but navigating that cleft is an essential part of becoming a pastor. I needed to learn how to shepherd other people's spiritual lives while staying authentic to my own. I have no idea how other ministers learn to do this. For me, it was one of the gifts of pregnancy.

———

There was still the matter of the foundational question for my Constructive Theology class. I had stewed on this for weeks.

After a lecture one day, we trooped down the stairs to the refectory with our lunch bags. Unwrapping a tuna sandwich, I asked one of my classmates, who also happened to be pregnant, if she had chosen her foundational question yet. She answered with a breezy, bright tone: "Oh, something about love, I suppose! Since God is love." Then she unwrapped her sandwich and a container of cottage cheese and dug in.

I bent back the spout on my little carton of milk. *God is love? Like pink Valentine hearts? That's it?*

I slurped down the milk with a feeling of defeat.

Oh, how I craved a steaming cup of coffee!

Seminary life included chapel services nearly every day. One day during a routine Prayer of Confession, I realized that I was silently confessing the fact that I was a rape victim. With a sense of shock, I realized that I frequently confessed this fact. But why? God had forgiven me long ago for the sins I committed during that period of my life. I didn't need some sort of special absolution because I'd been raped. Having been a victim wasn't some sort of permanent stain that I must repeatedly, and helplessly, scrub.

As if in a vision, I recognized that I did need to confess something—not having been raped, but my feelings of shame about having been raped. My shame was another brick in the wall that needed to crumble. I heard Jesus say to me, *Daughter, be healed.*

For that whole school year, my pregnancy served not only as a filter but also as a timetable. Sometimes I panicked. There was too much to think about and do, and not nearly enough time.

I would say to Doug, "What if I'm just not ready to be a mother?"

"You are. You're strong."

I'd say, "I don't feel strong. I feel scared."

Then he would say the thing I depended on hearing: "The hammer that shatters glass forges steel."

I would sigh deeply, to breathe in the words. I loved that image, and I loved that Doug believed they applied to me. I wanted to believe them too, that my ordeal had forged me, formed me, shaped me in positive ways. Through my husband's eyes, I dared to believe that maybe my whole story made sense. Look where it had led me: to him, to ministry, to motherhood. I tilted my chin down toward my belly and whispered, "You are precious, and your life is infinitely valuable, no matter what happens to you."

I realized that being a newlywed, and pregnant, was the perfect complement to seminary classes. I often pondered doctrines and couldn't think my way to the bottom of them. But I could always sink deeper into the experience of love.

When talk about God frustrated me—God so distant and unknowable and perfect—I could at least practice loving my husband, who was close and knowable and not perfect. Maybe it was the experience of our flawed love that opened my heart to a deeper love for a flawless God.

Ever since I had been plunged into sexual shame, which was reinforced by being raped—first by the hiker I trusted and then by a stranger at gunpoint—I'd had trouble believing that a perfect God loved me. Erasing words about shame is one thing, but erasing the feeling is another. Through my husband's loving eyes, I gradually came to see my imperfect self through God's loving eyes. And I learned to see my imperfect husband the same way.

Slowly, I eased up from my focus on doctrinal words. I would never get the words about God perfect. But theology was more than a litmus test. I wasn't losing my faith. But I was losing a certain obsession with pinning faith down.

In moments of worship and liturgy, I began to listen differently. We had studied the history of faith communities and how groups divided over the precise meaning of the sacrament—call it Mass or Eucharist or the Lord's Supper. The knowledge was surprisingly freeing. Instead of believing there was a perfect rendition of the doctrine of redemption that I must wrap my head around, I began to let the sacrament stand between me and the divine as a bridge. Sometimes I even glimpsed the meaning of grace in Christ's incarnation: love made flesh in Jesus of Nazareth.

32

I wrote that Constructive Theology paper. I wish I could say I definitively solved the problem of theodicy. But I was unable to reconcile God's sovereign power and the image of God in humans. At least I was unable to reconcile the conundrum like a mathematical formula. Each side of the equation was necessary and gave life comfort and meaning, though the two sides appeared to cancel each other out. But both sides are real and necessary. On the one side, God is all-powerful and loving, and God's will prevails. On the other side, humans are made in God's image and can exercise their will to make choices that matter, which God allows.

The way these two wills intersect—divine and human—is what creates the human story. I experienced the push and pull between God's will and my own, a push and pull that created energy as often as it generated friction. Hadn't God and I together kept racial hatred from lodging in my soul? Hadn't God's Spirit led me to enter seminary, a path I had been willing to follow? In preparing for ministry, weren't we together choosing to walk in the way of love rather than bitterness and fear? Weren't we together bringing a new life into the world?

When it was time to begin writing, I chose to shape my paper as a catechism. I had grown up on catechisms, and it felt powerful to frame questions and propose answers. I told myself that even John Calvin's systematic theology, written five centuries earlier, hadn't solved every conundrum. Instead of avoiding the contradictions, I called them "divine mysteries."

There were many mysteries. For instance, if God desired to save the whole world but had chosen the number of the elect, which was less than the full number of humans on earth, should I expect to understand or judge that discrepancy? If God sent Jesus into the world, divinity clothed in flesh, should I expect to understand the paradox housed in that God-Man, a paradox that councils of leaders over centuries of Christianity could not define? If God created the galaxies and caused the sea monsters to sport in the deep and the whirlwinds to blow through time, perhaps it was my turn to be quiet. Maybe I should fall silent and worship rather than pummel God with my words, no matter how diligently I'd written them.

Turning in that paper was the last act of the fall semester, and it felt supremely satisfying. Forty-six pages long, it was a clean document.

It began, after a few preliminaries, with this section called the "Overarching Perspective":

> At the outset of this statement of theology, I find it
> important to emphasize my understanding of God's tran-
> scendence and the recognition that humans will never
> fully understand who or what God is, or how God works.
> Human understanding is limited by our very creature-
> liness and our existence within history. Because of these
> limitations, much of what humans contemplate when we

contemplate theology—our reflection on the relationship between God and the human—appears paradoxical and contradictory. I do not ascribe this to the limitations of the divine-human relationship or of the life of faith, but to the limitations of the human mind. Were it possible for humans to understand all the workings of God, God would indeed be small and would cease to be God. While the study of theology is useful for shaping and articulating important ideas, it is necessary to recognize that the study of theology is inherently limited. When I run into a dead end or a paradox, then, I need make no excuse. I may have run into the vaguest shadow of God.

As part of the paper's introduction, I needed to include a section called "My Values." I said, in part,

The value that encompasses all the values is love. . . . My belief in a loving God originated in my childhood, largely because of parental and church instruction. A secondary but significant factor was the fact that the reality of my experience supported the notion that God is good and intends good for human life. My parents, who formed the focus of my life for many years, were consistently loving toward me and others.

This naive faith in a loving God was called into question when I ran headlong into an encounter with evil. Rather than doubting either my experience or the ultimate love and goodness of God, I came to a more realistic understanding of the interplay between a fallen world and a God who chooses not to exercise all of God's power and to allow evil events to happen. I found that my understanding of God and humans was able to expand sufficiently to include the reality of a broken world.

God is love. God is truth. We cannot know God, yet
we humans experience God-hunger. This is the motivating
force behind the study of theology, and a deeper experience
of the reality of this God of love is our goal.

In the fourth section I addressed "The Doctrine of God." After I
established the doctrine of providence, based on Romans 8:28, NRSV
("All things work together for good for those who love God, who
are called according to his purpose"), I went back and forth in the
catechetical form—questions followed by answers.

Q: But lots of times things don't go right for me.

A: God always works for growth. Growth is often
unpleasant, even painful. Yet anything that happens
can produce growth if the Spirit of God is welcomed
and allowed to operate. At the same time, anything that
happens can produce bitterness and decay if the Spirit
of God is perceived as being absent. Our orientation to
the Spirit of God determines whether we grow or decay.

Q: So who decides how our lives will shape up: God or us?

A: The shape of our lives depends upon many factors:
ourselves, the world around us, how God chooses to act
or not to act within that world. God has given humans
the gift of a will and the ability to make decisions. This is
a crucial aspect of the image of God within humans and
prevents us from living as automatons who could neither
grow nor decay. Whether our will conforms to the will of
God is an important factor in the shape of our lives.

Q: You still haven't proved the doctrine of providence.

A: I can't. To believe that God is ultimately in control
and desires good for human life is a faith statement. Yet
this belief in the providence of God is absolutely central
to my understanding of who God is and how I relate to
this God.

———

Then came January term, followed by spring semester. The baby
was due in April.

———

A friend of Doug's had given us a gift certificate to a famous downtown restaurant called Murray's, home of the "silver butter knife
steak." We knew we needed to use it before the baby came, but our
schedules were tight. My midsemester break fell during late March,
and we each squeezed in some extra work hours that week. We also
had to attend our last childbirth class that Thursday. But we made
a plan to meet at Murray's on Wednesday after Doug's shift at the
home for autistic adults and my shift at the law firm. I looked forward to the meal for weeks. We were living on cheap, easy food like
refried beans and tortillas, and the thought of a juicy steak made
me salivate.

On the Wednesday we were to meet at Murray's, the afternoon
sky went dark. The law office was abuzz as people moved from
office to office around the IDS tower, checking the sky from all four
directions. Rolling storm clouds were visible from every window.
As the building swayed noticeably, the radio announced a tornado
watch.

"Just a watch, not a warning," someone said.

"The building is designed for this," someone else said. "The
swaying is good."

"There's up to eighteen inches of sway." People loved to repeat
these things.

Still, folks cleared out early. When I brought some letters into the attorney's office for his signature, I noticed, over his shoulder, what might be construed as a funnel cloud in the distance. The attorney asked if I wanted to go home. I told him it would blow over. I had downtown dinner plans! We chatted about the eighteen inches of sway and then finished the paperwork.

A few hours later, I met Doug at Murray's, as planned. The dining room was elegant, with tall ceilings, white tablecloths, and waitresses in uniform. The restaurant was full, and the air was filled with electricity. It seemed that everyone who needed to wait out the storm downtown had come to Murray's.

The waitress brought our menus and a small dish with chunks of garlic toast. The buttery bits were too salty for a pregnant woman whose ankles were swelling. Still, I crunched one after another until the dish was empty. When our steaks were served, we cut them with our butter knives. Halfway through mine, I felt decidedly queasy, but I was determined to enjoy every mouthful. The beef would be good for me and the baby, if only I could squeeze it into my nine-months-pregnant body.

After the meal, Doug and I were barely back at our apartment when a pain twisted through me. Besides the shock of it, the pain scared me. Could this be a contraction? I was two weeks shy of my due date. It had never occurred to me that I might deliver early.

Not only was my stomach uncomfortably stuffed with steak, my heart was full of anxiety. "This can't happen!" I yelled to Doug. "We haven't had the last childbirth class yet!"

There were so many things I didn't know. I didn't know how big the baby was. I didn't know what the gender was. I didn't know if I had what it took to be a mother.

At my last appointment, the doctor had palpated my belly and said, "The baby's still on the small side. You should slow down. Stay home. Put your feet up. Relax."

Why hadn't I listened?

Doug drove us to Abbott Northwestern Hospital. Apparently every other pregnant woman in the Twin Cities area had arrived just ahead of us. The admitting clerk said it was the storm—a drop in barometric pressure can induce labor.

"It'll be a busy night," she predicted.

We filled out the paperwork and timed the contractions. They were disappointingly irregular. After an hour or so, the doctor breezed in. He was wearing tennis whites with a sweater knotted casually over his shoulders. He exuded a sense of irritation as he spoke to the nurse. Since my contractions had failed to progress, the doctor and nurse discussed the possibility of sending us home. Meanwhile, another nurse came in and asked Doug if he had parked in the correct lot. He hadn't. It was a common mistake, the nurse said, but he needed to move the car right away. Doug left to take care of it.

The doctor lifted my hospital gown and checked my dilation again. He spoke to the nurse and she handed him something, which he inserted into my vagina. He made a sudden pulling gesture. Fluid gushed out of me.

"That should help," the doctor said. Then he left the room.

When Doug returned a few minutes later, rainwater cascading from his jacket, he found me sitting in a puddle on the examining table. I was sobbing in anger, cursing the doctor, the nurses, the tennis whites, the hospital, the storm. Fortunately, my body was in control rather than my emotions, and my body knew just what it needed to do. My contractions quickly became more forceful and frequent. As each contraction rose, crested, and receded, I tried to breathe through it.

The force of the contractions shocked me. They consumed me. I'd never imagined that my body held such power. Everything spasmed and twisted at the same time. I felt as if my pelvic bones were being wrenched in opposite directions. My body seemed to be following a set of instructions I had never seen. Each contraction was a corkscrew. Why had no one told me? The baby wasn't going to be pushed out; it was going to be wrung from my body, the way a woman wrings out a dishcloth.

Hours passed, but I had no sense of time. Where were the painkillers? Doug spooned ice chips into my mouth and reminded me that I didn't want painkillers. I pushed him away. This was all his fault! I twisted in the bed.

Finally a nurse gave me a shot of Demerol. The effect was immediate. The pain was still there, but now I was watching it, like an interested bystander. As the nurse left the room, she paused by the small, square calendar that hung on the wall and ripped off a page. The new page was a number in bold type—the date. I stared at that number between contractions, trying to remember something. *26.*

Around five o'clock in the morning, our baby was born. A girl. Five pounds and three ounces of baby girl. The delivery nurse cried out, "A perfect little peanut!"

The baby was healthy—everyone said so. The doctor laid her on my stomach while Doug cut the umbilical cord. The baby lifted her head to look around, and the doctor laughed.

"Oh, you're in for it," he said.

I didn't know what he meant. "Is she okay?"

"Fine," he said. "Just fine. She's a very alert baby."

⌒

A couple of the nurses tended to the baby. Another nurse brought a warmed sheet and rolled me into it, as if I were the infant. I hadn't realized that I was bone cold. Being warm and swaddled felt rapturous.

We were transferred to a recovery room. The three of us were a family, a brand-new family. Our three heads pressed close together. Doug and I could only marvel and coo and wipe tears from our eyes. My heart felt as if it might explode with happiness. Our baby was here. A miniature human being.

I stroked her bald head and inhaled deeply. Other women had told me that newborn scent is what God smells like—this fleeting smell from the top of a baby's head. Her smell was indescribable, like nothing I'd ever smelled before, and I knew the women were right. This baby was fresh from God. Her eyes were open, a midnight-blue color, and her gaze seemed distant and wise, as if she had come from far away and knew things that the rest of us had forgotten.

Doug and I counted her tiny fingers and toes and stroked her cheek. I cautiously tugged at her blanket so we could inspect her umbilical cord with its plastic clamp. She seemed so breakable, and I knew I would do things wrong. I loved her, but I would do things wrong.

I remembered something I'd read in one of those pregnancy books: that baby girls are born with all the eggs their ovaries will ever produce. Those eggs would ripen and release over the course of a lifetime, but they were already there, formed in her tiny ovaries, at birth. That fact seemed almost too much to fathom. How could this helpless five-pound bundle be equipped, in some primal way, to procreate? It astounded me. It could only be proof that God intended for life to outlast death. Proof that the will to create is at least as elemental as the will to destroy.

We watched our baby's tiny nostrils flutter. Her little chest rose and fell with its unaccustomed breath. A heartbeat pulsed in her chest and throat and creased the soft spot at the top of her head. Everything about her five-pound body was bent on living. The gift of that overwhelmed me. I had no doubt that this life, this breath, this ferocious will to live came straight from the source of life Himself. What do we call this, if not love?

33

THE NURSES TRANSFERRED THE THREE OF US to a hospital room, with me in a wheelchair and the baby in a bassinet. When I was settled in bed, Doug gestured to a phone on the side table. "I suppose it's time to call our parents. They'll be awake soon anyway."

I suddenly realized why the "26" staring at me from the calendar had seemed so weighty. March 26 is a milestone for my family, on both sides. My father's mother was born on that date in 1895. My mother was born on that date in 1929. And a generation later, my sister Mary Lynn gave birth to her first daughter on our mother's fiftieth birthday.

Still, it had never occurred to me that my baby might also be born on this magical date. Now the coincidence seemed not only improbable but even a bit mystical.

Four generations of mothers had given birth to daughters on March 26. I had taken my place in a long line of laboring women and, like them, had been rewarded with an armful of daughter.

I knew, piercingly and beyond a doubt, that my mother had always loved me, just as I already loved my yet unnamed daughter.

Imperfectly, but fiercely. I felt a blessing descend on me like hands laid upon my head—hands from a community of women who transcended time.

At least I was pretty sure it was a blessing being conferred, and not just the aftereffects of the Demerol.

———

Doug made the phone calls: first his parents, then mine. I listened to him tell my mother, "Happy Birthday, Mom!"

I couldn't hear my mother's words, but I could hear her chuckle.

"I'm calling for Ruth," he told her, "because she's a bit busy right now."

A pause, then Doug spoke again.

"Well, we have a birthday gift for you, but we couldn't manage to get it wrapped and mailed." Doug winked at me and held the phone so I could hear my mother's response.

She was chuckling some more. "Oh that's fine, I know you two are plenty busy these days."

"Shall I just tell you what the gift is?" Doug asked.

"If you like, sure."

"It's a baby girl."

He didn't have to extend the phone for me to hear the whoops and hollers on the other end.

"I'm on a plane, I'm on a plane!" my mother said.

My heart was so full that it actually hurt. Doug handed me the phone, and my mother and I sniffled and exclaimed as I gazed at the baby. We didn't talk long because my mother had an airline ticket to buy.

———

Sandwiched between my husband and our baby, I could feel love in new places in my body. Love tingled in the tips of my fingers and pulsed in the base of my throat—that delicate, hollow spot between the ends of the collarbone. My heart seemed to still be beating with enough force for two instead of one. But I had been watching her precious heart beat on its own, her little lungs fill and expel. Now there was an entirely new body for me to love, a new body that needed to be constantly filled with breath. For the first time I understood what the word *vulnerable* meant.

How could I bear it if something or someone ever hurt this child? I was suddenly cognizant that there were innumerable ways that my world could be shattered now—ways I'd never imagined. I could count the number of minutes my daughter had been alive, and already I glimpsed that love holds in itself the seeds of great suffering.

A nurse appeared to show us how to care for the baby. With practiced hands, she showed us how to suction tiny nostrils with a blue vinyl bulb. She explained that this was important to prevent aspiration. She deftly rolled a blanket and laid it in the bassinet to be used as a prop behind the baby's back. She explained that this was to prevent crib death. Every one of her words and actions, meant to be reassuring, was terrifying.

The feeling of fear had been familiar to me in the past, but this was a different kind of fear, one that went beyond the borders of my own body. I saw something I'd missed when I wrote my Constructive Theology paper. The question isn't whether suffering or love is a more foundational concern, or how a sovereign God can will both. I had gotten so caught up in the matter of sin and evil that I had neglected to see another fundamental dynamic. It's not just evil that causes suffering; so does love.

Love and suffering are tied together. Maybe love is so tender that it leads to suffering. Or maybe suffering so softens us that it becomes a gateway to love. Or maybe love is simply unabated by suffering. Love is shown in flesh but persists beyond the limits of flesh. Yes, that is maybe the truest way to say it. And isn't that a guarantee of pain—something that is both limited and limitless? Isn't this the central message of the gospel, the meaning of grace?

In incarnation, love and suffering are bundled together in Christ's flesh. An infinite God chooses to become finite to embody love. How else could it be done?

How had I not seen this before—something so obvious and true? I had turned in my paper last semester, but I needed to add some sentences. A paragraph. Something. I needed to try. Then I saw that my theology would never be a clean document after all. And maybe that was all right.

———

We named the baby Hannah, after the biblical figure who pled with God. Hannah was barren, a fate she protested in prayer. She even had the temerity to bargain with God, promising that if He gave her a baby, she would give the baby back to Him. Her prayer changed God's mind, apparently. In one of Scripture's happy endings, Hannah gave birth to the baby she so deeply desired, named him Samuel, and dedicated him to be raised as a priest.

The legacy I wanted to pass on to our daughter was the courage to bargain with God. Although that did seem a bit much to bestow on an infant who weighed only five pounds.

———

That fall Doug and I juggled child care while he did his student teaching and I whittled away at my seminary requirements while continuing to work a few shifts each week as a legal secretary. Our weekly schedule was color coded: pink for the baby, yellow for the car, and blue for our jobs. Pink had to be a continuous line, yellow could never overlap, and blue was the most complicated of all, logistically. But by the spring, Doug had obtained his teaching credentials, and I had only one year of seminary left. Amazingly enough, we were on track.

Doug was unable to find a teaching position that fall, so he took a job working with severely disabled adults. He was disappointed not to get a job in his field but knew this was temporary. Plus, the job had good health benefits.

I plunged into my fourth and final year of seminary, which included a third and final internship. I was delighted to serve at our home church, Dayton Avenue, under the direction of the Reverend David Stewart, who had been installed shortly after I began seminary three years earlier. The church was thriving under Pastor David's leadership. The sanctuary had a new heating system, and the building bustled every day of the week.

As an intern, I gave guidance to the deacons, taught adult Sunday school classes, and preached once a month. The members of the congregation were kind. They showed up for the classes I taught. They offered positive, helpful feedback after every sermon. And they surrounded Doug and Hannah with love and attention. That congregation made it possible for me to have the seamless life I once envisioned, even if it turned out to be more chaotic than I had anticipated. A cup overflowing.

Still, it made sense to add to the family now rather than later. Those health benefits! When I graduated from seminary that May, I was two months pregnant. Once again I was living with one foot in the future. As soon as the baby was born, I would start looking for a church to serve. Someday soon I would be ordained.

⁓

Clara turned out to be a Sunday baby. She was born during the church hour, just before noon on the second Sunday of Advent. Exactly one week after her birth, our family of four went to church together for the first time. I dressed Clara in a red velour outfit that someone had given us, like a soft sleep sack with a hood. It was perfect for a Minnesota baby born in December. I wore my black maternity slacks and my favorite blouse: ivory crepe with a black notch collar and black covered buttons.

When we arrived at church, Doug took Hannah to the nursery,

which she loved, while I carried Clara into the fellowship hall—the same one Doug and I had first entered almost five years earlier, when we sat on folding chairs and heard a woman preach for the first time. Once again, Arthur was the first to greet me, which was no surprise. He was still spare and only slightly more bent than he'd been when I first met him. Then I was besieged by well-wishers. Any newborn is perfection, and Clara was a sleeping porcelain doll, with alabaster skin, pink petal lips, and long eyelashes adorning blue-tinged eyelids. I reveled in congratulations and joy.

Then it was time to go into the sanctuary for worship. Since it was Advent, the sanctuary was decorated with purple candles and red poinsettias and a tall, twinkling tree that reached toward the blue ceiling. On the pulpit stood a vase with a single red rose to bless the new baby. In the bulletin an announcement welcomed Clara to the world and congratulated all of us, including big sister Hannah.

Just a week postpartum, I was still sore and bleeding, but that only seemed right. Sitting in a pew beside Doug, holding our newborn, I felt like my life had come full circle. This was the church where I first felt welcomed as a woman, where Doug and I were married, where I preached my first sermon, where we had baptized one baby and soon would baptize another, where I had served in ministry. This was home.

"The light shines in the darkness, and the darkness has not overcome it" (John 1:5, NIV). I had recently written a paper on this passage, and each line of the reading resonated with meaning. As the service progressed, Doug and I passed Clara back and forth between us without needing to say a word. When she got hungry, I unbuttoned my blouse and Doug arranged a baby blanket over my shoulder. The choir began the anthem, accompanied by piano and bassoon.

Comfort, comfort, you my people.
Tell of peace, thus says our God.

Comfort those who sit in darkness,
Bowed beneath oppression's load.

As the music filled the sanctuary, I could hear the tiny sounds of my daughter suckling. I felt the pull of her taking what she needed from me, which my body was blessed to give.

Tell them that their sins I cover,
And their warfare now is over.

All of me had entered that sanctuary, and all had been received and welcomed. Body and spirit. Everything healed and everything unhealed. Past and present. Future and all that is yet to come.

EPILOGUE

A Letter to My Daughters

Dear Daughters,

The smell of curried cauliflower reminds me why I wrote this book. About a decade ago I was cooking supper and reading the newspaper when a news story filled me with passion. Hannah, you were away at college by then, and Clara, you were in high school.

Even years before that, I had suspected that I needed to tell this story. I just didn't know how, or when, or if I had the courage to write it down. I was a minister, preaching every week and counseling people. I felt competent and honored that I could serve in ministry. But as you became young women, I was filled with powerful, conflicting feelings—mainly pride, but also worry. You were both so beautiful, so confident, and moving about in the world so freely. But you were so vulnerable! What manner of things might reach out to hurt you? A piece of me was afraid all the time. Yet I didn't want my fear to taint you or to taint my interactions with you. In your childhood, I hadn't been a fearful mother. And I didn't want to become one. Still, I felt constantly torn between encouraging you to follow your dreams—"Go for it!"—and pulling you back to hold you close—"Be safe!"

I wondered why looming adulthood seemed so fearful, until I stopped and thought about my own experience. My own life felt ruined at age twenty, ripped apart. What did I know about navigating the passage into maturity? Yes, I had rebuilt a new life over a period of years, but my fears showed me that certain pieces of my past still needed mending. Maybe that's one of the gifts of being a parent— the chance to go through the stages of life again with different eyes. So in an effort to become a better mother, a more whole person, I delved more deeply into my past.

That soul searching is not a reflection on you, of course. I'm grateful to be your mother. You are both so courageous and kind and smart. There is no failing in you two that caused me to be fearful or searching, just as there was no failing in me that made me fall victim to a crime. Sometimes trauma just happens, which is a fearful thing. The world can be cruel to young women, no matter how courageous and kind and smart they might be. It's an act of faith to push past the fear.

As you were growing up, certain moments signaled that I should explore my past. Maybe you will remember this incident, Hannah. You were thirteen, and we were looking for something in my memorabilia box in the basement storage area. As we rooted through the box, a photocopy of a newspaper article fluttered out. I tensed when I saw the page.

You picked up the paper and read the headline aloud: "Heritage Hill Rapist-Robber Gets Long Term."

Then you asked me, "Mom, why do you have this?"

I remember looking at your sweet, confused face and feeling so unready for the moment. I wished I were the kind of person who had lots of papers crammed into random corners so I could pretend the page was inconsequential, even though my face probably said otherwise. Certainly I could have brushed the matter aside if I'd wanted to. Mothers have that power. But what if there was a reason we came across that paper at that moment? I didn't want to trample the opportunity. You were a young woman, after all. You had recently asked me, "Mom, do you have a secret?" I wondered what you meant. Had I become the kind of mother who seemed burdened and veiled by secrets? I never meant to become that woman.

Also, if I believed that being a victim of sexual violence wasn't unspeakable, then mustn't I be willing to speak about it? Maybe the time had come.

So I said, "I've kept that page all these years because the article is about my life, in a way. A long time ago I was the victim of a crime."

"Rapist-robber? Oh, Mom"—your face twisted up— "you mean you weren't a virgin when you married Dad! Poor you!"

It was a shock to realize that your understanding of sexual violence was being filtered through the language of sexual purity. I felt that I had failed you. The church had failed you. Women are not merely virgins or victims. There's more to living in a woman's skin than staying a virgin. So you and I had more conversations after that.

I began to wonder if I should be more overt about telling my story and what I had learned. Could I address my message to my daughters or to all the daughters out there—young women learning how to inhabit a woman's body in a world that is so often cruel? My heart is tender for all those who have to pass through the dark valleys of sexual assault. There are too many of us in that category: survivors, and those who love a survivor. I wanted to write a book that would stand as one woman's testimony: we are all more than what happens to us. We are all more than our worst decisions.

In some ways I'm sorry I had to write this book. It contains words that no one should have to associate with their mother. But I cannot change my history. None of us can. Instead we have to learn to love our histories, whatever they might be. Our histories give us our particular lens on the world. If life is a gift—if the lens is a gift—then I should be bold about using that lens.

I realized that my lens had value on a particular Monday afternoon in October 2006, nearly a decade ago.

Clara, you were a junior in high school at the time. A man entered an Amish school in Nickel Mines, Pennsylvania, with an arsenal of guns. He dismissed the boys and bound the girls by their hands and feet. Based on his supplies, it appeared that he was equipped for a siege. Possibly he intended to hold the girls hostage and rape them. But law enforcement arrived quickly. The gunman shot the girls in the back of their heads, one after the other.

I read all this as I was cooking supper and the smell of curried cauliflower filled the kitchen. The article captured the reaction of the father of one of the dead girls, who was grateful that his daughter had escaped "a worse fate." By which he meant that she had not been raped. Just executed. With a bullet to the back of the head.

When I read those words—"worse fate"—I was actually unable to breathe. I felt like the father had stepped on my chest with both feet and pushed all the air out of my lungs. It took an effort to suck in my breath again, and when I did, I bellowed. The sound I made must have been primal, like someone giving birth or someone dying. Maybe it was like the wail of watching a loved one die. Clara, you came running into the kitchen, terrified, and found me with the newspaper trembling in my hands. I could smell the cauliflower starting to burn, but I didn't care.

"Listen to me!" I yelled. "Listen to me! If you are ever attacked—which won't happen, but if it does—if you are ever attacked and it comes down to being raped or being killed, you must survive! It is your business to survive. Surviving is the *only* thing you must do. However you can. Because you will recover. You can recover from anything as long as you have breath in your body." I may have bellowed that entire speech without taking a breath.

In many ways, it was a strange response. Normally it would be my bent to stand by the side of another parent, especially a grieving parent in a tragic circumstance. And I did feel sorry for this father and the loss he had endured. But I didn't understand him. Or maybe I did. Maybe that was the problem. What he said was abhorrent to me. Could a parent think his child's survival was second to anything? Was he suggesting that his daughter's perceived bodily purity was more important than her retaining breath in that body? How could a father—whose own flesh had helped to create that flesh, that female flesh—prefer his daughter *dead* over damaged? What is this alleged "worse fate"?

Imagine saying such a thing about another injury— a broken bone or a punctured lung. Are those fates worse than death? Of course not! You would call an ambulance.

You would schedule surgery. You would remedy the damage. You would give thanks that the wounds were not fatal. So why is a violation of a female's sexual parts so much worse than a broken bone?

I could ask, rhetorically, "Since when has a woman's sexual purity been of more value than the breath in her body?" But I know the answer: since recorded history, and perhaps before that. The sad fact is that a woman's sexual purity has long been the measure of her worth. As a culture, we need to bury this worthless belief. A girl's or woman's value is not equal to her supposed sexual purity. That fallacy must die. Sometimes beliefs do die, though slowly. We no longer believe in Hippocrates's four humors, do we? We no longer use bloodletting to cure pneumonia. We no longer sanction racially segregated schools or facilities. It is time that this false belief in the supreme importance of women's sexual purity be cast into the grave of extinct beliefs.

The truth is that women who have been sexually violated have the same intrinsic value as women who have not been sexually violated. Period. Another human cannot damage a woman's sexual self and by doing so destroy her life.

Daughters, don't believe the lies! You are more than your virginity. You are more than your sexual history. You are more than what happens to you. You are immensely valuable. No wound can ever make you less than whole. Wounds become scars, and scars make a person beautiful. In fact, nothing is more washable than human skin. It is the most washable substance on earth. Thank God.

———

I rarely make curried cauliflower anymore. The smell reminds me of outrage and death, neither of which are particularly delicious. Still, outrage is valuable, and I don't reject it as worthless. That's why I make no apology for bellowing that day in the kitchen. There are things worth bellowing against. That's the lens I've been given by my history. You might even say that outrage is one of the gifts a person receives after enduring trauma. I want to pass on this gift to you, or at least prepare you to receive it. For trauma happens to everyone, sooner or later, to some degree.

Once you survive trauma, outrage is the warning bell that sounds when you hear truth being distorted by those who haven't passed through shadowed valleys. Because you have endured trauma, you can detect their lies. Maybe it's like having survived the measles or the flu. Your body now has some small measure of immunity and recognizes that same poison when it tries to invade again.

I wish you would never have to know trauma. But when trauma does appear in your path, don't fear it. There are things you can't fight. Still, by God's power, you will prevail. Our God brings life out of death. Sometimes there is no option except to let the waves of trauma engulf you for a time. Just trust that they will recede again. What's left in you will rise up afterward, and that will be enough. More than enough! There's more to you than you know. There is more to God than you know. Trust that the trauma will leave gifts in its wake—hard gifts like outrage and perspective. Maybe this is what faith is: this trusting that God will bring something new and beautiful out of the pain.

Love,
Mom

ACKNOWLEDGMENTS

I would like to acknowledge the extraordinary debt I owe to the other victims who share this story. On these pages they bear the names Marty, Teresa, Cheryl, and Karen. More than three decades after the crime, I attempted to reconnect with each of them. Our reunions were full of tears and healing, and they showed me how profoundly the crime had affected all of our lives. Our reconnection birthed the idea to write this memoir, and I am enormously grateful that they could tolerate having me write about the crime.

I am also humbled by the generosity and moral courage of my parents, Nick and Joan Huizenga, who allowed me to reflect honestly, and sometimes unflatteringly, on a faith tradition they cherish. Our relationship is proof of the healing power of love.

I am grateful to fellow writers who read drafts of this work and offered critique: Susan Okula, Kathy Lynch, Phyllis Langton, Christy Bergemann, Lygia Ballantyne, Elizabeth Hagan, Barbara Melosh, Leslie Klingensmith, Martha Spong, MaryAnn McKibben Dana, Hilary Barrett, Michael McGregor, Susan Baller-Shepard, Priscilla Little, David Little, Douglas Schuurman, Margaret DeRitter, Linda Bieze, Reinder VanTil, and others.

I am grateful to all those who gave me feedback that drew on their own memories: Mary Lynn Wesorick, Timothy Huizenga, Beth Huizenga, Susan Joy Cleveland, Annette Huizenga, Nicholas Huizenga, Joan Huizenga, John Kuiper, Joel Hoekstra, Julie Neraas, Barbara Bash, and others.

I am grateful to my agent, Chip MacGregor, and everyone at Tyndale House, especially my editors Carol Traver and Stephanie Rische, for using such tender care in helping me to get the words on the page and to bring the pages to readers.

My deepest gratitude is reserved for you readers, especially if your life has been touched by sexual violence—either because it happened to you or because it happened to someone you love. Thank you for traveling through my story with me. You didn't know what you'd find as you turned the pages, and yet you dared to keep reading. May you find recovery and healing for your own story. Remember that you are infinitely precious, no matter what happened to you.

"A touching memoir... Immensely inspiring."
KIRKUS REVIEWS

the tank man's son

A MEMOIR

MARK BOUMAN
WITH D. R. JACOBSEN

The time Mom met Hitler,
Frost came to dinner, and
I heard the Greatest Story ever told

a memoir

DIKKON EBERHART

SAVING MY 'ASSASSIN

A MEMOIR

VIRGINIA PRODAN

Enjoy these other *great memoirs* from Tyndale House Publishers

All But Normal
life on victory road
a memoir

SHAWN THORNTON
WITH JOEL KILPATRICK

Ruined

RUTH EVERHART
(a memoir)

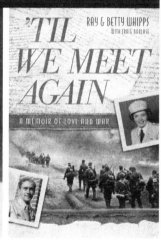

RAY & BETTY WHIPPS
WITH CRAIG BORLASE

'TIL WE MEET AGAIN

A MEMOIR OF LOVE AND WAR

To find out more about these and other great Tyndale memoirs, visit memoiraddict.com: ordinary people, extraordinary stories!

Love memoirs?

Find your next great read at MemoirAddict.com!

At Memoir Addict, we find ordinary people
with extraordinary stories.

Explore:

- updates on new releases
- additional stories from your favorite authors
- FREE first-chapter downloads
- discussion guides
- author videos and book trailers

- inspirational quotes to share on Pinterest, Twitter, and Facebook
- book reviews
- and so much more!

While you're there, check out our blog, featuring unique perspectives on memoirs from all facets of the publishing industry. From authors to acquisition directors to editors, we share our passion for storytelling. You'll get an insider's look at the craft of shaping a story into a captivating memoir.

Are you a memoir addict? Follow us on Twitter @MemoirAddict and on Facebook for updates on your favorite authors, free e-book promotions, contests, and more!

Plus, visit BookClubHub.net to

- download free discussion guides
- get book club recommendations
- sign up for Tyndale's book club and e-newsletters

MemoirAddict.com: ordinary people, extraordinary stories!

Online Discussion *guide*

TAKE *your* TYNDALE READING EXPERIENCE *to the* NEXT LEVEL

A FREE discussion guide for this book is available at bookclubhub.net, perfect for sparking conversations in your book group or for digging deeper into the text on your own.

www.bookclubhub.net

You'll also find free discussion guides for other Tyndale books, e-newsletters, e-mail devotionals, virtual book tours, and more!